Mythology For Dummies

W9-ASC-307

Cheat Sheet

A Timeline of World Civilizations

BCE	3300–1900	Beginning of Sumerian Civilization	CE	31 BCE–476 CE	Roman Empire
	2550–2150	Old Kingdom, Egypt		150–750	Teotihuacan: Central America
	1980–1640	Middle Kingdom, Egypt		27–30	Jesus of Nazareth preaches reforms in Palestine and is executed by the Roman governor Pontius Pilate.
	1792–1750	Hammurabi's reign, height of Babylonian Empire			
	1600–1100	Greek Bronze Age		35–62	Paul, a Diaspora Jew, founds a series of churches in Syria, Asia Minor, and Greece. Christianity separates from Judaism.
	1540–1070	New Kingdom, Egypt			
	1500–400	Olmec: Central America			
	1500	Aryans invade India; start of Vedic Age			
	1250	Moses leads Israelite slaves from Egypt, establishes worship of Yahweh at Mt. Sinai (formerly sacred to the moon god Sin)		400–499	Historical King Arthur might have lived
				250–900	Maya: Central America
				570–632	The Prophet Mohammed writes the *Qur'an* and founds the religion of Islam.
	1200–1000	Earliest Hindu Literature, the *Rigveda*		632–750	Islam spreads to the Near East, North Africa, Spain, and France.
	1100	Trojan War			
	800–700	Age of Homer		700–1000	Age of Vikings
	776	First Olympic Games in Greece, in honor of Zeus		900–1180	Toltec: Central America
	753	Founding of Rome		1000–1300	Apache and Navajo Indians move to Southwestern United States
	600–400	Age of Athenian Democracy			
	599–500	Lao-Tzu, founder of Taoism, active in China		1250	End of Anasazi culture, North America
	551–479	Confucius		1325–1521	Aztec empire: Central America
	563	Birth of Gautama (founder of Buddhism)		1438–1532	Inca empire: South America
	540	Birth of Vardhamana (founder of Jainism)		1492	Christopher Columbus lands in North America
	509–31	Roman Republic		1600–1700	North American Plains Indians incorporate horses
	365–323	Alexander the Great		1800–1899	North American Indians in United States mostly displaced by Europeans

Mythology For Dummies®

Cheat Sheet

Greek and Roman Counterparts

Greek Name	Roman Name	Description
Zeus	Jupiter	King of Gods
Hera	Juno	Goddess of Marriage
Poseidon	Neptune	God of the Sea
Saturn	Cronus	Youngest son of Uranus, Father of Zeus
Aphrodite	Venus	Goddess of Love
Hades	Pluto	God of the Underworld
Hephaistos	Vulcan	God of the Forge
Demeter	Ceres	Goddess of the Harvest
Apollo	Apollo	God of Music and Medicine
Athena	Minerva	Goddess of Wisdom
Artemis	Diana	Goddess of the Hunt
Ares	Mars	God of War
Hermes	Mercury	Messenger of the Gods
Dionysus	Bacchus	God of Wine
Persephone	Proserpine	Goddess of Underworld
Eros	Cupid	God of Love
Gaia	Gaea	Goddess of Earth

Hungry Minds™

For Dummies: Bestselling Book Series for Beginners

 ™

BESTSELLING BOOK SERIES

References for the Rest of Us!®

Do you find that traditional reference books are overloaded with technical details and advice you'll never use? Do you postpone important life decisions because you just don't want to deal with them? Then our *For Dummies*® business and general reference book series is for you.

For Dummies business and general reference books are written for those frustrated and hard-working souls who know they aren't dumb, but find that the myriad of personal and business issues and the accompanying horror stories make them feel helpless. *For Dummies* books use a lighthearted approach, a down-to-earth style, and even cartoons and humorous icons to dispel fears and build confidence. Lighthearted but not lightweight, these books are perfect survival guides to solve your everyday personal and business problems.

> "More than a publishing phenomenon, 'Dummies' is a sign of the times."
>
> — The New York Times

> "A world of detailed and authoritative information is packed into them…"
>
> — U.S. News and World Report

> "…you won't go wrong buying them."
>
> — Walter Mossberg, Wall Street Journal, on For Dummies books

Already, millions of satisfied readers agree. They have made For Dummies the #1 introductory level computer book series and a best-selling business book series. They have written asking for more. So, if you're looking for the best and easiest way to learn about business and other general reference topics, look to For Dummies to give you a helping hand.

Hungry Minds™

Christopher W. Blackwell
and Amy Hackney Blackwell

Hungry Minds™

Best-Selling Books • Digital Downloads • e-Books • Answer Networks • e-Newsletters • Branded Web Sites • e-Learning

New York, NY ◆ Cleveland, OH ◆ Indianapolis, IN

Mythology For Dummies®

Published by:
Hungry Minds, Inc.
909 Third Avenue
New York, NY 10022
www.hungryminds.com
www.dummies.com

Library of Congress Control Number: 2002102449

ISBN: 0-7645-5432-8

Printed in the United States of America

10 9 8 7 6 5 4 3 2

1B/RX/QV/QS/IN

Distributed in the United States by Hungry Minds, Inc.

Distributed by CDG Books Canada Inc. for Canada; by Transworld Publishers Limited in the United Kingdom; by IDG Norge Books for Norway; by IDG Sweden Books for Sweden; by IDG Books Australia Publishing Corporation Pty. Ltd. for Australia and New Zealand; by TransQuest Publishers Pte Ltd. for Singapore, Malaysia, Thailand, Indonesia, and Hong Kong; by Gotop Information Inc. for Taiwan; by ICG Muse, Inc. for Japan; by Intersoft for South Africa; by Eyrolles for France; by International Thomson Publishing for Germany, Austria and Switzerland; by Distribuidora Cuspide for Argentina; by LR International for Brazil; by Galileo Libros for Chile; by Ediciones ZETA S.C.R. Ltda. for Peru; by WS Computer Publishing Corporation, Inc., for the Philippines; by Contemporanea de Ediciones for Venezuela; by Express Computer Distributors for the Caribbean and West Indies; by Micronesia Media Distributor, Inc. for Micronesia; by Chips Computadoras S.A. de C.V. for Mexico; by Editorial Norma de Panama S.A. for Panama; by American Bookshops for Finland.

For general information on Hungry Minds' products and services please contact our Customer Care department; within the U.S. at 800-762-2974, outside the U.S. at 317-572-3993 or fax 317-572-4002.

For sales inquiries and resellers information, including discounts, premium and bulk quantity sales and foreign language translations please contact our Customer Care department at 800-434-3422, fax 317-572-4002 or write to Hungry Minds, Inc., Attn: Customer Care department, 10475 Crosspoint Boulevard, Indianapolis, IN 46256.

For information on licensing foreign or domestic rights, please contact our Sub-Rights Customer Care department at 212-884-5000.

For information on using Hungry Minds' products and services in the classroom or for ordering examination copies, please contact our Educational Sales department at 800-434-2086 or fax 317-572-4005.

Please contact our Public Relations department at 212-884-5163 for press review copies or 212-884-5000 for author interviews and other publicity information or fax 212-884-5400.

For authorization to photocopy items for corporate, personal, or educational use, please contact Copyright Clearance Center, 222 Rosewood Drive, Danvers, MA 01923, or fax 978-750-4470.

About the Authors

Christopher W. Blackwell earned a BA in Classics from Marlboro College in Vermont and a PhD in Classics from Duke University in North Carolina. He is the author of a book on the political history of Greece in the fourth century BCE — *In the Absence of Alexander* (Peter Lang, New York, 1999) — and is an editor and contributor to several ongoing projects aimed at bringing the ancient world to wide audiences via the World Wide Web. He is currently a professor of Classics at Furman University in Greenville, South Carolina, and gets to spend his days exploring the language, history, literature, and mythology of the ancient world with some very smart young people.

Amy Hackney Blackwell has degrees in Medieval and Renaissance History from Duke and Vanderbilt Universities. She also has a JD from the University of Virginia, but has given up the practice of law for the more interesting (if less lucrative) practice of writing — not surprisingly, most of what she writes is either on history or law. She has lived and worked all over Europe and Asia, including two years in rural Japan, and speaks several foreign languages. She and Chris enjoy skydiving and scuba diving, but not at the same time.

Dedication

This book is dedicated to Will and Zoe.

Authors' Acknowledgments

We would like to thank our agent, Grace Freedson, for all her help with this project. Kudos to all the editors and hard workers at Hungry Minds, Inc., who got this thing put together on time. Chris thanks his colleagues in the Department of Classics at Furman University, and especially Richard Prior, Associate Professor of Classics, who had a lot to do with us getting to write *Mythology For Dummies,* and who can produce out of his head anything anyone would want to know about the ancient languages and civilizations of Italy. We would both like to acknowledge the excellent librarians at the Furman University and Greenville Libraries. Amy thanks Favignana for her constant presence and support, and both of us thank our parents and brothers and sisters for their enthusiasm about this project.

Publisher's Acknowledgments

We're proud of this book; please send us your comments through our Hungry Minds Online Registration Form located at www.dummies.com.

Some of the people who helped bring this book to market include the following:

Acquisitions, Editorial, and Media Development

Project Editor: Sherri Fugit

Acquisitions Editor: Greg Tubach

Copy Editor: Robert Annis

Technical Editors: William Hansen, Professor and Chair, Classical Studies Co-Director, Program in Mythology Studies, Indiana University, Bloomington, Indiana; Anthony Leonardis, St. Richard's School, Indianapolis, Indiana; Janet Withers

Senior Permissions Editor: Carmen Krikorian

Editorial Manager: Jennifer Ehrlich

Editorial Assistant: Nivea C. Strickland

Production

Project Coordinator: Jennifer Bingham

Layout and Graphics: Karl Brandt, Kelly Hardesty, LeAndra Johnson, Stephanie D. Jumper, Tiffany Muth, Jackie Nicholas, Brent Savage, Betty Schulte, Rashell Smith, Jeremey Unger, Mary J. Virgin, Erin Zeltner

Proofreaders: John Greenough, Andy Hollandbeck, Susan Moritz, Carl Pierce, TECHBOOKS Production Services

Indexer: TECHBOOKS Production Services

Special Help

Chrissy Guthrie, Neil Johnson

Cover Photos: © Mimmo Jodice/Corbis

General and Administrative

Hungry Minds Consumer Reference Group

Business: Kathleen Nebenhaus, Vice President and Publisher; Kevin Thornton, Acquisitions Manager

Cooking/Gardening: Jennifer Feldman, Associate Vice President and Publisher; Anne Ficklen, Executive Editor; Kristi Hart, Managing Editor

Education/Reference: Diane Graves Steele, Vice President and Publisher

Lifestyles: Kathleen Nebenhaus, Vice President and Publisher; Tracy Boggier, Managing Editor

Pets: Kathleen Nebenhaus, Vice President and Publisher; Tracy Boggier, Managing Editor

Travel: Michael Spring, Vice President and Publisher; Brice Gosnell, Publishing Director; Suzanne Jannetta, Editorial Director

Hungry Minds Consumer Editorial Services: Kathleen Nebenhaus, Vice President and Publisher; Kristin A. Cocks, Editorial Director; Cindy Kitchel, Editorial Director

Hungry Minds Consumer Production: Debbie Stailey, Production Director

Contents at a Glance

Cartoons at a Glance

By Rich Tennant

page 5

page 185

page 129

page 231

page 27

page 329

Cartoon Information:
Fax: 978-546-7747
E-Mail: richtennant@the5thwave.com
World Wide Web: www.the5thwave.com

Table of Contents

· ·

Chapter 18: Land of a Thousand Gods: India 261

Chapter 19: China: Tao . . . Wow! 275

Chapter 20: Japan: Myths from the Land of the Rising Sun 289

Introduction

• •

This book is about mythology, the stories people tell that really matter. It can be argued that that the telling of myths is one of the most important things human beings do. Everyone tells myths. Every culture of every time produces myths. Put together all of these myths and you come up with the subject of "mythology," a vast body of stories about heroes, gods, monsters, and forces of nature.

To understand mythology is to understand human beings. That's why myths are worth thinking about. Just like human beings, myths can be stirring, inspirational, funny, and beautiful. On the other hand, (just like human beings) myths can be complicated, cruel, violent, obscene, or just (seemingly) absurd.

This book offers explanations wherever it can, but if you like quick, unambiguous answers, mythology is probably going to drive you crazy. Myths exist, you see, to answer those human questions that do not have quick, unambiguous answers.

One important thing to remember: Mythology is religion. Some of the myths in this book are stories from religions no one practices anymore; others are myths from religions that millions of people the world over practice today.

About This Book

This book is meant to be a quick reference for anyone who wants to learn the basics of world mythology. It's organized into chapters that deal with specific topics; if you have a particular interest, you can just read the pertinent chapters and not bother with the rest of the book. Or you can read the whole thing but in any order you like. Though we devote about half the book to classical mythology — Greek and Roman — we also cover myths from the rest of Europe and the rest of the world.

Conventions Used in This Book

In this book, dates are in terms of "BCE" and "CE". You may be more familiar with "BC" and "AD." Don't worry! 19 BCE was the same year as 19 BC, and not only did we write this book in AD 2002, we also wrote it in 2002 CE. *CE* stands for *Common Era,* and *BCE* stands for *Before the Common Era.* Most scholars refer to dates in this way instead of BC (Before Christ) and AD (*Anno Domini*, or, "In the Year of Our Lord"). The new abbreviations are more considerate in an age when scholars of different religious faiths (or no religious faith) work together.

We generally use the word *deities* to refer to gods and goddesses together. We may occasionally use "gods" to mean "gods and goddesses."

This book is in English, but most myths were not told originally in English. We have often had to choose among different but equally okay ways of rendering human or divine names into English. Was the hero of the Trojan War called Achilles, or Akhilleus? Was the founder of Taoism named Lao Tse, or Lao Tzu? We've tried to make good decisions, but don't be surprised if you see some of the names spelled very differently in other books.

How This Book Is Organized

This book is divided into five parts, each of which contains several chapters. The first part is an overview of mythology. Each of the next four parts focuses on a particular geographical area and its mythology: Greece, the Roman Empire, northern Europe, and the rest of the world. Each chapter is about 10 to 14 pages and deals with specific topics such as Greek goddesses, Homeric stories, or Egyptian mythology.

Part I: Mythology and the Cradle of Civilization

This part is an overview of mythology. Chapter 1 describes what mythology is, some of the theories people have formed about the subject, and the common types of myth and mythical figures. Chapter 2 discusses some of the ways in which myths have appeared in culture throughout the ages and into the present day.

Part II: It Started Here, Folks: Greek Mythology

When most Americans think "mythology," they immediately think about Greek mythology for good reason. The gods, goddesses, heroes, and monsters of ancient Greek mythology are especially vivid to us. The Greeks wrote a lot of very good literature, much of it on mythological subjects, so some very exciting versions of Greek myths survive from ancient times. Also, the artists and thinkers of the European Renaissance fell in love with the Greeks and helped those stories survive. This part describes the Greek gods and goddesses and where they came from (which is not a pretty story). It retells the adventures of the more famous heroes of Greek mythology — Heracles (also known as Hercules), Perseus, Theseus, and Jason. It also tells the long, involved story of the Trojan War and the body of myths that were the subject of some of the more famous Greek Tragedies.

Part III: The Cultural Spoils of an Empire: Roman Mythology

It's well known that the Romans used most of the Greek gods and goddesses with occasional name changes. This part explains why they did that, who those Roman gods were, and how Romans integrated these borrowed deities with their own home-grown ones. You can also read a chapter about Roman origin myths, as presented in the *Aeneid* and the tale of Romulus and Remus. There is also a chapter about popular Roman mythological stories.

Part IV: One Big Family Feud: Northern European Mythology

Though myths from the Mediterranean region are better known, the folks who lived in northern Europe also had deities and stories about them. This part discusses Norse myths, including the sagas of Beowulf and the Volsungs. It also has a chapter on one of the most famous mythical heroes: King Arthur.

Part V: Some Sunblock, a Sacrifice, a Monster, and Thou: Non-European Mythology

Westerners tend to assume that "mythology" means Western mythology, but people all over the world have their own bodies of myths. This part covers the Middle East, Egypt, China, India, Japan, and the Americas. Hopefully this book will whet people's appetites for learning about myths and lead them to finding out more about the mythologies of the world.

Part VI: The Part of Tens

Have some fun reading these lists, an integral part of any *For Dummies* book. See if your favorite mythological place or monster made the cut.

Icons Used in This Book

Along the way, we have included some extra information and marked it with these four icons. The book should make sense even if you skip over all of these, but it may be more fun if you don't.

This icon marks places where we tie bits of mythological theory with myths — pointing out what kind of myth you're looking at.

Trivia is trivia — little odds and ends of information that aren't terribly important in themselves but can mean the difference between winning and losing a quiz bowl or can make someone seem really, really smart. Myths tend to produce lots of trivial information.

This is historical or scholarly information; things that the professionals who study this stuff care about.

Enrich your word power! Myths and their characters have provided tons of words to the English language.

Where to Go from Here

This book isn't linear; it'll make sense even if you don't start at the beginning. If you have a burning interest in Egyptian myths, you can safely skip the Ancient Greece part.

A few chapters in the beginning of the book can help you with an overall understanding of mythology. Chapters 1 through 3 are overviews about the field of mythology and the role that myths have played through the ages. Start there if you want to know what mythology is all about. Or check out the Part of Tens at the end — it's a good place to start for fun and makes a nice light introduction for folks who are primarily interested in myths for their entertainment value. Otherwise, start anywhere and jump around as you like.

Part I
Mythology and the Cradle of Civilization

The 5th Wave   By Rich Tennant

"It's a myth, of course."

In this part . . .

So what the heck is mythology anyway? Why should anyone care about it? Well, aside from helping students write essays or young professionals sound scintillatingly witty and well-read at cocktail parties, a knowledge of mythology can help people understand their own culture and the cultures of other places. This part discusses the basics of mythology as a field of study and some of the effects mythology has had on the world.

Chapter 1

The Truth About Myths

First things first. Before you read any more of this book, we want you to know this: We take myths very seriously.

Now, we're not saying that myths aren't funny — many myths are really funny, and they're supposed to be. Neither are we saying that our entire discussion of myths will be serious, because it won't. This book is supposed to be engaging and entertaining, so we plan to have fun talking about mythology with the hope that you have fun reading about mythology.

But when we say that something is a myth, we're *not* saying that it's false or wrong. In other words, we don't think that science and history belong on the one correct side and mythology belongs on the other. (We don't have anything against science and history. They teach the world a great deal, and we profit from them every day; we just don't think people should elevate them above myths simply because they seem more verifiable.)

When we were growing up, we were taught that people used myths to explain the world before science became an established field. The assumption was that once people became rational, they didn't need myths. We know better now.

Mythology is a way of understanding the world, and it is just as important and just as "true" as the scientific or historical ways. In fact, science, history, and other logical ways of thinking simply fail to describe some very important things — things that we think are true. But myths can do the job.

Chris's father was lucky enough to have known Paul Tillich, a Christian thinker who fled from Nazi Germany and ended up at Harvard University. Tillich, who really knew a thing or two about what is important, used to say: "Never say something is *only* a myth. Say, rather, it is *nothing less than* a myth."

That's what we think — that myths are important and worth taking seriously. And anything worth taking seriously should be fun to think about as well. So, here we go. . . .

How to Spot a Myth a Mile Away

A myth is a story. The Greek word "mythos" means "story." That's the basic concept. But, of course, not just any old story can be a myth. Amy (one of the authors of this book) was served a whole pig's head for dinner in Thailand — this is a good story and one worth telling, but it isn't a myth. Chris (the other author of this book) once got shot at by some lunatics in the woods — another good story, but not up to the standards of mythology. You may know a myth when you see it, but you still need some kind of definition before you can get down to the business of fully appreciating myths.

Experts love to argue about difficult, hard-to-define subjects, and mythology has been a popular topic for argument for the last two centuries. Scholars argue about what is a "true" myth as opposed to some other kind. They insist, however, that no one confuse myths with other similar types of stories, such as legends, sagas, and folktales.

Specifics of mythological proportions

So what's special about a myth? Well, *myths* are stories about gods and goddesses and supernatural entities and human relationships with them. This definition can expand to include stories that explain universal truths or values and stories that help groups of people (such as Americans) identify themselves and define their values. Myths help validate the social order, such as hereditary kingships or social class structures. They also can provide a "history" of a kingdom that makes it seem inevitable.

Because myths are about humans and the gods, then they're also always about religion. Every myth in this book was or still is part of a religion that people practiced seriously.

The word "myth" has come to mean "untrue" in some contexts; people say something is "just a myth" if no factual basis exists for it. But myths do have their own truths. They provide people with a view of the world and a set of values that can be as important as any scientifically verifiable fact. (For some examples, see Chapter 3.)

Legends

Legends are similar to the myth, but they're based on history. It doesn't have to have much of a historical basis — lots of legends hardly jibe with the historical versions at all. A legend or saga, however, does have to include something that may actually have happened. For example, the story of King Arthur is a legend because there (probably) was an actual man who served as the basis for the King Arthur we know of today.

Folktales

A *folktale* is a traditional tale that is primarily a form of entertainment or in some cases is used to instruct. Folktales involve adventures and heroes and magical happenings, but they don't usually try to explain human relationships with the divine.

Most stories known as myths have elements of legend or folktale in them and vice versa. These terms are useful in helping decide what is a myth and what isn't, but you shouldn't get too hung up on them.

 Fairy tales look like myths and folktales, but they're a little different. Fairy tales came out of the Romantic Movement of the nineteenth century, when people such as the Brothers Grimm collected stories from local people and wrote them up in romanticized versions. The Grimm fairy tales, however, are nothing like the sanitized, modern ones — the original versions are full of blood and brutality.

Which Came First, the People or the Myths?

People haven't always had access to big books of Greek mythology or world mythology to refer to for mythological information. But these myths nevertheless have moved down through the ages through the spoken word and through art. After writing was invented, people preserved the myths on paper. What could be more interesting — for authors in antiquity or even yesterday — than writing stories from myths?

The oral tradition

Myths are stories, and stories get told. Stories that are passed down from one generation to the next are stories told in the oral tradition.

In places and times where people don't use written language, oral tradition is one of only two ways of preserving knowledge from one generation to the next (the other is art, which we talk about in a minute).

In cultures with oral traditions, people tend to have better memories. In cultures that write down their material, people don't need particularly good memories because they have books, self-stick notes, and other ways of reminding themselves of things that they otherwise might forget. Societies with oral traditions often turn stories into poems or songs, which are easier to remember and to repeat word for word.

This is the most traditional way for myths to start, to spread, and to develop. Because each generation that tells a myth has its own unique needs and its own unique experiences, myths tend to evolve over time and tend to exist in different versions.

One modern equivalent to the oral tradition is the material that passes from person to person by e-mail. Stories can spread across the world from computer user to computer user, changing slightly all the while. Some of these tales may become the myths of the twenty-first century.

Archaeological evidence

People who don't read or write can tell stories, and they can make art. Art is another way that myths can survive from generation to generation, even if they aren't written down.

Art can survive long after the people who made it have died, enabling archaeologists to uncover, restore, and interpret it. Art that helps preserve myths doesn't have to be fancy or sophisticated art. Ordinary household objects often feature decorations that can tell modern archaeologists a lot about a society.

Literature

Eventually, of course, people put myths in writing. The poetry of Homer, a great source for Greek mythology, began life as an oral tradition of songs that singers would perform publicly. Those poems ended up as written text for people to read. In the case of Homer, scholars argue endlessly about how the oral material came to be preserved on paper in one specific version.

Mythographers existed even in ancient times. They recorded myths for later generations.

Myths can serve as the inspiration for other kinds of literature. Greek tragedies, written texts intended to be performed as plays, often take their plots from Greek mythology. William Shakespeare used mythological themes for many of his plays, borrowing from the mythology of the Mediterranean world and from northern European myths. For example, *A Midsummer Night's Dream* is set at the court of the Greek hero Theseus during his marriage to the Amazon queen Hippolyta (read about him in Chapter 7); and *Romeo and Juliet* is based on the story of Pyramus and Thisbe in Ovid's *Metamorphoses* (see Chapter 13 for that).

In more recent times, people have sought out oral traditions to record in writing for the purpose of study. So anthropologists might visit the indigenous people of Brazil or the people who live in the Sea Island community in South Carolina to listen to their stories and write them down. This written documentation helps preserve a culture and can provide insight into how myths evolve.

Looking at the Different Types of Myths

Myths are tricky. Myths from around the world, from long ago and from recent times, often seem similar. Most myths appear to fall into certain categories, regardless of whether different cultures had much to do with each other. Why? What's up with that?

Comparative Mythology 101

Any time that scholars find several factors that appear to follow a pattern, they try to find the rules that govern the pattern. During the twentieth century, several scholars tried to explain what myths were all about and answer the age-old question: What is the purpose of all these stories? Because that truly is an unanswerable question, they devised several different theories, which gradually were incorporated into the fields of psychology, comparative literature, and anthropology.

Here's a quick summary of some of the more important theories about myths:

- ✔ Myths define social customs and beliefs.
- ✔ Myths are the same as ritual.

- Myths are allegories, similar to parables in the Christian Bible.

- Myths explain natural phenomena.

- Myths explain psychological phenomenon such as love, sex, and anger toward one's parents. (Sigmund Freud bought into this theory.)

- Myths contain archetypes that reveal the collective unconscious of the human race. (Carl Jung bought into this theory.)

- Myths are a way of communicating and helping people work together, or they're a way for people to talk about things that cause anxiety. (The theory of "structuralism," which was first observed by Claude Levi-Strauss, falls into this category.)

Not too much thought is needed to figure out that not one of these approaches explains each and every myth. But, taken together, they can make thinking about myths more fun. (We tend to find the symbolic/allegorical theory of myths to be most satisfactory, mainly because it covers almost all of the others, without being too narrow.)

Major types of myths

One reason so many scholars have tried pinning down the definition of myths is that myths can be similar across cultures, even in distant cultures. For example, Greece and Japan have stories about men who visit the underworld to retrieve their dead wives. The coincidence is freaky, as if some universal knowledge resides in human memory from the days when all people lived in caves.

Anyway, some stories frequently recur in all cultures. Here are a few of them:

- **Creation myths:** Everybody wants to know where the world and its creatures came from. Generally the world emerges from primordial darkness, often in the shape of an egg, through the work of a creator deity.

- **Cosmogeny:** Many myths describe the way the world, the heavens, the sea, and the underworld are put together and how the sun and moon travel around them.

- **The origin of humanity:** Humans had to come from somewhere, and many mythologies describe their origin. They're often the pet creation of a deity dabbling in mud.

- **Flood stories:** Many mythologies have a story about gods who were unhappy with their first version of humans and destroyed the world with floods to get a clean start. Usually one man and one woman survive.

- **The introduction of disease and death:** Myths often describe the first humans as living in a paradise that is marred when someone introduces unhappiness. The Greek story of Pandora's box is one of the best-known myths.

✔ **Afterlife:** Many people think that the soul continues to exist after the body dies; myths explain what happens to the soul.

✔ **The presence of supernatural beings:** Every body of mythology features deities and other supernatural entities. Individual deities often are in charge of particular aspects of the world or human life. Some supernatural beings are good, and some are evil; humans and the good gods fight the evil ones.

✔ **The end of the world:** Although the world has already ended at least once in most mythologies (usually through a great flood), some myths also have a plan for how it will end in the future.

✔ **The dawn of civilization:** Humans had to learn to live like people, not animals, and often the gods helped them. A common story tells of the theft of fire by a deity who brings it to humans.

✔ **Foundation myths:** People who founded empires like to believe that historical reasons help to explain why it was inevitable that they vanquished their enemies and built a city in a certain place. A myth can help explain these reasons.

One reason that myths recur is that people have always moved around and talked with one another, even in the days before they started writing things down. People carried myths to one another just as they brought trade goods and disease. For example, many North American Indians have flood stories as part of their mythologies. Some of the first Europeans they encountered were Christian missionaries, who told them Christian stories, including, no doubt, the biblical story of Noah and the flood. The North American Indians may not have heard of the idea of the destruction of the world in a great flood before being exposed to Europeans, but instead they may have borrowed the story from the Europeans.

The details of these stories are significant and have had far-reaching consequences. For example, many people have used myths to justify male domination of women (think of Eve emerging from Adam's rib in the Bible — he was there first). Myths also have been used to justify the oppression of one social group by another, and it's still happening today.

A Who's Who of Mythological Players

Myths have a fairly standard cast of characters. They always include divine beings, called deities or gods. Also present are humans who interact with gods; some of the extraspecial humans get to be heroes. Magical animals and tricksters, who live to stir things up, complete the list of players.

Deities

All bodies of myth have supernatural entities that hold power over the world and the people in it. These entities often are called gods and goddesses — the word *deity* is a neutral term that means god or goddess. Some cultures have many deities, and some have only one. Generally a culture has at least one creator deity and several other divine beings who divide up jobs such as driving the sun and moon, herding the dead, making crops grow, and so on. With this division of labor, people automatically knew which deity to ask for help — for example, a woman seeking help in childbirth knew not to waste her time praying to the rain god.

Antigods

The supernatural world isn't home only to benevolent deities; negative beings also live there and walk the earth with humans. Myths contain stories of devils, demons, dragons, monsters, and giants; these creatures fight both the gods and humans.

Heroes

Many myths feature heroes, who perform amazing feats of daring, strength, or cleverness. Some heroes are human, some are gods, and some are half-and-half; they're usually male. One feature common of mythological heroes is that their definitive characteristics are evident from childhood.

Culture heroes appear in myths bringing specific benefits to humans; for example, Prometheus was a culture hero to the ancient Greeks because he gave humans fire. See Chapter 7 for more on about this ancient Greek. In the mythology of Native Americans, the man who discovered tobacco on the spot where he had (earlier) discovered sex was doubly a culture hero. Chapter 23 has the complete lowdown.

Other heroes served as models of human accomplishment; for example, the Greek hero Heracles (also known as Hercules) was the biggest, strongest, most heroic guy ever. You can read more about him in Chapter 7. Heroes often played a role in *foundation myths,* myths that explain how kingdoms came to be where they are and why the people who lived there before don't deserve to live there anymore.

Tricksters

Myths are full of trickster characters. Some of these tricksters are helpful to people by outwitting their enemies and bringing them gifts such as fire. Others are not so nice — Loki in Norse myths is sometimes downright evil. See Chapter 14 for more about him. Tricksters subvert the social order, stirring things up either to thwart someone or for their own entertainment.

Tricksters are popular mythical characters. Native American tricksters were often animals that also could seem human-like; they were ambiguous creatures. Examples include the Coyote in the Southwest, the Mink in the Pacific Northwest, and Wisakedjak, or Whiskey Jack to the Europeans, a rabbit trickster hero known to Eastern tribes. Whiskey Jack may well be the mythological ancestor to Br'er Rabbit. Br'er Rabbit may also have had an African ancestor; in many parts of Africa, myths feature a rabbit trickster. See Chapter 23 for more about North American Indian myths.

Two American Myths

Some myths are firmly rooted in historical fact, and others are entirely made up. The easiest way to see the difference is to look at two American myths. One of these myths is based on a historical character and his historical actions. And another one is entirely fictional but an important myth nevertheless.

Johnny Appleseed, a cultural hero

Johnny Appleseed is a figure of mythology. He is also 100 percent historically factual. His real name was John Chapman, and he was a professional nurseryman (that is, he grew plants and sold them). He collected apple seeds from cider-making operations in Pennsylvania and then moved westward, planting a series of orchards between the Allegheny Mountains and Ohio. He gave away seeds to pioneers, but he also made a tidy profit off his enterprise.

But none of these historical facts are nearly as important as the mythological "truth" of Johnny Appleseed. As a figure of myth, he represents the pioneering spirit of the early history of the United States as people moved west to settle in new lands. He represents the conquest of the wilderness as settlers turned wild forests into productive farms. And he represents a set of values that Americans like to associate with the early builders of the nation: piety, charity, closeness to the earth, and independence.

Br'er Rabbit, American trickster

The myth of Br'er Rabbit is entirely fictional. Br'er (that is, "Brother") Rabbit (see Figure 1-1) and his tricks and adventures first appeared in print in 1879 in an Atlanta newspaper. This was the first of a number of stories about the tricky rabbit who outsmarts Mr. Fox, Mrs. Cow, and others again and again.

Figure 1-1:
Br'er Rabbit could have taught some human heroes a thing or two.

These stories were part of the folklore of the American Southeast before the Civil War and during the period of Reconstruction. All segments of the population, particularly African-American communities, enjoyed these stories. The Br'er Rabbit tales can be called myths because they convey important truths. For the slaves, Br'er Rabbit represented a hero who won, again and again, despite being in the power of others. When Joel Chandler Harris brought these stories to the attention of a wider American audience, Br'er Rabbit became a shared American myth. Americans like to root for underdogs and to believe that a hero can use his wits and his initiative to overcome obstacles. Br'er Rabbit never existed, of course, but he represents truths that are important to Americans' ideas about themselves.

Chapter 2

That's Our Story and We're Sticking to It: The Legacy

In This Chapter

▶ Discovering mythological elements in our culture

▶ Getting starry-eyed

▶ Celebrating the holidays

▶ Finding mythology in all types of art

▶ Turning myths into movies

Myths describe important truths by using symbols. The truths are things that ordinary language doesn't describe well: the relationship between humans and the divine, the nature of love, what happens after we die, and so on. The symbols are things from everyday life: women and men, sons and daughters and fathers and mothers, gifts, storms, animals, plants. This combination — really important stuff in stories about ordinary things — is magical, and that's why myths stick around.

Many myths have managed to survive for thousands of years, long after the death of the civilization that created them. Myths travel across continents and oceans. Even today, in a world that supposedly is rational and scientific, myths are everywhere, and still very powerful. People want heroes; they want to believe in monsters; they want stories that explain how the world works.

Mythology has always been everywhere in the art and literature of the world, and this is particularly true of Greek and Roman mythology in the art and literature of Europe. For this reason, things that recall those myths often seem familiar, important, or just plain classy.

This chapter mentions some of the ways these myths are still with us today. Along the way, it should become clear to you why mythology is worth knowing.

Around the Block and Through the Wringer: The Journey of One Myth

Myths can stick around for thousands of years, serving different people's needs at different times and changing all the while. Myths don't have one "true" version; stories and characters can be different things to different people, while still retaining their mythical stature.

Troilus's journey from obscurity to fame

As an example of a myth that has grown through the ages, here's the long, long journey of the myth of Troilus, Prince of Troy. Troilus started out as a very minor character in Homer's *Iliad,* but through time and the work of different authors who took an interest in him, he turned into a major Shakespearean hero whose girlfriend's name is familiar to most Americans today (read on to see how!).

The pathetic Trojan prince

Troilus didn't start in the mythological Big League. He first shows up in Homer's poem, the *Iliad,* which tells the story of part of the Trojan War. The full details of this story appear in Chapter 7, but Troilus in Homer is so insignificant that we don't even mention him there! Troilus was one of the (many, many) sons of Priam, King of Troy. He appeared very briefly in the *Iliad* mostly as a literary device: Achilles killed him right away, which set up Achilles as the destroyer of Troy and foreshadowed his murder of Hector, Troilus's more important older brother.

Later Greek and Roman writers added to Troilus's story — they either made up new parts of it or wrote down other pre-existing versions of the myth that differed from what Homer wrote. In these versions, a prophecy said that if Troilus reached the age of 20, then the Greeks would never defeat Troy. But Achilles killed Troilus in a temple of the god Apollo. This turned him into a kind of "savior" of Troy, except that he died so he didn't save the city.

Early pulp romance: Medieval authors rediscover Troilus

Now jump about 1,500 years into the future to the twelfth century CE. During the "High Middle Ages," a French writer named Benoît de Sainte-Maure, picked up the story of Troilus and turned it into a romance: the *Roman de Troie* ("The Romance of Troy"). De Sainte-Maure portrayed Troilus as an innocent young man, and he also gave the young Trojan hero a girlfriend:

Briseida. (In Homer, Briseis was Achilles's girlfriend; de Sainte-Maure thought it would be nice to give her to Troilus instead with a slight name change.)

His story emphasized the tragedy of a lover betrayed. Troilus and Briseida were deeply in love and made all sorts of promises to each other. But then Briseida was captured by the Greeks and fell in love with the Greek hero Diomedes. Poor Troilus, his heart broken, was killed by Achilles. So Troilus served to tell a moving story of romantic love and tragic innocence.

On to Italy and England

Giovanni Boccaccio, a medieval Italian writer, retold the story of Troilus around 1338 in his work *Il Filostrato* ("The Guy Betrayed by Love") and changed the girlfriend's name to Cressida — presumably to help keep her straight from Achilles's woman Briseis. Geoffrey Chaucer told it again, in English, a few years later, as "Troilus and Criseyde." Both of these writers also emphasized the romantic tragedy of the story.

William Shakespeare, in 1601 or 1602, wrote the most famous version of the story, in his *Tragedie of Troylus and Cressida*. Shakespeare followed de Sainte-Maure, Boccaccio, and Chaucer (for the most part) in his plot, but he used the story for a different purpose, which was to show how "heroic" characters can act like completely despicable jerks. He wrote this play during a time when politics in England were somewhat chaotic, and he used this old, old myth of Troilus (originally from the eighth century BCE) to say something important about politics in the world of the seventeenth century CE.

Troilus and Cressida are still around

Troilus and Cressida live on in our world because people still find Shakespeare's play to be enlightening and meaningful and in more everyday ways as well. For example, in the 1990s, Toyota made a car called the Cressida — though it would be possible to question the wisdom of this, given the fact that Cressida is famous for betraying her lover and leaving him to die. In 1986, when the Voyager II spaceship flew by Uranus and discovered a new moon orbiting that planet, this new heavenly body — only 67 kilometers in diameter — assumed the name Cressida.

And that is how myths survive and change. Troilus wasn't even important originally, but his name and story served Homer and the other Greeks and Romans, then the French, Italian, and English writers of the Middle Ages. After 1,500 years, he got a girlfriend, whose name changed a few times, and she survived on to our own time, as a car and as a tiny moon around a far-away planet.

Pop Culture

Myths are stories about important things — life, death, immortality, power, love, nature — so the names in myths are powerful. These names, even if they are from very ancient and very foreign myths, still evoke emotions. Myths are symbols, and the folks who sell stuff — cars, trinkets, books, movies — give them names that, they hope, will symbolize things you like.

They're out on the street

Driving down the street, going on vacation — you can't avoid the impact of myths. They're everywhere! Some of it comes from marketing to emotions; some of it is because myths are just cool and people like to buy stuff with mythical names.

Driving it all home

If your Toyota Cressida should betray you (see above) — and we doubt that it will, because our family is fanatically loyal to Toyotas — you can probably hitch a ride in another mythologically named car, perhaps even a Legend (from Acura).

Driving a Toyota Avalon should make you feel like King Arthur himself, and you should feel very, very rich in a Cadillac El Dorado. And a trip to the beach with the kids might feel like it takes twenty years, like the journey of Odysseus, but unlike that Greek hero in his ship, you'll have lots of cup holders in a Honda Odyssey.

Jewelry and baubles

The symbolism of myths isn't limited to cars. Any tourist to the American Southwest will have no trouble coming home with a dozen T-shirts featuring Kokopelli, the flute-playing trickster from North American Indian mythology (for more on him, check out Chapter 22). He symbolizes the ancient art and culture of the region, a spirit of lively independence from the straight-and-narrow, and he has come to be an easily recognized symbol of that part of the country in general.

People all over the place wear necklaces with pendants in the shape of an ankh (like a cross but with an oval top). This symbol comes from the mythology of Egypt and symbolized (for many thousands of years, back into deep antiquity) life and happiness. The famous King Tut incorporated it into his name, which in its fullest form is TutANKHamun). The ankh still symbolized life and happiness, and is especially popular as a symbol of the Coptic Church. The Ankh is also a modern symbol of Africa and its contributions to world culture (contributions which much of the world spent a lot of time and energy ignoring or disparaging).

Up in the sky . . . it's a bird . . . it's a plane . . . no, it's a myth!

The sky is chock-full of myths. The Greek and Roman gods lived in the sky (well, way high up on Mount Olympus, at least), and many mortals who had done something important got to go live there, too. So people looked for those gods and heroes in the patterns of stars, and they found them!

The gods are in the stars shining brightly

Even rational, scientific astronomers of the twenty-first century see myths in the night sky in the form of constellations. Pegasus, the winged horse that was born from the blood of the monstrous Medusa, is up there, as is the half-man, half-horse Centaur. During the winter in the Northern Hemisphere, Orion the Hunter is one of the most obvious constellations — easy to find because of his bright belt of three stars. Orion, in Greek mythology, died after being stung by a scorpion, but he is safe in the sky, because he sets in the west just as Scorpio rises in the east. Folks in the Southern Hemisphere can see the Argo, the ship that Jason and the Argonauts sailed to Colchis, to steal the Golden Fleece. (For more on Jason, see Chapter 6.)

All the planets are named after Greek and Roman gods (including Earth, who was Gaia to the Greeks): Mercury, the messenger; Venus, the goddess of love; Mars, the war-god; Jupiter, the king; Saturn, the father of the gods; Neptune, god of the sea; Uranus, the ancient sky-god; and dark Pluto, god of the dead. (For more on these gods, see Chapters 4, 5, and 10.)

The stars weren't just Greek

One easy-to-find constellation (or, technically, "star cluster," since it doesn't actually make a picture) is the *Pleiades,* or the "Seven Sisters." The Greeks said these were the daughters of Atlas: Alcyone, Merope, Celaeno, Taygeta, Maia, Electra, and Asterope.

But the Greeks didn't have a monopoly on myths, of course, and they don't have a monopoly on constellations, either. The Egyptians knew these seven stars, too, and some scholars think that the seven chambers of the Great Pyramid intentionally echo those seven stars. The Blackfoot Indians in North America knew this group of stars as the "six brothers" (one of the seven stars is not very clear, which the Greeks noted as well). The Blackfoot story tells of six boys who were too poor to wear nice buffalo robes, and when their friends laughed at them, they told everyone to get lost and moved up into the sky. In the southern islands of the Pacific, the Polynesians know these seven stars as *Mata-riki,* or the "Little Eyes."

NASA loves mythology, too

Because of all the mythological names already up there, it made sense for NASA to choose mythological names for the programs and machines that got humans to the moon. The first part of the U.S. space program was Project Mercury, named after the messenger god of the Greeks; this was to "send a message" to the Soviet Union that America was in the race. The Mercury (see Chapter 10) capsules were launched with Atlas (see Chapter 3) rocket boosters, named after the Titan who held up the sky.

Project Gemini was next, named after the twins (see Chapter 6) Castor and Pollux ("twins" in Latin is *gemini*), because the Gemini capsules held two astronauts. The Gemini astronauts rode into space atop Titan rockets. Finally, human beings made it to the moon with Project Apollo, named after the Greek god — in the mentality of the Cold War, a victory in the "space race" by the United States represented "light" winning over communist "darkness." Apollo astronauts rode atop Saturn rockets. Saturn was the "big daddy" of the Titans.

Myths on the Page, on the Wall, and in the Concert Hall

When ancient people, anywhere in the world, painted anything or sculpted anything, they usually chose subjects from their own mythology. When people learned to write, they started by writing down their myths. But myths stick around, and the myths of the ancient world keep showing up in art and literature right up to the present day.

Art without myth? Impossible!

The mythology of Greece and Rome has been painted and sculpted for three thousand years, and not always by Greeks and Romans. After the fall of the Roman Empire in Western Europe, the old pagan myths took a vacation from art for a few centuries. This was for two reasons:

- ✔ In the north, where Christianity was dominant, artists tended to focus on Christian themes and avoided non-Christian ones.

- ✔ In the south around the Mediterranean, where Islam had enjoyed its rapid rise, artists did not do figurative art (that is, art that looked like people, animals, plants, or anything real) at all. This was because the Koran (and the Hebrew and Christian Bibles, for that matter) forbade the making of "graven images." So Islamic artists focused on abstract decorations and calligraphy (incredibly fancy letters).

But then the Renaissance came to Europe. *Renaissance* means "rebirth," and in this case what was "reborn" was the knowledge of the ancient, pre-Christian Greek and Roman world. In the world of art, the Renaissance led artists to pay more attention to the natural world (as opposed to the world of the divine) and to include more Greek and Roman mythological content in their works.

So Michelangelo painted pagan prophets on the ceiling of the Sistine Chapel, right alongside prophets from the Christian Bible. This illustrates (literally!) the fact that mythologies tend to pile up, rather than replacing each other. Bernini sculpted David, a figure from Hebrew history and mythology, and Perseus from Greek mythology.

Myths are darn good stories

The same tendency went on in the world of literature. Myths make good foundations for books. Myths are symbolic ways of telling the truth, and (better yet) they are *shared* symbols. This makes myths useful for writers, who need to take their own, private, ideas and relate them to important truths that readers can recognize. So behind many (if not most) good books, readers can find a good myth (or two, or a dozen)!

The divine Dante

Dante Alighieri lived in Florence, Italy, during the thirteenth century. Dante's most well known work is his *Comedy,* more famously known as the *Divine Comedy.* This is a very long poem in three parts that describes how the poet was given a tour of hell, purgatory, and heaven; the three parts are named after those three places, "Inferno" (hell), "Purgatorio" (purgatory), and "Paradiso" (heaven).

The poem is a "comedy," by the way, because the main character starts off in a bad situation (a midlife crisis) and ends up in a good situation (aware of the full glory of God).

Like Michelangelo with the Sistine Chapel, Dante populates his poem with images from Christian mythology and Greek and Roman mythology. His guide through hell and purgatory is Virgil, the Roman poet who wrote the Aeneid, which tells the foundation myth of the Roman people. Hell is particularly full, of course, with (a) people Dante knew personally in Florence, (b) corrupt Church officials and politicians, (c) figures from history, and (d) mythological characters. Odysseus is down there (for lying), as is the warrior Achilles (for being "wrathful"). Dante even used Greek mythology to describe the lay of the land in his Christian vision of hell and heaven: Before crossing from purgatory to heaven, Dante crosses Lethe (pronounced "lee-thee"), which in Greek mythology was the "river of forgetfulness" that caused the dead to forget what it was like to live.

Myths in English literature

In England, folks generally didn't know how to read ancient Greek until the 1700s. William Shakespeare used stuff from Greek myths in his plays in the 1600s, but he got his material from mostly Latin and Italian sources.

Between 1713 and 1720 Alexander Pope translated Homer's *Iliad* and *Odyssey* from Greek into English. This made Pope really, really rich (he got £10,000 for this book, and that was in 1713 money!). It also made ordinary folks who knew only English aware of all of the mythology contained in Homer's poetry. It also set Pope up for another famous poem, this one a parody of Greek epic called the *Dunciad*. Because the *Iliad* is the "Poem about Ilium," the *Dunciad* is the "Poem about a Dunce;" this poem was Pope's chance to poke fun at all of his critics.

In the 1800s, English poets and painters, particularly those known as *the Romantics,* produced a lot of art about mythological themes. Alfred, Lord Tennyson, was a particularly popular poet of the Victorian period, and his first published volume of poetry contained two mythological works: "The Lotus Eaters," was based on one of the adventures that the Greek hero Odysseus had on his journey home from Troy; and "The Lady of Shalott" is based on the mythology of Arthur and the Knights of the Round Table. One of Tennyson's most famous poems is "Ulysses," named after the Roman name of Odysseus. In this poem, Odysseus has grown old and, after complaining about how boring his life is, plans his last adventure. Its last words — " . . . to strive, to seek, to find, and not to yield" — are quoted every spring in thousands of graduation speeches.

Modern mythical literature

In the twentieth century, artists were just as likely to use stories from mythology, but often with some sort of twist. George Bernard Shaw wrote a play called *Pygmalion* in 1913 that was based on the myth of the woman-hating artist who made a sculpture of a woman, then fell in love with his own creation. But in Shaw's play — which was later turned into a musical, *My Fair Lady* — the artist becomes a professor of *phonetics* (he studied the sounds that make up language) who takes a woman from the lower classes, teaches her to speak the speech of the upper classes, then falls in love with her.

After the First World War, writers were more likely to put an ironic twist on mythological themes. So W. H. Auden's poem "The Shield of Achilles" contrasts the ethics of war in Homer's poetry with the horrors of war in the twentieth century. And Arthur Miller's play, *Death of a Salesman,* uses Greek tragedies, which were almost all about mythological themes, as its model. However, it has a very un-heroic main character, a traveling salesman, as its "tragic hero."

They've got the music

Composers of music in the 1800s and into the early twentieth century loved mythological themes. Richard Wagner, the German composer, is probably most famous for this, with his sequence of four operas about Germanic myths: *Das Rheingold* (The Rhine-gold), *Die Walküre* (The Valkyrie); *Der Junge Siegfried* (The Young Siegfried), and *Götterdämmerung* (The Twilight of the

Gods). These are, collectively, called *Der Ring des Nibelungen* (*The Ring of the Nibelung*). Another German Richard, Richard Strauss, at the end of the nineteenth century wrote music based on the Greek myths of Theseus and Ariadne, and Electra.

It's a denim-tie occasion

Mythology in art isn't always something you have to rent formalwear to see. The other day, when we were reading Maurice Sendak's book *Where the Wild Things Are* (published by Harper Collins Juvenile Books) to our 3-year-old, we noticed that this children's story is essentially Homer's *Odyssey* in a very short form: The Hero is mischievous and banished from normal life against his will; on his journey, he faces danger and overcomes it through force of character; he is offered a position of great honor in a faraway land; but he chooses to return home, even if that means facing the problems he left there; in the end, all is well. A good story for our kid, and a good story for people for the last three millennia.

Movies are a good place to go looking for myths. Walt Disney's classic *Snow White,* for example, will seem very familiar to anyone who knows the Greek story of Persephone. Persephone was separated from her mother, the kind goddess Demeter, and kidnapped by the god of the underworld. Ultimately, she has to spend part of the year "dead" (married to the underworld god) and part of the year alive. Disney's story follows this pattern, but makes the female characters (except for the heroine) bad, and the male characters good. Snow White flees from her evil stepmother and comes to live with dwarves (who work underground). In the end, her mother "kills" her, but she is "awakened" by a passing prince. If you watch the movie closely, you can see Snow White actually falls into the underworld before meeting up with the dwarves!

Back in the 1980s, the controversial film *Angel Heart* retold the (controversial) Greek tragedy of Oedipus. And more recently, the Cohen Brothers' film, *O Brother Where Art Thou?,* retold Homer's *Odyssey,* more or less (the main character is even named Ulysses, the Roman name for Odysseus).

Mythical themes can be found in lots of other movies; try to look for them!

Learn Your Myths, Earn $461,000,000!

The fact is, myths are important, perhaps ultimately important. People know that some things that are true can't be described with scientific or theological language. Those truths have to come through symbolic stories. When people find stories that contain symbols that point to those important truths, they respond.

George Lucas knew that, which is why his first *Star Wars* film grossed $461 million dollars (and those were 1977 dollars!). *Star Wars* tells a story that is strongly mythological. Rather than give away all of the secrets, try this challenge (on the reasonable assumption that you are not one of the eight people in the world who has not seen the original *Star Wars* film): Read the rest of this book and find all of the different myths that resonate in George Lucas's film about a young man who leaves his family's farm to get involved in events of universal significance.

May the Force be with you!

Part II
It Started Here, Folks: Greek Mythology

The 5th Wave   By Rich Tennant

©RICHTENNANT

"It says here that because Persephone ate a
pomegranate seed she had to spend all year
in the Underworld except for 4 months each
year that she spent with her mother. Some
scholars say it was 6 months. It probably
just _felt_ like 6 months."

In this part . . .

Ah, the Greeks — the culture that forms the foundation of Western Civilization. In this part, you learn about the Greek gods and goddesses and some of the best known stories about them. Then you walk through a quick survey of Homer's *Iliad* and *Odyssey* and the famous Greek tragedies everyone reads in high school. If you need help getting the Oedipus story straight, this is the place to look.

Chapter 3

Greek Creation Myths and Really Ancient Greek Gods

• •

In This Chapter

▶ Creating the world, violently

▶ Watching to see which gods come out on top

▶ Making humans: making humans warm, making humans miserable

• •

The ancient Greeks were not particularly uptight about keeping their collection of myths consistent. We find completely contradictory versions of certain stories living happily side-by-side, with no one seeming to mind. This is one feature of myth — it isn't science; you don't have to get *the* right answer, only *a* right answer. On Tuesday it may be useful to think that a Titan made humans out of mud; on Wednesday, metal may seem more appropriate.

One thing that is consistent across Greek myths about the world's creations is that the business wasn't pretty. All of the nastiness that goes on between human beings also went on between human beings and the gods, and between the gods themselves, according to the Greeks. It was all about getting, keeping, or getting back the upper hand.

The short version of the creation of the world, according to the Greeks, would go like this: Scary old gods came first; they got stomped down by their kids, who were better looking, younger gods, who then created humans; humans and gods jockeyed for advantage; humans won a few rounds, but got more and more miserable.

The earliest versions of these stories come from the seventh century BCE. Life must have been pretty rough then, so it isn't surprising to see creation myths that paint a pretty dark picture.

Here Comes the Sun (and a Whole Mess of Other Stuff): Creation At Last!

The most complete version of the Greek creation myths that survives is a poem called the *Theogony* ("Birth of the Gods") by a poet named Hesiod, who lived in the late eighth or early seventh century BCE (that is, the low-numbered 700s or high-numbered 600s BCE). Not much is known about Hesiod except that his dad lost all of his money when his ship sank, and his brother tried to rob him of his inheritance. These two facts may account for the tone of what you're about to read.

Remember that what we're about to describe is just one version of the Greek creation myth — a particularly good and complete one, but by no means the only one.

In the beginning, there was Chaos. Darkness covered the earth. Hesiod's creation story doesn't involve something being created from nothing; there was stuff (Chaos), but it was shapeless, mixed-up, and dark.

The first generation of gods

After Chaos, five divinities came into being (it isn't clear how) and began giving shape to things, separating the muddle into specific places and times, and to set the stage for more creation. The divinities were: Gaia (the mother Earth), Tartarus (the underworld), Erebus (the darkness that covers the underworld), Night (darkness that covers Earth), and Eros (Love).

Night and Erebus got together and had some children: Hemera (Day), Phôs (Light), and (a cheery set of quintuplets) Doom, Death, Misery, Deceit, and Discord.

Discord later gave birth to the following other forces: Murder, Slaughter, Battle, and Crime.

The earth is born

Earth held the Sky up above itself. Or maybe we should say "herself," because Earth, called "Gaia," was female and the Sky, called "Uranus" (Earth's child) was male.

Gifts of the Stork: The Offspring of Mother Earth and Father Sky

Gaia and Uranus had a bunch of kids. First they had a bunch of monsters; then, perhaps having worked out the kinks in the system, they produced some gods known as Titans.

Our children are real monsters!

Gaia and Uranus's first three kids were monsters with100 hands (Hekatoncheires) and 50 heads each, which must have been a bit surprising to their parents.

The next three were the *Cyclopes,* giants with one eye in the middle of their foreheads. They were as big as mountains and immensely strong (and not to be confused with another batch of Giants that show up later). The three Cyclopes were

- ✔ Brontes ("Thunderer")
- ✔ Steropes ("Lightning Flash")
- ✔ Arges ("Shining Guy")

Eventually, these three would get jobs manufacturing the thunderbolts that Zeus (their nephew who hadn't been born yet) used to blow folks up.

The word *"Cyclops"* means round-eyed or wheel-eyed. The first part of the word is in the modern words "cycle," "bicycle," and "encyclopedia;" the second part gives us words such as "optical," "optician," and *"myopia"* (near-sightedness). If you have only one of these round-eyed monsters, you have a "Cyclops," which rhymes with "high-tops"; if you have a bunch of them, you have "Cyclopes," which rhymes with "high-top, please."

A Cyclops named Polyphemus also appears in the *Odyssey.* In that poem, the Cyclopes are the sons of the sea god Poseidon.

Meet the Titans, the second generation of gods

Uranus and Gaia gave birth to many more children, but their most famous batch of kids were the *Titans.* They were big and strong, too. Uranus hated all of these kids, and as each one was born, he shoved it back up into Gaia. Gaia didn't like that. Nevertheless, the Titans, their six sons and six daughters, were

- ✔ **Oceanus:** God of the Sea.
- ✔ **Thetis:** Sister and wife of Oceanus.
- ✔ **Hyperion:** God of the Sun.
- ✔ **Theia:** Sister and wife of Hyperion.
- ✔ **Themis:** An earth goddess.
- ✔ **Rhea:** An earth goddess.
- ✔ **Mnemosyne:** Goddess of Memory.
- ✔ **Iapetus:** No notable responsibilities.
- ✔ **Coeus:** No notable responsibilities.
- ✔ **Phoebe:** No notable responsibilities.
- ✔ **Crius:** No notable responsibilities.
- ✔ **Cronos:** The brightest, strongest, and cleverest of all.

These Titans were the generation before the better-known Olympian gods — Zeus and others — who are discussed in the following section.

Gaia's sweet revenge and the prodigal son

Gaia was understandably mad about Uranus shoving her kids back up into her body (they were still alive in there), so she asked her other children, the Cyclopes and the Titans, to help her out. One of her sons, the Titan Cronos, agreed to attack his dad for her. Gaia made a huge sickle out of flint, and gave it to Cronos with some pretty explicit instructions.

When Uranus came to have sex with Gaia, he found a nasty surprise waiting for him. Cronos (who was, remember, inside Gaia's womb) reached out with the sickle and attacked Uranus, or specifically, that part of Uranus that was nearest at hand. Cronos cut off his father's genitals and threw them into the sea. From the blood were born several more monsters: the Giants and the Furies. (See Chapter 5 for more on the Furies.) The full family tree of all the Greek gods can be found in Figure 3-1.

As Uranus's genitals fell into the water, the sea foamed up like certain headache remedies, and the foam produced the goddess Aphrodite. Her name means "gift of the sea-foam." She floated around in the sea for a while, and then came to shore on the island of Cyprus, which is why she is often called Cyprian Aphrodite.

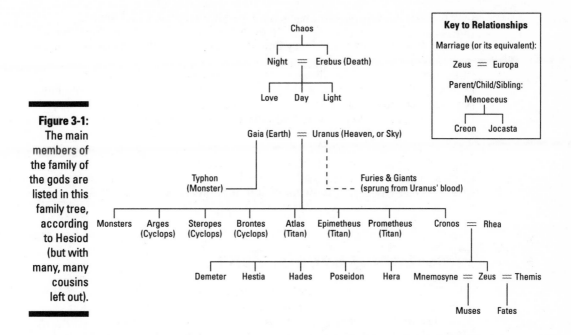

Figure 3-1:
The main members of the family of the gods are listed in this family tree, according to Hesiod (but with many, many cousins left out).

Because Aphrodite became the goddess of love, the circumstances of her birth — the result of a nasty bit of domestic violence — are somewhat ironic. Additionally, in the order of things here in Hesiod, Eros is an ancient god, older than Aphrodite; however, in subsequent Greek myths, Eros shows up as Aphrodite's son, a young man. And in another mythological paradox, some Greek myths say that Aphrodite was the daughter of the goddess Dione and the Titan Oceanus. This kind of inconsistency didn't bother the Greeks, so you shouldn't let it bother you. (For more about Aphrodite, see Chapter 5.)

Hesiod doesn't say so, but the marital spat between Gaia and Uranus is probably why, in other myths, the Titan Atlas, and not Earth herself, holds up the sky.

The Third Generation of Gods: The Olympians

Now we're getting closer to the birth of the more familiar Greek gods, the third generation of gods who were known as the Olympian Gods, because they eventually made their home on Mount Olympus.

After Cronos castrated his father Uranus (see preceding section for more about this), Cronos set himself up as king of Heaven. He married his sister, the Titan Rhea, and they had a bunch of kids.

Like his father, Cronos didn't want all of his kids to live. He had heard a prophecy that one of his sons would dethrone him and he had no intention of allowing that to happen. So every time Rhea had a baby, he swallowed it whole.

Rhea, like Gaia, wasn't at all happy to see all of her children eaten by their father. So she did what we would expect a young bride to do: She asked her parents, Gaia and Uranus, for help. Gaia and Uranus had some experience in these matters (and apparently had gotten over any lasting bitterness from their own marital difficulties), so they came up with a plan.

When Rhea had her sixth child, Zeus, she smuggled him away to the island of Crete and gave her husband a baby-sized rock wrapped in a blanket instead. Cronos obviously didn't know much about babies, because he swallowed the stone and never gave it another thought.

First among equals: Zeus

After his mother smuggled him away (see preceding section) Zeus grew up safely on Crete. The Nymphs gave him milk from a magical goat named Amalthea, and the *Curetes,* minor gods who had the job of protecting him, banged their spears against their swords every time baby Zeus cried, and that way Cronos never heard him. (See Chapter 5 for more about nymphs.)

Zeus grew up. He had no particular reason to love his dad, so he got together with his grandmother Gaia and they made Cronos throw up the children he had eaten. The first thing Cronos tossed was the stone Rhea had given him instead of Zeus, so he knew he had been tricked. The other five babies had grown up in his belly, and they emerged as full-fledged deities. These deities were the *Olympians:*

- **Hera:** Goddess of marriage.
- **Poseidon:** God of the sea.
- **Hades:** God of the underworld.
- **Hestia:** Goddess of the hearth.
- **Demeter:** Goddess of crops and the harvest.

The Olympians clash with the Titans

During his fight with his father, Zeus cut off Cronos' genitals — like father like son! — which dropped into the sea just as Uranus's privates had.

Dirty Harry feels lucky: Zeus punishes the Titans and battles the Giants

After castrating his father Cronos (details in the preceding section), Zeus bound the Titans in *Tartarus,* the underworld. He sentenced Atlas, Prometheus's brother, to hold up the sky on his shoulders.

Zeus gets his thunderbolts

Gaia had one more baby, the monster Typhon. *Typhon* had 100 heads and was covered with flame. But Zeus by now had taken control of thunder and lightning, and shot down Typhon with his thunderbolt. Typhon's hopes of terrorizing the universe were ended, but he still needed a job, so he moved to Sicily, where he supplied the volcanic magma for Mount Etna.

Cool thrones for everybody!

After this, the Giants (the ones born when Cronos cut off Uranus's testicles) rebelled against Zeus's control. Zeus and his siblings, aided by the hero Heracles, beat the Giants and sent them down to the underworld. Now Zeus and his brothers and sisters were the ultimate rulers of heaven and earth.

Zeus really showed his stuff in the way he escaped the fate of his father, Cronos, and his grandfather, Uranus. After the dust had settled from the Battle with the Titans, Zeus married Metis (a goddess who was the personification of "Cunning Intelligence").

Just like his father before him, Zeus received a prophecy that his wife would bear a child who would become King of the Gods. Instead of waiting for the child to be born, Zeus was proactive, and swallowed his wife. The child was born anyway, but it came out of Zeus's head — thus avoiding the important detail of the prophecy that Metis would bear the child. The baby was Athena, the wise goddess, who, although she was Daddy's girl, had a lot of her mom's cunning intelligence in her.

The Creation of People

The most common Greek story of the creation of humans (recounted by the author Pausanias) says that the Titan Prometheus and his brother Epimetheus got the job of creating all the creatures on the earth. Prometheus was wise; his name means "forethought." Epimetheus, on the other hand, was scatter-brained; his name means "afterthought."

Prometheus sat down and made creatures out of mud. Epimetheus gave them gifts of skills, abilities, and protection — he gave the birds wings, the lions and tigers claws and teeth, hard shells to turtles and snails — get the idea? But silly Epimetheus didn't plan ahead, so he ran out of gifts just before Prometheus created humans.

The Greeks said that Prometheus had made humans in the image of the gods. The main difference between animals and humans was that animals turn their faces down to look at the ground while humans walk upright and turn their faces up toward the sky. (We say "humans," but really the myths say "men." The ancients didn't go in much for gender equality.)

The Love-Hate Triangle: Prometheus, People, and Zeus

Zeus also was angry because Prometheus had arranged things so that whenever humans sacrificed animals to the gods, they'd get the best part and the gods would get the leftovers. Prometheus had cut up an ox and divided it into two parts. He put the meat inside the skin and piled the guts on top of it, and then he took the bones and wrapped them in the delectable fat, and asked Zeus to pick the pile he wanted. Zeus picked the fat (fat was valuable in those days . . . lots of calories to keep you warm) and the humans kept the meat. Zeus was aggravated.

However, forever after when people made a sacrifice, they burned the bones and fat for the gods and kept the edible parts. This was convenient, because humans got to have a good barbeque even as they honored the gods — a better deal for folks who had a hard enough time feeding themselves, much less burning up whole animals just for the gods.

Playing with fire

When the race of humans was young, the gods tried to keep the use of fire a secret. Prometheus decided to give his pet creation a technological boost by delivering the tool of fire into human hands. Even more exciting was that he stole it. He went up to heaven, lit his torch in the sun, hid the burning torch in a stalk of giant fennel, and smuggled it down to earth

Fire made humans more than a match for other animals — they could cook their food, warm their homes, make metal tools and weapons, and coin money. It was the ultimate tool for creating civilization. But boy was Zeus mad when he found out!

Prometheus bound (and tortured)

After the fire-stealing escapade, Zeus had it in for Prometheus. He captured him, dragged him to the Caucasus Mountains, and chained him to a rock. Every day an eagle came and tore out Prometheus's liver, which evidently grew back every night.

Prometheus the tragic psychic

Eagles constantly pecking Prometheus's belly wasn't punishment just for giving fire to humans. Zeus also had heard a prophecy that one of his sons would overthrow him. Prometheus was the only one who could tell him who that boy's mother would be. After being bound and tortured for a while, Prometheus agreed to give up his secret — the mother of the child who would overthrow Zeus was Metis. Zeus could now act to preserve his reign.

Heracles to the rescue

After Prometheus told Zeus the secret, Zeus arranged to set Prometheus free and increase the reputation of one of Zeus' favorite sons, Heracles. When Heracles was wandering the Earth — he traveled a great deal on his way to various tasks during his life (see Chapter 6) — he found Prometheus chained to his rock. He killed the eagle and let Prometheus go. Zeus approved, Prometheus was a free man (well . . . a free Titan), and Heracles got the bragging rights.

The World People Lived in, Courtesy of the Gods

After everything was created, the Greeks also developed their own ideas about geography. The Greeks thought the Earth was a round disk divided by the Mediterranean and Black Seas, as you can see by checking out Figure 3-2.

The Greeks called the Black Sea the *Euxine Sea,* meaning the Friendly to Guests Sea; this may have been a named based on wishful thinking, because archaeologists have found many ancient shipwrecks at the bottom of the Black Sea. The word "Mediterranean" is Latin for "in the middle of the lands."

The great river Oceanos flowed around the rim of the world.

Permanent vacation: The Hyperboreans

Up north of Oceanos was the land of the *Hyperboreans,* which some people think was Great Britain. It was a land of perpetual dancing, music, and happiness. The Muses lived near there, the locals were said to live for 1,000 years, and the god Apollo vacationed there in the winter.

Celebrity dinner parties: The Ethiopians

To the south of the Greeks was Ethiopia. The people of Ethiopia were, according to mythology, on good terms with the gods and liked to entertain. When the gods have meetings in Greek myths, one or another of them were often absent, off having dinner with the Ethiopians.

Evil wrapped up all pretty: Pandora, the first woman

Remember how Zeus was upset about Prometheus stealing fire and giving it to humans? He had punished Prometheus by chaining him to a rock — see "Prometheus bound (and tortured)" earlier in this chapter — but Zeus still had to do something to put the humans in their place.

So Zeus created a woman named Pandora. All the gods gave her cool presents such as beauty (from Aphrodite), persuasion (from Hermes), and musical talent (from Apollo). Her name means "the gift of all," or possibly "having all gifts." However, the big deal here was that she was created to be curious. They sent her to earth and gave her to Epimetheus.

Pandora's box (or jar) and the human condition

Gullible Epimetheus was thrilled with his new wife, even though his brother Prometheus had told him never to accept gifts from the gods. And Prometheus had been right. Pandora had brought another present with her, a jar that the gods had given her, telling her not to open it. But Pandora was so curious that she couldn't stand not knowing what was inside the jar, and one day she opened it.

In English today, we call Pandora's container a box, but in ancient Greek it was a jar.

That was a big mistake! As soon as she lifted the lid, hundreds of horrible monsters flew out, all the plagues and torments that have bothered humans ever after. Pandora slammed the lid down, but she was too late to stop the evils from flying out. She managed, however, to keep one last thing inside the jar — hope.

Is the jar half full or is it half empty?

You can view Pandora's jar two ways:

- ✓ The nice version is that hope remains the possession of people, helping us deal with all the nastiness of the world.

- ✓ On the other hand, given the general pessimistic tone of the Greek creation myths, we need to consider another way of reading this myth. Pandora let evils loose in the world but kept hope in the box. So violence, plague, famine, poverty, and hard labor are among us, *but hope isn't.*

The phrase "Pandora's Box" has come to mean anything best left unopened or not discussed for fear of what might come out of it.

A Flood and Rebirth Story

The Greeks had a myth about a great flood that killed everybody except a virtuous few, just like the Hebrews and the Mesopotamians (see Chapter 16 for more about those myths). The Greek flood story fits the general pattern of flood myths, which have a universal flood killing everyone except for one couple chosen by the gods.

We get the best version of the Greek flood story from the poet Ovid. He was Roman, from the first century BCE, but his long poem *Metamorphoses* is full of Greek myths. The theme of that poem is "things changing into other things," and a great flood was terrific material for him; he describes dolphins swimming through fields of grain, people rowing boats where they used to plow, and fish building nests in tall trees.

Human guest friendship goes awry

The story goes that Zeus, sensing that evil among human beings had gotten completely out of control, took a tour to see for himself. When he visited a certain tyrant named Lycaon, he saw that the rumors hadn't been even close to the truth. Zeus arrived at Lycaon's palace and announced that he was the god, Zeus, and asked to be invited for dinner. All the people bowed to worship him, but Lycaon laughed in Zeus's face and said, "A god, huh? We'll see about that!" Then he set out to test this so-called "god." He killed one of his prisoners of war, a guy from Molossia in Northern Greece, cooked him, and served him to Zeus for dinner. His assumption was that if his guest weren't a god, then he wouldn't notice that he was eating a Molossian P.O.W. The assumption was valid, but Lycaon evidently didn't take into account the possibility that his guest really was a god.

Zeus makes an executive decision

Zeus, to whom hospitality (the proper relationship between guests and hosts) was especially important, took one look at the entrée, blew Lycaon and his palace to bits with his lightning, canceled the rest of his fact-finding mission, and returned to Olympus.

The detail Ovid gives about the unfortunate man who ended up on Lycaon's menu — that he was Molossian — probably serves to make the tyrant's crime even worse, as far as Zeus was concerned. The people of Molossia had a special relationship with Zeus. There was an oracle of Zeus at Dodona, in Molossia. This was an old oak tree; people could ask their questions to the tree, and Zeus would give them answers. Alexander the Great was Molossian on his mother's side and used that fact to help his claim that he was the son of Zeus.

Zeus's task force: Let it rain good, honey

Zeus got his brother, the sea god Poseidon, to help him churn up a huge thunderstorm and flood the earth. It rained for nine days and nights. Water covered the land and only the top of Mount Parnassus stuck out. Almost everyone drowned. But Prometheus had protected his own family. He had told his son, Deucalion, to build a wooden chest and fill it with food and then get in it with his wife, Pyrrha, the daughter of Epimetheus and Pandora.

Deucalion and Pyrrha save the human race

Deucalion and Pyrrha finally landed on top of Mount Parnassus. The waters drained away, and they walked down the mountain until they found a temple. They heard a voice tell them to veil their heads and throw the bones of their mother behind themselves. Pyrrha was shocked, because it would be sacrilegious to desecrate her mother's bones. Surely no god would ask them to do that! They thought about this, and decided their "mother" was Gaia, the earth, and that her "bones" must be stones. So they threw some stones, and these turned into people.

So in the end, Gaia gave birth not only to all the gods, but to a new generation of people, too!

Chapter 4

Taller, Younger, and Better Looking Than You: The Olympian Gods

• •

In This Chapter

▶ Kickin' it with Zeus, king of the gods

▶ Peeking in on Poseidon, god of the sea

▶ Going down under with Hades, god of the underworld

▶ Hanging with the new, younger gods: Apollo, Hephaestus, Hermes, Ares, and Dionysus

• •

Most of the Greek gods supposedly lived on Mount Olympus. This mountain still exists in Northern Greece; the gods probably picked it because it's really tall and, therefore, close to heaven. Also, its top is often shrouded in clouds, making it mysterious.

The Greeks saw the world as divided into several parts: sky, earth, ocean, and underworld. They had deities to handle all of these. The gods divided the universe among themselves, but Zeus was the supreme king. Other gods handled various aspects of human existence — medicine, music, love, wine, and the sun. Everything considered, they kept things running for humans, and occasionally interfered in mortal lives.

This chapter hits the main gods, but other folks turn up in myths from time to time. Sometimes old gods got subsumed into new ones but didn't always lose their names. Suffice it to say that there were many, many deities — someone for everyone.

Zeus, Poseidon, and Hades: Big Daddy and His Brothers

According to most ancient writers, Zeus, Poseidon, and Hades were brothers, the sons of Rhea and Cronos. After they conquered the Titans and other monsters (see Chapter 3), they divided up the world among themselves. They did so by drawing lots, which is like drawing straws or throwing dice. Here is how they came out:

- Poseidon got the oceans and seas.
- Hades got the underworld and all the dead people.
- Zeus got the skies.

Because Zeus got the skies, that made him king of all the gods.

Much of this information comes from a poem called *Theogony* ("Birth of the Gods"), by a man named Hesiod.

King Zeus, lover of women and thunderbolts

As king of heaven, Zeus controlled thunder, lightning, clouds, and rain. He was known as the sky god, and like every god or goddess, he had a special symbol — the eagle/oak grove. The Greeks believed that lightning happened when Zeus hurled his thunderbolt down from heaven like a javelin.

You can call me Ray, or you can call me Jay . . .

Zeus, like most of the Greek Gods, had various *epithets* — second names, similar to nicknames only more seriously intended — depending on what a person expected him to do. Here are a few:

- **Zeus Xenios:** Means "Guest Zeus." Using this name, travelers looking for a place to stay prayed to him, because he made sure that hosts treated their guests right.
- **Zeus the Thunderer:** If someone were looking for some rain, Zeus the Thunderer was a better choice.
- **Zeus Eleutherios:** Means "Freedom Zeus." Athenians living under a democratic government who found themselves in a war against the King of Persia prayed to him for strength in battle.
- **Zeus Nephelegereta:** Means "Zeus the Cloud Gatherer." This was Zeus when he was sending thunderstorms. Along those same lines was *Zeus Keraunos*, or "Thunderbolt Zeus."

The Greeks knew that other cultures had different names for gods, but they assumed that any king of the gods, whatever his name, was Zeus. So they used the names of foreign gods as epithets for Zeus. Ammon was chief god of the Egyptian city of Thebes. (A city the Greeks found impressive.) So, the Greeks referred to him as *Zeus-Ammon*. This was a good way for them to cover all their bases.

Scholars believe that Zeus actually was a combination of gods from various ancient lands. Whenever the worship of Zeus arrived in a city that already had a god, the two were joined together under Zeus's name. That may be one reason why Zeus had so many affairs with mortal women — cities liked to claim that their rulers were descended from a god, and Zeus eventually ended up with all the credit.

Does he pass the wedding-ring finger check?

Zeus was married to the goddess Hera. Hera was a complicated goddess, sometimes worshipped as a goddess of the countryside (and gardens and wild animals), sometimes worshipped as a protector of cities (especially the city of Argos). But after her marriage to Zeus, she mostly represents royalty, and *Queen Hera* is her most common epithet. Marriage was one human institution associated with Hera, which is somewhat ironic, given the extent to which her marriage to Zeus was usually on the rocks. See Chapter 5 for some of stories about Hera's relationship with her husband; those two would have been welcome guests on certain TV talk shows.

Yeah, baby, I'm a god . . . so what's your sign?

Zeus loved human women and visited those of his choosing quite often. He liked to change his shape so that people couldn't spot him; some of his disguises were pretty weird. These couplings usually resulted in semidivine offspring and Hera going off the deep end with violent jealousy. Here are a few of his more well-known lovers:

- **Danaë:** He visited her in the form of a golden shower. She gave birth to the hero Perseus.

- **Alcmena:** The mother of Heracles, Zeus came to her in the shape of her husband. He spent the night with her, and then her husband came home and was surprised to find his wife not very enthusiastic in bed — she must have been worn out! She gave birth to twins; Heracles was Zeus's son, and the other baby was her husband's.

- **Leda:** Zeus turned into a swan to visit Leda, wife of King Tyndareus of Sparta. She had two immortal children with him:

  - Helen of Troy

  - Pollux, of the duo Castor and Pollux

Because of the form Zeus took for his affair with Leda, these kids were hatched out of an egg! (See Chapter 7 for more about Helen.)

- **Io:** With the beautiful Io, Zeus tried disguising his lover instead of himself, and turned the girl into a beautiful white cow. His jealous wife Hera asked Zeus to give her the Io-cow as a present and then sent a biting fly to plague her. Io eventually turned back into a woman and became the ancestress of Heracles. The Ionian Sea is named after her. The Roman poet Ovid tells the story of poor Io (who really didn't ask for all the strange things that happened to her) in his *Metamorphoses*.

- ✔ **Europa:** Zeus turned himself into a beautiful bull and carried Europa over the Aegean Sea to Crete. One of her sons was King Minos of Crete. Europe is named after her.

- ✔ **Ganymede:** Not all of Zeus's mortal lovers were female. Ganymede was a beautiful Trojan prince. Zeus changed into an eagle and carried him to Olympus to serve him wine and do him other favors. Ganymede's father got some mighty fine horses in return.

It's not easy being king

Zeus was king, but he wasn't all-powerful. Not only did he get grief from his wife, but in some stories he was tied by Fate just like any mortal. For example, during the Trojan War (see Chapter 7), one of Zeus's many illegitimate sons, Sarpedon, was a warrior on the Trojan side. In the *Iliad*, Zeus learns that Sarpedon is about to get killed in battle. He tells Hera that he is tempted to save the man. Hera says, "Do whatever you want, but the rest of us gods won't obey you anymore if you go against Fate." So it seems that Zeus *could* defy Fate, but not without losing his authority.

Poseidon, god of the sea and full-time macho man

Poseidon was god of the sea. He was also in charge of horses and earthquakes, and sometimes bulls. He caused storms and could also calm the waters if he so chose. His wife was Amphitrite, one of the 50 daughters of the river god Nereus — they had a daughter named Benthesicyme.

Why the sea god was also associated with horses is anybody's guess. Some scholars have suggested that the worship of Poseidon arrived in Greece at the same time as horses. The Greeks sacrificed horses to him, especially stallions (Poseidon also had a reputation for extreme masculinity). The winged horse Pegasus was his offspring, emerging from the sea after Medusa's blood fell on it. (See Chapter 6 for more about Pegasus.)

That's his name, don't wear it out

Poseidon's epithet was Earth-shaker — appropriate for the patron of earthquakes. Other epithets for this god include Wave-dashing, Earth-holding, Hippius ("Horsey"), Horse-tending, Nurturer, Overseer, Securer, Pelagaeus ("Oceany").

A fishy audience

Sailors and fishermen worshipped Poseidon, for obvious reasons. Many coastal towns named themselves Poseidonia after him and took him as their sponsor.

Figure 4-1 *might* show Poseidon, who was often depicted carrying a trident or a three-pronged spear. Fishermen used tridents to spear fish.

Figure 4-1:
Whatever
this god
actually was
throwing
would
explain
a lot — a
thunderbolt
(indicating
Zeus) or a
trident
(indicating
Poseidon).

© Glan Berto Vanni/CORBIS

TECHNICAL STUFF

Ancients could identify statues and other artistic renditions of gods and goddesses by the things they wore or carried. For example, a middle-aged man with a thunderbolt was Zeus, but if he held a trident, he was Poseidon. A handsome young man with a crown of laurel leaves was Apollo; if he wore ivy, he was Dionysus.

But I wanted that city!

Poseidon once got into a bidding war with Athena over which god would get to be the protector of the city of Athens (which didn't have a name yet). Poseidon promised horses and made a spring of salt water flow from the hill of the Acropolis in the center of town. Athena promised them lots of olive trees. Now, horses don't do well in countryside as rocky as the land around Athens, and a spring of salt water is not especially handy. On the other hand, olive trees are great; even before the invention of the martini, olives were incredibly useful, mainly for their oil. People burned it in lamps, made it into soap, conditioned their hair with it, and ate it (yummy, loaded with calories, and cheaper than meat). So Athena won, and today the capital of modern Greece (or *Hellas* as the Greeks call it) is "Athens," not "Poseidonia."

Not always a happy guy

Poseidon bore a grudge against the mortal hero Odysseus because Odysseus had blinded his son, the Cyclops Polyphemus (see Chapter 6). Another of his sons was the giant hunter Orion, whom Artemis killed. Orion the Hunter is now one of the most prominent constellations in the North American sky: The three bright stars of Orion's belt are especially obvious, and their appearance in the sky means that winter is coming.

Hades, god of the underworld: The land down under (like way under!)

Hades was god of the underworld, and king of the dead. His domain was often called Hades, too. Evidently running the underworld was a full-time job, because Hades didn't have a long list of responsibilities like his brothers Zeus and Poseidon.

The underworld in Greek mythology should properly be called Hades's, with an "'s" at the end, meaning The [place] of [the god] Hades. But, just like with Valentines Day (which used to be "Saint Valentine's Day"), people stopped bothering with the apostrophe long ago.

The gates of the underworld were guarded by a three-headed dog named *Cerberus.* Cerberus wagged his tail to greet new arrivals but ate anyone who tried to leave. The underworld itself was cold, dark, and just no fun. Don't expect any picnics in the park here, folks!

Death may not take a holiday, but he does take different names

Hades was often called Pluto, a name related to the Greek word "plutos," which means wealth. Gold, silver, and precious stones come out of the ground, and that is out of Hades's realm. Sometimes Hades is called Golden Reined, in reference to the chariot he drove around in. And he has the epithet The Warder because he is in charge of keeping the dead in the underworld. These epithets indicate that while Hades was not everyone's favorite god, he wasn't actually evil — he wasn't a Greek version of Satan, and his realm wasn't like the Christian concept of hell.

The road to nowhere

The road to the underworld was the same for everyone; good and bad people didn't have separate facilities, although certain bad people were singled out for special punishments.

The great Persephone heist

Hades was married to Persephone, Demeter's daughter. He didn't exactly ask Persephone to marry him; instead, he snatched her up while she was picking flowers with her friends and dragged her back to the underworld with him. After her mother Demeter had spent a year refusing to work, Zeus told Hades that he had to return Persephone to her mother.

Before she left, however, he asked her to remember him fondly and gave her a pomegranate to eat. The *pomegranate* was the special food of the dead, and Persephone swallowed four (or six) seeds from it before she left. Because she had eaten while in the underworld, she was doomed to spend four (or six) months out of every year there with Hades. During that time her mother mourned her absence, once again took a vacation from work, and the earth experienced winter.

Deader than a doornail

Despite their unpromising start, Hades and Persephone appear to have had a relatively peaceful marriage, and Persephone was known as queen of the dead. They never had children — kids would never have fit in there anyway.

The Boys in the Band: Studly Young Gods

Apart from the Big Three of Zeus, Poseidon, and Hades, there were other male gods: Apollo, Hephaestus, Hermes, Ares, and Dionysus. With the exception of Hephaestus, they were all young and good-looking. In fact, when the Greeks thought of their gods and goddesses, they seemed to picture them as being, simply, perfect humans. The gods had certain powers and didn't die — that's what *immortal* means. They remained in the prime of life forever but in other ways were pretty much like normal folks.

As with Zeus and Poseidon, these other guy-gods had their own various areas of expertise and authority.

Apollo, handsome jukebox hero

Apollo, son of Zeus and Leto, was also Artemis's twin brother. Artemis was born first and helped her mother deliver Apollo.

Apollo was gorgeous. He was always portrayed as an extremely handsome young man. He was the god of light, truth, and healing. He was also an athlete. The laurel tree was his special plant, and victorious athletes would receive a crown of laurels as their prize for winning competitions.

Ancient psychic hotline: Visit now! First five minutes free!

One of Apollo's most important roles was as sponsor of the oracle at Delphi. Delphi was like the center of the world for ancient people; anyone who wanted their fortune told went there to get a message from the priestess, who inhaled the vapors from a crack in the earth and then revealed the messages that the god sent her.

Playing a lyre or playing a liar?

Apollo was famous for music, and often played on a lyre, a kind of stringed instrument that probably sounded nothing like a modern guitar. The Greeks thought of the lyre as a refined, orderly instrument in contrast to the wild pipes that the followers of Dionysus preferred.

Despite being a god of music, he wasn't the kindest of musical competitors. Once a satyr (for more about satyrs, see the "E-Z do-it-yourself wine cellar: If you're nice, I'll show you how" section later in the chapter) named Marsyas challenged him to a musical contest. For the prize, the winner could do whatever he liked to the loser. Apollo played his lyre and Marsyas played the pipes that Athena had thrown away because she didn't like the way they made her face look. During the competition, Apollo turned his lyre upside down and challenged Marsyas to do the same thing with his pipes. Marsyas couldn't, so he lost the contest. Apollo then killed him by hanging him on a pine tree and stripping off his skin.

Sun, medicine, and other jobs

Apollo was sometimes called the god of the sun, who drove his chariot across the sky every day, pulling the sun from east to west. Other stories said that the sun god was named Helios.

Medicine and purification were also Apollo's provinces. When Orestes killed his mother (because she had killed his father), the young man fled to Delphi to get Apollo to purify him. Anyone who killed a parent, even by accident, got covered by *miasma,* a kind of pollution that was invisible but nasty enough to prevent the murderer from associating with unpolluted people. Apollo, and his priests, knew the rituals that would clean off the miasma and allow the repentant killer to return to normal society.

Apollo was also the guardian of epic poets, and sometimes was said to be the leader of the Muses.

You gotta stand for something: Apollo's symbols

Apollo had various symbols. The lyre, a Greek harp, was one, because he invented it. The laurel tree (whose leaves are the *bay leaves* sold in grocery stores) was so named because (at least according to the Roman poet Ovid) a young woman named Laurel (well, Daphne in Greek) turned into a tree rather than have sex with Apollo (the whole story is told in the "Daphne and the origin of the laurel tree" section later in this chapter). The dolphin is another symbol — Apollo once sent a dolphin to save the life of a young harpist named Arion, who was about to be thrown off of a ship by some evil sailors.

The bright trickster with the suntan

Like some of the other gods, Apollo has a lot of epithets that he goes by as well. Some of the more popular ones are:

- **Phoebus Apollo** or just **Phoebus:** Phoebus means bright.

- **Delian Apollo:** After the island of Delos where he was born.

- **Pythian Apollo:** Apollo learned the art of prophecy from Pan. He went to the oracle at Delphi, which was guarded by the snake *Python*. Python tried to stop him from approaching, but he killed the snake.

- **Apollo Smintheus** or **Rat Apollo:** This is the manifestation of the god who sent plagues, like the one at the beginning of the *Iliad*. This epithet may also come from the particular worship of Apollo in the city of Sminthe, which is near Troy.

- **Loxias:** This means tricky because the prophetesses spoke in tongues.

Apollo consulted prophetesses known as *sibyls*. (Sybil still happens to be a fairly common name today). The most famous sibyl was the high priestess in Delphi named *Pythia* (after that snake, the python). Pythia inhaled fumes of burning bay leaves or vapors coming up from cracks in the rocks, get really high, and then tell people their fortunes. It was a profitable business.

Daphne and the origin of the laurel tree

Daphne was the daughter of a river god. She was incredibly beautiful but had no interest in men, preferring to run free in the woods.

One day, Apollo saw her and immediately fell in love. He went after her, but she ran from him. He chased her through the woods, yelling to her that he was a god and he loved her and wouldn't she please stop so they could make sweet love. But Daphne kept running.

She finally reached her father's riverbank at the same moment that Apollo caught up to her. Just as he reached out for her, she called to her father to help her. He obliged by turning her into a laurel tree ("laurel" is *daphnê* in Greek); in Figure 4-2, Apollo finds himself embracing a tree trunk.

As a sort of consolation prize to himself, Apollo then declared that the laurel would always be his special tree. And Daphne didn't have to give herself up.

Figure 4-2: Daphne's transformation either saved her virginity or (the pessimistic view) put her completely in Apollo's power. In Bernini's sculpture, she already is transforming just as Apollo catches her.

Hephaestus: He has a great personality . . .

Hephaestus was the god of fire and the forge, the big fiery pit used by blacksmiths to work metal. He was extremely skillful and could make absolutely anything he wanted — any god who wanted something special, like super armor, got Hephaestus to make it. Hera, queen of the gods, gave birth to him by herself to retaliate against Zeus for having created Athena on his own. (See Chapter 5 for how that worked.)

Not one of the beautiful people

Hephaestus was ugly and crippled. Some ancient accounts attribute this to the fact that Hera produced him by herself. To the male-dominated Greek society, it made sense that if a man produces a child all by himself, the child would be wonderful (such as Athena, Zeus's solo effort — see Chapter 5), but if a woman tried it, the result would be inferior.

Other versions say that he was born ugly, but became crippled when Hera, upon seeing how ugly he was, tried to abandon him by throwing him out of heaven. Still others say that nothing in particular was wrong with baby Hephaestus until Zeus got his hands on him. The King of the Gods, angry with

Hera for having an illegitimate child, threw Hephaestus off of Olympus. Hephaestus was, according to this version, crippled and uglified from the fall. (Other stories say that he was born crippled, and Hera threw him out of the sky when she saw his deformity — nice mommy!)

In any case, by the time Olympus was in full swing, Hephaestus lived in heaven with the rest of the deities and enjoyed a certain amount of respect. In a huge irony, the ugly god Hephaestus was married to the beautiful Aphrodite.

The only god with a real job

Hephaestus spent his time making armor and weapons and building houses and furniture for his fellow gods. He had lovely female assistants made out of gold who helped him in his work. The Greeks said that his forge was under a volcano and that volcanic eruptions were a sign that the god was at work. Achilles's mom, the goddess Thetis, commissioned Hephaestus to make new armor for her son, including the fabulous "Shield of Achilles" described in Homer's *Iliad* (see Chapter 7).

The Olympian gods, with the possible exception of Ares (see the following section for the explanation), liked Hephaestus, who worked hard to keep everyone happy and to stop arguments among the gods. Homer describes how, when quarreling broke out during a feast of the gods, Hephaestus grabbed the wine pitcher and went around the table refilling everyone's cup; the sight of the gentle, ugly god hobbling around busily made all the gods laugh and forget their fight.

The Athenians loved Hephaestus, too, because he was peaceful, kind, and a patron of craftsmen. A large temple in ancient Athens was built in his honor and called the *Hephaestion*.

Ares, god of war

Ares was god of war. His parents were Zeus and Hera, neither one of whom liked him very much (at least according to Homer).

Ares embodied the destructive forces of war, the part that people don't really like. The goddess Athena, on the other hand, was also a war goddess, but she was in charge of the intelligent and orderly use of war to defend the city.

Wasn't voted most popular in high school

As a result of this difference in violent proclivity, the Greek people didn't like Ares much. Homer has him fighting on the Trojan side in the *Iliad,* while Athena fights for the Greeks. Ares was ferocious and loud and generally unpleasant to be around. On the other hand, the Greeks definitely admired brave warriors and courage in battle, so this gave him a certain measure of popularity. A hill in Athens named *Areopagus,* which means "hill of Ares," was where Ares was tried for murder and acquitted (see Chapter 8). An important political council used to meet on the hill, perhaps to discuss war, which also would account for the name.

Even the other gods didn't like Ares. In the *Iliad*, his own father, Zeus, tells him that he is the "most hateful of the gods" — right to his face!

All's fair in love and war

Although Aphrodite was married to Hephaestus, Ares was Aphrodite's lover. Some scholars have suggested that the two of them got together because they both represented wild impulses that subvert order and organization; people crazed with lust or crazed with war don't make the sensible decisions that a practical goddess such as Athena would have preferred. This union managed to produce three sons:

- Eros (Love)
- Deimus (Fear)
- Phobus (Panic)

A pretty funny scene in the *Iliad* tells of Ares and Aphrodite getting caught in bed together. Aphrodite's husband Hephaestus hung a golden net over the bed, and when the two got busy, he dropped it on them and then called all the other gods and goddesses to come laugh at them. His revenge wasn't that successful, though, because most of the gods agreed that it would be worth getting caught in a net to go to bed with Aphrodite.

Eros, god of sex

Eros was the force that drove people together with physical desire, heterosexual or homosexual. He was often said to be Aphrodite's son, and possibly even the son of Ares, although in Hesiod, he was around from the beginning of the world. He was full of mischief and loved to play tricks on humans and gods, making them fall in love suddenly. In his later depiction, he was a beautiful young man with a bow and arrows and wings on his back; the arrows made people fall in love. Eros was a pretty popular god in ancient Greece and lots of people belonged to his cults. His name is the root of the English word "erotic." The Romans knew Eros as Cupid, but the Greek version and the Roman version are different. Cupid is a cute, pudgy baby, but Eros is a malevolent, dangerous teenager, whose arrows are real and can kill!

Hermes, fleet of foot and mind

Hermes was the messenger of the gods. He was the son of Zeus and Maia, the daughter of the Titan Atlas. He was a beautiful young man. He wore a cap and sandals with wings on them, and also carried a staff wrapped with snakes — the *caduceus,* the same thing that doctors use as their symbol now. The caduceus, which is shown in Figure 4-3, was the symbol of heralds in the ancient world.

Figure 4-3: Note the varied symbolism of the caduceus since the 16th century: medical sciences, postal service, and ambassadorial services.

Always on the run

Hermes had a huge number of jobs. Apparently his swiftness enabled him to accomplish many different things at once. Here is how a typical business day stacked up for Hermes:

- He was god of commerce and traders.
- He guided the dead into the underworld.
- He acted as Zeus's go-between for delicate negotiations (such as the purchase of the Trojan Prince Ganymede), ran errands for him, and arranged his amorous liaisons.
- He was a patron of children and heroes and transported divine children to safety (he brought baby Dionysus to the nymphs at Nysa).
- He guided shepherds and travelers along the proper paths. He was a patron of herdsman and a god of fertility and prosperity.
- He was also a god of athletes and the gymnasium.
- He was the god of thieves.

Symbols: Gimme a stick to carry

Hermes' symbols are his famous winged sandals, his "caduceus" (the staff carried by a herald with two snakes twisting around it), and a shepherd's crook, useful for shepherding folks on their journeys and driving dead souls down to the underworld.

A hero to the heroes

Hermes' epithets include "Argus Slayer" (after the monster he killed as a kid), and "Psychopompos" or "Soul Leader," after his role in bringing the dead down to Hades. The Athenian comedian Aristophanes pokes fun at his own culture's tendency to give each god a million epithets. In the play *The Frogs,* two characters have a comic argument over whether it is better to pray on behalf of a dead father to Hermes Patrios (Ancestor Hermes) or Hermes Chthonios (Underworld Hermes).

A single father who got around

Hermes didn't have a wife of his own, though he did have children. Pan was his son. The deity Hermaphroditus, half male and half female, was the child of Hermes and Aphrodite. He (she?) had female breasts and male genitals.

This gives us the word *hermaphrodite,* meaning having both male and female sexual characteristics.

The invention of the lyre

Hermes was extremely clever and cunning from his earliest days. When he was one day old, he stole all of Apollo's cattle. He led them away walking backwards to disguise the direction they had walked, sacrificed two of them, and hid the rest in a cave. He and Apollo made up after Hermes gave back the cattle and presented Apollo with the first lyre, which he had just invented by killing a turtle and stretching strings across its shell. They made a pleasant twanging sound. Apollo loved the instrument, and apparently became quite skilled at drawing music out of it.

Herms

Ancient Athens was full of statues of penises, called *Herms* after Hermes. Herms were marble or bronze pillars, often with male genitals on them that served as road and boundary markers. They protected the city and houses and the Athenians took them very seriously. In the fifth century, an Athenian guy named Alcibiades and his buddies knocked down a bunch of them; the people of Athens got so angry they exiled Alcibiades and confiscated all of his property.

Dionysus, the party god

Dionysus, god of wine and of vegetation in general, was a latecomer to Olympian deities.

Dionysus was the son of Zeus and the Theban princess Semele, which made Dionysus the only god with one human parent. He also achieved divinity during his lifetime unlike another, Heracles (see Chapter 6), who also had one divine parent. But his birth was very weird. When Semele was pregnant, Zeus promised her, swearing his oath on the river Styx, that he would do anything she asked him to. She asked to see him in his full glory. Zeus was dismayed — no human could see him that way and live. But he had promised, so he showed himself to her in flame and splendor.

As he knew would happen, Semele dropped dead immediately. Zeus snatched out her unborn baby Dionysus and hid him in his own body in his thigh (we don't know how this worked, but it's too bad for women that the technology hasn't survived).

After Dionysus was born, Hermes took the baby to be raised by the nymphs (or, depending on the story, by Athamas and Ino) in the beautiful valley of Nysa. Later, Dionysus missed the mother he had never known and went to ask Hades if he could have her back. Hades agreed, and Dionysus brought Semele up to Olympus to live with the gods. Hera, Zeus' wife, was understandably upset, and made Dionysus *and* Athamas and Ino temporarily insane. She evidently relented after a while, and they all got their wits back.

Really fun symbols: Some handy paraphernalia

The most common symbol associated with Dionysus, by far, is the vine, either the grape vine (the source of wine), or ivy (which makes nice garlands to wear on the head while drinking wine). The masks that actors wore in tragedies and comedies also symbolize Dionysus.

The born again pagan

Dionysus' childhood history gave him the epithet "Twice Born." Other epithets reflect his identity as a party god: Acratophorus ("Bringer of Unmixed Wine"), Nocturnal, and Torch-bearing. Others have to do with fertility or the natural world: Flowery, Ivy, or Of the Black Goatskin. Perhaps because of the magical properties of wine, he has the epithets Savior and Deliverer. And because he was a sort of "Joe Six Pack" god, he occasionally sports the nickname Citizen Dionysus.

E-Z do-it-yourself wine cellar: If you're nice, I'll show you how

When Dionysus was grown, he spent his time wandering the earth teaching people how to grow grapes and turn them into wine.

Dionysus traveled with an exclusive entourage of his own long before today's celebrities started doing it. They were unusual creatures and included the following:

- **Maenads:** These were the female worshippers of Dionysus, his "Fly Girls."

- **Satyrs:** Pan and his buddies, the satyrs (called *fauns* in Rome), were men up top and goats below the waist. They danced around playing pipes, drinking, and having wild sex with each other and the woodland nymphs. Satyrs were often painted with enormous erections or playing with giant dildos. Pan himself was the son of Hermes, born in Arcadia. He loved woodlands and mountains and was the god of goatherds and shepherds. The word *panic* comes from his name — when people heard his sounds in the woods at night, they would lose control.

- **Seileni:** In some ancient sources, these guys are half human, half horse, and chummed around with Dionysus and Hephaestus. But as time went by, "Silenus" came to be a synonym for satyr.

An example of one of his tantrums

Although Dionysus was just a boy, folks shouldn't have messed with him. One day some pirates spotted him and decided to capture him — he looked like a beautiful black-haired young man with a fancy purple cloak, and they thought he must be the son of a king who could pay a good ransom. They grabbed him and dragged him onto the boat, but whenever they tried to tie him up, the ropes refused to hold together.

The captain ordered the sailors to raise the sails and take the ship out to sea, but the boat refused to move. Instead, vines started to grow all over it and wine flowed down the deck. Dionysus turned into a lion and roared at the sailors; they all jumped overboard and turned into dolphins.

Setting up shop: Worship me and worship me now!

The ancients had mixed feelings about worshipping Dionysus. On the one hand, everyone loved the happy feeling they got from drinking wine — it made them brave and eloquent and confident. On the other, when people drank too much, they sometimes did crazy things.

One form of Dionysian worship was pretty gruesome. Women called *maenads* (*bacchantes* in Latin) would drink themselves into a frenzy, and then run through the woods ripping apart animals and (at least in the plot of one Greek tragedy) people with their bare hands and teeth.

One king in Thrace, Lycurgus, opposed the worship of Dionysus. The god imprisoned him in a cave, and Zeus struck him blind. He died not long afterward. It didn't pay to oppose the gods.

When Dionysus tried to bring his religion to Thebes, the king there, Pentheus (who happened to be Dionysus's first cousin) didn't believe that Dionysus was a god and didn't like the wild dancing and singing that the maenads were doing. He told his soldiers to arrest them all. The soldiers brought in Dionysus, who had come willingly, but confessed that the maenads had all escaped because the ropes couldn't hold them. Pentheus still refused to believe that his guest was a god, and threw him in prison.

Dionysus immediately escaped and got his revenge. When Pentheus went up to the hills to chase the maenads, Dionysus made all the Theban women crazy. Convinced that Pentheus was a mountain lion, they tore him to pieces with their hands and teeth, with Pentheus's own mother leading the charge. As soon as they were done, they realized their mistake and were pretty upset, but they could do nothing about it.

Friedrich Nietzsche, the German philosopher, got a lot of mileage out of describing all of ancient Greek culture as a competition between Apollo (rational, reasonable, orderly) and Dionysus (drunk, crazed, chaotic). You probably can't categorize a whole culture like this, but people still find it useful to talk about aspects of a culture as being either *Apollonian* or *Dionysian*.

Chapter 5

The Fairest and Meanest of Them All: The Greek Goddesses

● ●

In This Chapter

▶ Meeting the wives: Hera and Aphrodite

▶ Visiting Mother Nature: Demeter

▶ Encountering the virgin goddesses Athena and Artemis

▶ Getting to know the Muses, Fates, Furies, and Graces

● ●

When the Greeks thought of goddesses, just like when they thought of gods, they pictured powerful, beautiful, immortal versions of normal human beings. So the goddesses, even though they were powerful, beautiful, and immortal, did the things that mortal women did: some got married (a few never did), occasionally had affairs, had kids, fought with their husbands and lovers, made up with their husbands and lovers, and often resented how the male gods got to make up all the rules.

As with the gods, there were more goddesses than most people bothered to keep track of. There were goddesses of victory, strife, and the dawn, just to mention a few, but they ordinarily didn't get a lot of attention.

Hera, Aphrodite, and Demeter: The Dueling Diva Goddesses

Most Greek women spent much of their lives as wives and mothers, as indeed women always have. Likewise, some of the more important goddesses were wives and mothers.

Queen Hera, protector of marriage (except her own)

Hera was Zeus's wife. She was also his sister, but that didn't bother anyone. Hera and Zeus were children of Rhea and Cronos.

Don't let the incest that occurred among the gods and goddesses give you the wrong idea. Incest was forbidden in Greece just like it was in most other cultures.

Hera was the female equivalent of Zeus, queen of heaven. Greek women worshipped Hera as the goddess of marriage and the home. Hera's daughter Ilithyia helped women in childbirth. Greek women sometimes saw in Hera all the stages of women's lives: girlhood, matrimony, motherhood, and widowhood. Hera was definitely royal — she was noble and beautiful and often depicted sitting in a throne. Hera also protected cities and some social groups.

Hera's other children were Ares, Hebe, and Hephaestus, the latter of whom she bore all on her own (with no help from Zeus) in revenge for Zeus's giving birth to Athena by himself. (See Chapter 4.) In some accounts, she also gave birth to the monster Typhon by herself.

Imperial displays for only a special few

Hera's symbols were the peacock, because it was fancy and flashy and fit for a queen, and the cow (she turned at least one of her husband's girlfriends into a cow).

Like a natural woman

Hera had some obvious epithets: "Protectress" (especially in Argos, which was her special city), "Bride," and "Olympian" (just like her husband Zeus). Others seem stranger: "Full-grown" and "Ox-eating." The Stymphalian people even knew her as "Hera the Widow," an ironic epithet that refers to the frequency with which Zeus cheated on her.

That no-good man of mine

Hera spent a lot of time pursuing Zeus's human mistresses and illegitimate children. For example, when Zeus fell in love and fathered a son with the girl Callisto, Hera turned her into a bear. When Callisto's son grew up, Hera sent the Callisto-bear in front of him while he was out hunting. Zeus snatched up Callisto before their son could accidentally kill his mother and turned her into a constellation of stars — the Big Bear. Callisto's son later became a constellation himself, the Little Bear. Whatever the rationale for Zeus's continual gallivanting (see Chapter 4), Greek women probably enjoyed hearing about the punishments the goddess inflicted on her rivals.

Nymphs

What the heck were *nymphs?* They were lovely nubile women who gallivanted around the woods scantily attired. Greek mythology did not limit itself to the main Olympian gods; sometimes it seemed that every rock, tree, and body of water had its own guardian spirit. Today, a nymph is an immature insect. Charming. The word also denotes sexy young girls, though it's sometimes diminutized to *nymphette.*

One time, Hera was angry with Zeus for some reason, and he consulted a wise man on how to win her back. The man told him to make a wooden statue of a woman, drape it with cloth, and announce that she was his bride. Zeus did as he was told, Hera heard about it and raced to the scene, tore off the drapery, and was delighted to find a wooden statue instead of a flesh-and-blood woman. They were reconciled with one another and that was the start of a regular festival involving wooden statues.

Mad enough to start a war

Hera was vain, the way most Greek goddesses seem to have been, and on one notable occasion, her vanity (combined with the vanity of Athena and Aphrodite) caused a war. During a wedding reception, the goddess of strife, Eris, threw down an apple labeled, "To the Fairest." The three most powerful goddesses each claimed to be the fairest and, thus, the most deserving of the apple. For complicated reasons — the whole story appears in Chapter 7 — a young Trojan man named Paris found himself with the job of judging the relative beauty of the three goddesses. Each resorted to bribery, and Aphrodite's bribe — marriage to the most beautiful woman in the world — carried the day.

Hera was so angry that she swore revenge on Paris and his entire nation. Her reaction led to the Trojan War (source of about a thousand mythological stories), the deaths of many heroes, and even the founding of the Roman people (see Chapter 11).

Hera and Heracles: 'Til death do you annoy me

Hera didn't limit her vengeance on Zeus's girlfriends. When he had an affair with Alcmena, who bore a baby son, Heracles, Hera took an immediate dislike to the baby. In fact, the name "Heracles" means either "the fame of Hera" or perhaps "famous because of Hera."

Hera's anger was certainly caused by this further evidence of her husband's infidelity, but Zeus didn't help matters. In a typically tactless moment, Zeus asked Hera if she would mind breast-feeding his new illegitimate son to make him immortal. Hera's answer to this tacky request was to arrange to have the baby killed.

In one account, Zeus actually brought baby Heracles to Hera while she was sleeping so that he could nurse on the sly. She woke up and pushed him away. Milk shot out of her nipple and turned into the Milky Way.

Hera sent two snakes to kill the boy in his crib. See Chapter 6 for the rest of that story. Later, Hera made grown-up Heracles go crazy and kill his wife and sons, and she riled up the Amazons against him.

After Heracles died, Hera apparently relented. She agreed to give him her daughter Hebe (goddess of youth) as his wife and even let him come live with the gods on Olympus.

Aphrodite, fertile femme fatale

Ah, Aphrodite. The goddess of love. Aphrodite was born out of the sea where Uranus's genitals fell in after Cronos cut them off. Sandro Botticelli's famous painting *Birth of a Virgin* (see Figure 5-1) showed her coming ashore in Cyprus on half of a giant shell. (In Homer, though, she is the daughter of Zeus and Dione.)

Aphrodite was beautiful and sexy and lived to make people fall in love with her and each other. She stood for all the good and bad aspects of female nature: seductive charm, desire for children, and a capacity for deception. She was the goddess of erotic love — of whatever variety — and of fertility.

She's from the seashell by the seashore

Aphrodite's symbols include the shell on which she rode to shore after being born of the sea, the swan, sparrow, and dove, and the myrtle tree (all pretty things that can symbolize love).

Land ahoy!

Aphrodite often went by the epithet Cyprian, after the island of Cyprus where she beached her seashell after her birth. Other epithets include Bridal Aphrodite, Aphrodite of the Deep Sea, Heavenly Aphrodite, and Aphrodite Victorious. The most interesting epithet for her is Black, perhaps referring to the fertility of the black earth, or for her power over, ahem, things that go on at night.

Probably voted most popular in high school

Aphrodite was one of the more popular goddesses. The Greeks worshipped her as the person in charge of sexuality and reproduction — both fun and necessary to keep the community going. Brides made sacrifices to Aphrodite to help make their first sexual experience a good one. Prostitutes worshipped her. She had a lot to do with fertility of the land as well. Poets loved her and her power of love.

Figure 5-1:
Note Botticelli's depiction of Aphrodite's half-hearted attempt at modesty in his painting *Birth of a Virgin.*

© Francis G. Mayer/CORBIS

In a cosmic joke, the lovely Aphrodite was married to ugly Hephaestus. Why they got together is anybody's guess, but they don't seem to have gotten along very well. Aphrodite's real love was Ares, the god of war. See Chapter 4 for more about their affair.

In Virgil's epic poem, the *Aeneid,* Aphrodite (going by her Roman name Venus) is the hero Aeneas's best pal, just like Athena is to the Greek hero Odysseus in Homer's *Odyssey.* That made sense, because she happened to be his mother, too.

Aphrodite's son was named Eros. (Hesiod mentions an Eros born from Chaos, but this Eros seems quite different from the little boy described by later writers.) He was a beautiful young boy who went around with a bow and arrows. Whenever he shot someone with an arrow, they fell in love with someone else. Aphrodite and the other gods sometimes got him to shoot particular targets — Aphrodite had him shoot Zeus to make him fall in love with Europa, and Hera persuaded him to shoot Medea and make her fall in love with Jason.

Eros is the root of the word *erotic,* meaning sexy. An *aphrodisiac,* from the name Aphrodite, is a substance that puts someone in the mood for love.

Just another beauty contest: The judgment of Paris

Aphrodite was the winner of the beauty contest that started the Trojan War. She, Athena, and Hera competed for the title of "The Fairest" and each resorted to bribing the judge, a young Trojan good-for-nothing prince named Paris. Athena's offer of victory in battle and Hera's offer of political power amounted to nothing compared to Aphrodite's bribe of the most beautiful woman in the world. Paris then got Helen of Troy, the most beautiful woman in the world, and a whole mess of stuff resulted from it (like the Trojan War). See Chapter 7.

Part-time lover: Adonis

Adonis was a human man. Aphrodite fell in love with him the moment he was born. She took him away from his family and brought him down to Persephone, queen of the underworld, for safekeeping.

Persephone fell in love with him, too, and refused to give him back to Aphrodite. The two goddesses fought about this, and finally Zeus stepped in to referee. He decided that Adonis would spend autumn and winter with Persephone and spring and summer with Aphrodite.

This compromise was pretty good and must have helped poor Persephone cope. She was doomed to spend those cold months in the world of the dead but was allowed to spend her springs and summers in the living world with her mom Demeter. Persephone's story can be found in the "Rape of Persephone and the seasons" section later in this chapter.

Adonis spent most of his time hunting, and Aphrodite liked to dress up as a huntress and go with him. One day, however, he was hunting alone and tried to kill a wild boar with his spear. Unfortunately, he only wounded it, and the enraged beast gored him with its tusks.

Aphrodite heard him scream and flew to him. He was rapidly bleeding to death, and the goddess couldn't help him. So she kissed him as he died, and everywhere his blood touched the ground, blood-red *anemones*, or windflowers, sprang up.

Demeter, Mother Nature and master gardener

Demeter was in a class by herself, an earth goddess who didn't live on Mount Olympus with the rest of the immortals. She was the daughter of Cronos and Rhea and was the goddess who made grain grow in the fields. She wasn't the goddess of the earth — that was Gaia — but she was much more important to most Greeks because of her role in agriculture and nature.

A corny symbol?

Demeter's symbols are the things of the harvest: ears of grain, little cakes (which folks placed on her altar), and the tools used in the harvest, scythes and sickles.

Jinxed!

One of Demeter's more interesting epithets was The Unnamed Maiden, suggesting that it was unlucky to name such a powerful goddess. She often appears as Eleusinian Demeter, after the town of Eleusis, near Athens, which was an important center of Demeter worship. Other epithets name her power over growing things: Fruit-bearer, Sender-of-Gifts, Green, and Black (after the black, and therefore fertile, soil).

Rape of Persephone and the seasons

Demeter had one daughter, Persephone. She loved her daughter to distraction.

One day Hades, King of the Dead, got a glimpse of Persephone and decided to steal her. He got Zeus to help him by creating a beautiful flower, the narcissus, and planting it in some rocks. (This contradicts another story about the origin of the narcissus, the one with Echo and Narcissus. That's the way mythology is.)

Persephone saw the flower and wandered away from her friends to pick it. See Chapter 4 to find out how this story turned out — suffice it to say Persephone became his wife.

Demeter went on strike — all plants stopped growing and said she wouldn't go back to work until she had her daughter back. Zeus hadn't worried about Persephone or thought his brother Hades had done anything bad until he talked to Demeter, but then he decided that Hades would have to give up the girl. He sent Hermes down to the underworld to bring her back.

Hades realized he would have to return his "wife" to her mother. But before she left, he gave her a pomegranate, and she ate four (or maybe six) seeds out of it. (For more about Hades, god of the dead, see Chapter 4.)

Hermes brought Persephone back to Demeter, and the two had a fond reunion. But Demeter got worried when Persephone told her about the pomegranate. And she was right to worry.

Zeus's mother Rhea came to visit Demeter and informed her that because Persephone had eaten those pomegranate seeds, she would have to go back to Hades for part of every year. Demeter consented, though she didn't want to give up her daughter again. After that, Demeter was happy for the part of the year when Persephone was with her and made plants grow, but when her daughter went back to Hades, Demeter mourned and stopped working. That's where winter comes from.

The strange nurse

While Demeter was wandering around missing Persephone, she disguised herself as an old woman. One day she sat down to rest beside a well in a town called Eleusis. Four young sisters saw her and asked her what she was doing there. She said that she had escaped from pirates who wanted to sell her as a slave.

The girls brought Demeter home to their mother, Metanaira, who hired the goddess as a wet nurse for her baby boy.

Wet-nursing, hiring a woman to breast-feed a baby instead of its mother, was extremely common in the ancient world. Many women who could afford to preferred to hire a nurse rather than breast-feed their babies themselves.

Demeter loved the baby, and decided to make him immortal. So every night when the family was asleep, she put him in the fire, which evidently would have made him immortal if she could have finished the job. But Metanaira saw her do this one night, and grabbed her baby in a panic.

Demeter got mad, and yelled at the poor woman that she would have saved her son from old age and death, but now it was too late. Then she revealed her true identity and demanded that Metanaira and her town build her a temple. All the townspeople pitched in, and when the temple was done, Demeter went and sat there missing her daughter.

Look but Don't Touch!: The Virgin Goddesses

Some goddesses were virgins. This was probably just as well, since things never seemed to work out well for men (divine or mortal) who became sexually involved with goddesses — Aphrodite cheated on Hephaestus with Ares, for example, and both male gods were publicly humiliated in the process; Zeus' marriage to Hera was tense, to say the least; and the mortal Peleus was prematurely aged by having sex with his divine wife, Thetis. But two goddesses, in particular, were known for their virginity. Artemis was the sexy kind of virgin; men who saw her lusted after her, but never got anywhere (except in big trouble). Athena was most famous for her virginity — the most famous temple in Greece, the Parthenon in Athens, bears her epithet *Parthenos,* which means virgin. Virtually no myth about Athena suggests, however, that men lusted after her — she was too powerful, too impressive, and too scary.

Athena, the real GI Jane

One day Zeus came down with a terrible headache. He called the blacksmith Hephaestus over and asked him to split his head open with an ax. Out sprang Athena, full-grown and fully armed.

So how did Athena come to be inside Zeus's skull? Well, Zeus had sex with Metis, who was one of those feminine abstractions treated as goddesses — the embodiment of practical wisdom or cunning. Whatever she was, she didn't want to have sex with Zeus and kept changing shapes while he was at it. After he was done, his grandmother Gaia told him that after Metis had the daughter he had impregnated her with, she would have a son who would overthrow him and become king of heaven. So Zeus swallowed Metis whole and baby Athena gestated inside his head. This made Athena the parthenogenetic equivalent of Hephaestus, who Hera had by herself (*parthenogenesis* is having a baby by oneself, without a member of the opposite sex to get things started). See Chapter 4 for Hephaestus's story.

Athena was a goddess of war; she wore a helmet and breastplate and carried a shield with the head of Medusa on it. In addition to her shield, she had the considerable honor of carrying Zeus's *aegis,* which was like a poncho made of goatskin, with a fringe. That doesn't sound all that nice, but this particular aegis was more like a Kevlar vest, impervious to any weapon, even Zeus's own lightning.

The United States Navy has a class of warships armed with and incredibly powerful combination of radar, computers, rapid-fire guns, and guided missiles. These ships exist to protect aircraft carriers from harm, and they're named Aegis Combat System cruisers after Athena's divine shield.

A real smarty

Among Athena's symbols is the owl representing her wisdom — an owl graced the silver coins of Athens, Athena's special city. She also was accompanied by her pet snake — snakes are often symbols of powerful female divinities, and the Athenians believed that Athena's snake protected their city. And the most famous statue of Athena, in the Parthenon in Athens, showed her holding a tiny, winged Nike (Goddess of Victory) in her hand.

Quite the good girl

Like many of the other gods and goddesses, Athena had certain epithets. Here they are:

- **Pallas Athena:** Pallas is just a name; perhaps Pallas Athena represents the coming together of two really ancient goddesses into one.
- **Athena Parthenos:** *Parthenon* means "Temple of the Virgin."
- **Gray-eyed:** Athena was famous for her wisdom and her gray eyes.
- **Aegis-bearing Athena:** Because she carried Zeus's aegis.
- **Athena Polias:** Athena who protects the city (*polis* in Greek).
- **Athena Pronaos:** In Delphi, there was a statue of Athena in front of the temple of Apollo, so visitors to Delphi would offer sacrifices to Athena Pronaos, or Athena-in-Front-of-the-Temple.

Her pet city, though, was Athens (which is obviously named after her). She protected the city, encouraged crafts and agriculture, and taught humans to tame wild horses.

Athena's temple in Athens is the famous Parthenon on the Acropolis. She was not the sexy, drive-guys-crazy kind of virgin-goddess that Artemis was; she was more of the don't-even-think-about-it kind of virgin goddess.

Stick to your day job

In one story, Athena gave music a shot, playing the pipes. But after she caught a glimpse of her reflection with her cheeks all puffed out, she threw away the pipes in disgust. Marsyas, son of Olympus, picked them up and engaged in a musical contest with Apollo, the results of which are detailed in Chapter 4.

Divinely nice favors

Athena pops up all the time in the course of Homer's poem the *Odyssey*. Athena also helped Perseus in his quest to kill Medusa, lending him her shiny shield so that he could see to cut off the Gorgon's head without looking straight at her and turning to stone. (This shiny shield was not the aegis, which Athena probably wasn't supposed to lend out to just anyone.)

Artemis, the pretty huntress

Artemis was Apollo's twin sister, the daughter of Zeus and the Titan Leto. When Leto was in labor for the twins, Hera chased her all over the earth and no place would allow her to give birth to the babies. Finally, Leto came to the town of Delos. The people there gave her permission to give birth provided that Delos would then be the sacred location of a temple to Apollo. Leto finally gave birth to Artemis, who immediately helped deliver her brother, Apollo.

The outdoorsy type

Artemis loved the woods and wild animals and was the goddess of the hunt. She carried her bow and arrows everywhere. She watched over young animals.

Artemis was a very important goddess. She presided over women's transitions — from virgin to adult woman, and from woman to mother, helping women give birth and raise their children. Ironically, for a goddess who protected women, she also brought women sudden death; Apollo did the same favor for men.

Artemis's symbols are the moon (because she is sister to Apollo, the sun god, and because she was associated with women's monthly cycles), the stag (because of her perpetual hunting), and the cypress tree.

Artemis was a complicated goddess, worshipped for different things in different places. Sometimes she represents feminine things; at others she sides with masculine things. A short list of her many epithets shows how varied people's impressions of Artemis were. (This list is by no means exhaustive — none of the lists of epithets for gods in this book are — and it especially excludes epithets that merely identify Artemis with particular places, like Persian Artemis, Mysian Artemis, and so on): Best One, Cedar Goddess, Child-rearer, Correct One, First-seated, Friend of Youth, of Good Fame, Horsefinder, Huntress, Hymnia, Lady of the Lake, Leader, Light-bringing, Market, Paternal, of Persuasion, of the Portal, Priestess, Saviour, of the Steep Place, the Strangled One, and Wolfish. So Artemis came in a lot of flavors.

In the *Iliad,* Artemis heavily favored the Trojan side, and she demanded that Agamemnon sacrifice his young daughter Iphigenia. In Sparta, she took charge of men's transition to adulthood and handled hunting and some aspects of war.

In some stories, Artemis is the goddess who pulls the moon across the sky every night. The moon goddess is also sometimes called Selene, the sister of Helios, the sun god, with whom Apollo was sometimes confused.

Oh, I'll just have to kill you

Artemis was not a goddess anyone wanted to cross. Whenever she got mad, her revenge was swift and straightforward. Niobe, queen of Thebes, had seven sons and seven daughters, and made the mistake of bragging that she was better than Leto, who only had two. Artemis killed all the girls and Apollo killed all the boys, and then Niobe had none.

Acteon was a hapless hunter who was strolling through the woods with his dogs, minding his own business, when he happened upon a woodland pond. Unfortunately for him, Artemis was buck naked, bathing in that pond. Furious that Acteon had seen her without her clothes on, she turned him into a stag. His own dogs ripped him apart.

Artemis couldn't stand for any of her young female companions to lose their virginity. Zeus fell in love with her beautiful attendant Callisto, who gave birth to a son named Arcas. Some stories say that Artemis killed Callisto with an arrow; others say that she or Hera changed Callisto into a bear. Zeus eventually turned bear-Callisto and her son into constellations in the stars; they became the Big Bear and the Little Bear.

Hestia, goddess of good fire

Hestia, the firstborn daughter of Cronos and Rhea, was the goddess of the hearth. The hearth was the center of the home, so Hestia had authority over the home, and by extension the family and the entire community. She didn't really feature in any myths (she couldn't leave the house, so she never had the opportunity), but she was pretty important to the Greek people and also to the Romans in her later incarnation as Vesta (as in "Vestal Virgins," her priestesses).

The hearth is where the home is

The *hearth* was the symbolic heart of the home, and families made daily offerings to Hestia, kind of like saying grace before meals.

New members of the family — brides, babies, and slaves mostly — were initiated into the household by rituals around the hearth. Each city in Greece had a public hearth dedicated to Hestia, and the fire was never allowed to go out. In fact, the sacred hearth may actually have defined a city; when Theseus (according to Athenian myth) was unifying the territory of Attica and making all the independent villages part of a larger city of Athens by removing all of the village public hearths until only one was left in Athens.

Flicker, flame, or by some other name?

Hestia didn't have any epithets, as far as we can tell. The poet Homer (a good source of epithets) doesn't seem to know about Hestia (when Homer says "hestia" in the *Iliad* and Odyssey, he simply means fireplace.) For what it's worth, the people of Scythia called her Tabiti.

A few other goddesses

In the Greek language, abstract ideas — strife, necessity, victory, peace, madness — are grammatically feminine. In Greek literature, these abstract ideas are often mentioned as though they are gods, or actually, goddesses. Here are a few:

Strife (Eris)

Eris means "strife" in Greek, and because strife is a powerful actor in human affairs, it was only reasonable to speak of it as a divinity. So, the poet Hesiod begins his poem *Works and Days* by saying that two kinds of strife are found among people:

- The bad kind, which causes wars
- The good kind, which causes free enterprise

But he talks about Strife (Eris) as if she were a goddess.

In the Trojan War myth, Eris (Strife) definitely *is* a goddess. She's the one who wasn't invited to the wedding of Peleus and Thetis, and with the golden apple started the whole thing. (See Chapter 7 for more about how she started the Trojan War.)

Victory (Nike)

Another abstract idea that appears as a concrete goddess is Victory, which is *Nike* in Greek (and which rhymes with "spikey"). A temple can be found in honor of Nike on the Acropolis in Athens. Representations of Athena often show her holding a tiny Nike goddess in her hand.

Nike often had wings, except at Athens. The Athenians were especially fond of their Wingless Victory, because she couldn't fly away!

Wisdom

This Greek tendency didn't end with the rise of Christianity, either. The great Christian church of Constantinople is called *Hagia Sophia,* or "The Church of Holy Wisdom," ("wisdom" in Greek is "Sophia") yet another example of a feminine abstraction turning up as a Greek divinity.

Goddess Gangs: A Motley Crew

Some of the more minor goddesses appear in teams, such as the nine Muses ("Mousai" in Greek), the three Graces ("Charites" in Greek), the three Fates ("Moirai" in Greek), and varying numbers of Furies ("Erinyes" in Greek). The tendency toward groups or even multiples of three is probably no accident. Three seems to be important in many cultures.

Muses

The *Muses* were the daughters of Zeus and Mnemosyne, or memory. They handled artistic endeavors. Poets and other artists depended on them for help with their creations. They were popular subjects for sculptors. These inspiring ladies include (various sources differ regarding the precise number of Muses and their specific areas of responsibility, but we'll give one standard version):

- **Polyhymnia:** The sponsor of hymns to the gods
- **Urania:** The Muse of astronomy
- **Calliope:** The Muse of epic poetry
- **Thalia:** The Muse of comedy
- **Terpsichore:** The Muse of choral singing (lyric poetry) and dancing
- **Clio:** The Muse of history
- **Euterpe:** The Muse of flute playing

- **Melpomene:** The Muse of tragedy
- **Erato:** The Muse of poetry not accompanied by dancing, specially love poetry — hence her name

All epic poets claim that their inspiration comes from the Muses. Homer's first words in the *Iliad* are "Sing, Goddess, of the wrath of Achilles," and there can be no doubt that this "goddess" is a Muse. He opens the *Odyssey* with "Muse, tell me about a man of many ways. . . ." The Roman poet Virgil is a little more self-centered. His *Aenead* begins "I sing of arms and of a man. . . ." and he gets around to invoking the Muses only later.

Graces

The three *Graces* were the daughters of Zeus and Eurynome, the daughter of the Titan Oceanus. They brought grace and beauty everywhere they went, and no party was complete without them. They were closely associated with Aphrodite. Here they are:

- **Aglaia:** The Grace of splendor or radiance
- **Euphrosyne:** The Grace of joy and mirth
- **Thalia:** The Grace of good cheer (and flowering)

The Graces, as shown in Figure 5-2, liked poetry, singing, and dancing and sometimes performed at divine weddings. They made flowers grow, especially roses. They could bestow all kinds of beauty and charm, including physical, moral, and artistic.

Fates

The *Fates* were another trio of women. They were the daughters of Zeus and Themis (or of Night). The Fates decided the course of every person's life from birth to death by spinning thread, which symbolized the person's life.

Here are the fates along with their specialties:

- **Clotho (Spinner and Twister):** She spun the thread. She was depicted as a beautiful young woman.
- **Lachesis (the Lot Caster):** She determined the course of a person's life. She was a middle-aged woman, like the mother of a family.
- **Atropos (The Unyielding One):** This dreaded lady cut the thread with her scissors, ending the person's life. She was an old hag.

Figure 5-2:
Three
graceful
Graces.

The image of a person's fate as a piece of string is important. In Homer's poetry, it seems clear that a person's fate determines when she or he will die, but it doesn't determine what will happen in the meantime. Folks die when they get to the end of their string, and that is that. So, the Trojan warrior Hector can tell his wife, "Don't worry! If today is my day to die, I'll die whether I stay home or go out and fight. If today is not my day, I'll be perfectly safe in the middle of the battle." (See Chapter 7.)

The Olympian gods seemed powerless against the forces of the Fates; in the *Iliad,* Zeus tries to save his favorite heroes, but Hera and Athena won't let him upset the natural order of things. (For a little more detail about this story, see Chapter 4.)

Furies

The *Furies* sprang from the blood that fell into the sea when Cronos cut off Uranus's genitals. They were sometimes depicted with snakes for hair. They punished anyone who had incurred *miasma,* which included anyone who killed relatives, people in temples, or murdered a host. They also protected beggars and assured the "natural order" of things, such as the birthright of an eldest son.

Although authorities differ on how many Furies there were, the tragedian Aeschylus wrote a play about them, the *Eumenides,* which referred to just a whole bunch of Furies. Eventually, however, writers narrowed them down to these three:

- ✔ Tisiphone
- ✔ Allecto
- ✔ Megaera

The Greeks believed in divine retribution and in the proper natural order of things; the Furies filled in the gaps when human law failed.

Chapter 6

So Fine and Half Divine: Heroes

*H*eroes have left their mark all over Western culture. Everyone has heard of Hercules (or Heracles, as he's sometimes referred to), the strongest hero of all; he even had his own TV show. Heroes live in English vocabulary: a *Herculean task* is a job that seems too huge for anyone to accomplish. The word *labyrinth,* a kind of maze, comes from the story of Theseus. The Argonauts who went with Jason on the quest for the Golden Fleece were the inspiration for the word *astronaut* and its Russian counterpart *cosmonaut.*

Heroes were humans but larger than life. Most of them were sons of a god (usually Zeus) and a mortal woman, most of them were bigger and stronger than everyone else (a few were cleverer) and they all had adventures involving monsters, gods, and fantastic creatures. The "Age of Heroes" was (according to ancient Greek reckoning) the generation before the time of the Trojan War. By our reckoning, this was around 1500-1200 BCE, otherwise known as the Bronze Age.

What made a man a hero? Having a divine daddy was a start, but doing deeds beyond the ability of normal mortals clinched it. Heroes were not uniformly good people. Many of them murdered innocent victims, and few of them knew how to treat a woman right. Though they were often rulers, they were not always very good at government, preferring to spend their time in heroic exploits.

This chapter describes four of the most important Greek heroes and why they're still remembered today. Perseus killed Medusa. Heracles was the biggest, strongest guy ever. Theseus killed the Minotaur and turned Athens into a great city-state. Jason led the Argonauts to the Golden Fleece. They all did great things, but they were only human, too.

We mention several writers who were the sources of these myths. Pausanius lived during the second century CE, when the Greek world was under the rule of the Roman Empire; he was a travel writer and his book, *Description of Greece* is much like a travel guide you might buy today. Apollodorus was a scholar in Alexandria and in Egypt, during the second century BCE; he was, by specialty, a *mythographer,* or someone who collected and wrote down myths. Ovid was a Roman poet in the first century BCE whose famous, long poem, the *Metamorphoses,* is full of myths. Herodotus was a Greek historian who lived in the fifth century BCE; he was smart enough to know that what people believe influences how they act, so he includes in his history many mythological stories. Why do we get Greek myths from Roman sources? The Romans loved Greek culture, and scholars have to work with what survives today.

Perseus, a Real Prince of a Guy

Perseus was perhaps the most "heroic" of the Greek heroes, in the sense that he mostly did things such as kill monsters and rescue helpless maidens and then marry them, just like a prince in a fairy tale. His grandfather's story has a lesson, too: What goes around comes around.

The story of Perseus was popular in ancient Greece. Homer called him the "most renowned of men." The Roman authors Apollodorus and Ovid told full-length versions of his tale, and Pausanius and Herodotus mentioned him. The Greek playwrights Aeschylus, Sophocles, and Euripides wrote plays about him. Artists loved to depict him cutting off Medusa's head or with the beautiful Andromeda.

Perseus was one of Zeus's many sons. His mother's name was Danaë. She was the only child of King Acrisius of Argos. Acrisius was nervous about her because a priestess at an oracle had told him that not only would he never have a son of his own, but that his daughter would have a son who would kill him.

An *oracle* was a place where people could go ask gods questions. For a fee, a priestess inhaled burning bay leaves to become inspired and blurted out vaguely worded predictions. They always came true, just like the insights from fortune cookies. Later, *oracle* came to refer to the answer that the priestess gave as well as the priestess herself. So you could go to an oracle, to ask the oracle to give you an oracle.

Uh oh, here comes trouble

You can't get around a prophecy, but Acrisius gave it his best shot. He shut Danaë in an underground house open only to the sky and had her guarded day and night. But that didn't stop Zeus; he visited her from the sky in the form of a golden shower and impregnated her with Perseus. (We don't know what a golden shower is or how it can get someone pregnant, but that's how the myth goes.)

Danaë had her baby and hid him from her father for a while, but eventually Acrisius discovered him. He refused to believe that Zeus was the father. More to the point, he didn't want the kid around to kill him one day. So he shut Danaë and the baby in a trunk and set it adrift on the sea. By doing this, he hoped to get rid of her for good without being personally responsible for her death: The ol' "she was fine when I left her!" idea.

A good hot meal and salvation at last

But Zeus saw to it that Danaë and the baby didn't die; he sent the chest with mother and child to an island beach, where a fisherman named Dictys found them and took them home with him. Danaë and Perseus lived with Dictys and his wife for years. Dictys's brother, Polydectes, was the ruler of the island. Around the time that Perseus grew up, Polydectes noticed that Danaë was still looked pretty good and decided that he must have her. Danaë didn't want anything to do with him, and her son would have thwarted any attempts to take her by force. So Polydectes decided he had to get rid of Perseus.

So Polydectes came up with a rather far-fetched plan. He announced that he was getting married and invited all his friends, including Perseus. He told everyone to bring horses, which he was collecting as a bridal gift. But Polydectes knew that Perseus would have to salvage his pride some sort of way, and the only thing a strong young man like him could do was to conduct some heroic exploit. And that's exactly what Perseus did: He announced that he was going to go kill Medusa and bring back her head as a gift. The king was more than happy to give his approval to this foolhardy mission — in fact, Apollodorus says Polydectes ordered him to go.

Medusa was one of the three *Gorgons,* or scary women with the hair of snakes. Anyone who looked at her face turned to stone. Medusa could be killed, but the other two Gorgons were immortal.

On the trail of the Gorgons

Polydectes expected that Perseus would go off and get himself killed trying to kill Medusa, and then Danaë would be all his. Boy, was he wrong!

No one knew where to find the Gorgons. Perseus went off to the oracle at Delphi (see the "Perseus, A Real Prince of a Guy" section earlier in this chapter) without stopping to say goodbye to his Mom, but the priestess was of no help. The talking oak trees at Dodona didn't know either. So he wandered around for a while.

He gets by with a little help from his friends (divine, that is)

Eventually, Hermes (often known as Zeus's personal assistant) and Athena stepped in to get things going. They told Perseus that if he wanted to kill Medusa, first he needed to get some equipment from the nymphs of the North. And the only people who knew where the nymphs lived were the Gray Women. Probably worried that Perseus would never find the Gray Women on his own, Hermes said he would take him to them.

First, Hermes gave Perseus a magical sword that wouldn't break on the Gorgon's scaly neck. Athena lent Perseus her highly polished bronze shield. She told him he could use it as a mirror, so that he could see Medusa to attack her without actually looking at her face and turning to stone. Perseus took his gifts, and he and Hermes set off together to find the Gray Women.

The *Gray Women* were three old crones who looked like swans with human heads, hands, and arms under their wings; they were the Gorgons' sisters. They had one eye for the three of them and took turns using it. Perseus waited until he saw one of them take the eye out of her head and pass it to her sister; then he jumped up and grabbed it. He told them that they could have their eye back as soon as they told him how to find the nymphs of the North, and they sensibly told him right away. Returning the eye, he and Hermes set off again.

This time, Perseus arrived at the charmed land of the *Hyperboreans* (the name means "People who live really far north," and sometimes refers to the inhabitants of Britain), an earthly paradise of feasts and music and dancing. The Hyperboreans gave him three gifts:

- Winged sandals
- A cap to make him invisible
- A bag that would hold whatever was put in it, no matter what size it was

Now he was set.

Hermes actually knew where the Gorgons lived, and he and Perseus flew over the ocean to their island where Athena met them. The three monsters were asleep, and Perseus took a good look at them in the reflection on his shield. Athena told him which one was Medusa. Perseus flew over her on his winged sandals, chopped off her head (Athena helped him aim), swooped down to grab it, and dropped it into his magic bag. (Don't be afraid to look, now, Figure 6-1 shows Perseus and Medusa.) The other two Gorgons woke up and tried to get him, but Perseus put on his cap of invisibility and flew away safely.

Figure 6-1:
Perseus and
Medusa.
Evidently
once she
was dead,
you could
look at her
head.

Perseus finds true love and another battle

Perseus flew through Ethiopia on the way home. There he found a beautiful maiden about to be eaten by a sea monster. Her name was Andromeda.

Andromeda's mother, Casseiopeia, had boasted that she was more beautiful than the daughters of the sea god. The angry deity sent the sea monster to Ethiopia, where it terrorized the people by eating them. An oracle said that the only way to make it go away was for Casseiopeia's daughter to be given to the monster, so Andromeda's dad chained her to a rock and waited for the monster to eat her.

Perseus instantly fell in love. He waited for the sea monster to surface and then cut off its head. Perseus took Andromeda back home and asked her parents if he could marry her. They said yes. Of course, a girl like Andromeda hadn't gone unnoticed before, and it happened that she already was engaged to a guy named Phineas. Phineas plotted against Perseus, but Perseus gave the Medusa head a tryout and turned his rival to stone. Then he married the princess.

Here's your gift!

Perseus and his bride sailed back to his island home. They discovered that his mother had rejected Polydectes's advances, and she and Dictys had run away to hide. Some accounts say they hid at the altars of the gods where no harm could come to them. Meanwhile, Polydectes was having a party with all his buddies that evening. Perseus walked into the banquet hall, announced that he had brought the promised bride-gift, pulled out Medusa's head, and turned Polydectes and his cronies to stone.

Of ironies and oracles. . . .

Dictys became king of the island. Perseus, Andromeda, and Danaë went back to Argos to try to make up with Danaë's father Acrisius. When they got there, they learned that he left the city and no one knew where he was. What had happened was that Acrisius had heard of Perseus's great exploits and had run away, fearing that Argos would be the new hero's next stop.

Perseus heard about a track meet that was being held in Larissa. Having nothing else to do, he decided to participate. As it happened, Acrisius had come to watch the same event. Perseus accidentally threw the discus into the stands, which hit his grandfather on the foot and killed him, just as the oracle had said so many years ago. And no, we don't know how getting hit on the foot can kill someone instantly — maybe he had a heart attack. Pausanias tells a different version — Perseus had gone to Larissa looking for his grandfather to make up with him. He decided to give a little discus display, and Acrisius accidentally walked into the path of the discus.

Perseus and Andromeda lived happily ever after. They had a son named Electryon, who became Heracles' grandfather. Perseus gave Medusa's head to Athena. She put it onto her shield so she could turn people to stone whenever she wanted.

Box Office Gold of the Ancients: Heracles

Heracles, better known as Hercules (his Roman name), was the mightiest of the mighty. He was strong and sexy and knew that he was hotter than any other guy. He usually relied on brute strength — who cares about brains when you're the hugest — but occasionally he displayed flashes of brilliance, such as when he persuaded two rivers to divert their courses into the Augean stables.

Heracles (see Figure 6-2) was *extremely* popular with the ancient Greeks. Homer mentioned him, and storytellers constantly added to his legend. Apollodorus and Pausanius wrote a ton of stuff about him, and so did the historian Herodotus. The Greeks worshipped their mythological heroes with small *hero shrines*. Heracles had more shrines than any other hero. Maybe the reason he had so many shrines is that he dedicated his life to useful work and suffered a great deal while helping folks.

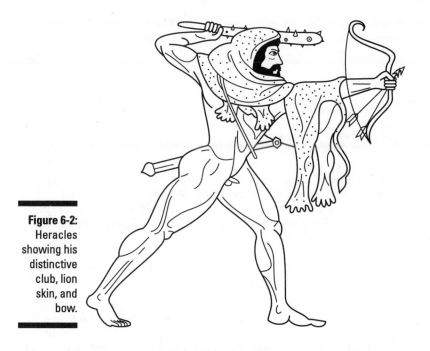

Figure 6-2:
Heracles
showing his
distinctive
club, lion
skin, and
bow.

Zeus strikes again

Zeus was Heracles's father. Zeus had gotten the hots for a woman named Alcmena and disguised himself as her husband so she would have sex with him. Alcmena got pregnant and had twin boys. One was her husband's child and only human, and the other was Heracles.

Zeus's jealous wife Hera had it in for Heracles all his life. (The name "Heracles" means "Fame of Hera" or "Famous because of Hera.") When Heracles was a baby, Hera sent two snakes to kill him in his crib. Little Heracles grabbed each one around the neck and strangled them; his mother rushed in to find her toddler laughing with two dead snakes in his hands.

When Heracles was 18, he killed the Thespian lion, whose skin he wore as a cloak for the rest of his life. (Or he got the skin from the Nemean lion, who he killed as the first of his twelve labors — see the next section for that story.) He then fought and destroyed the Minyans, who had been demanding tribute from Thebes. The grateful citizens gave him a princess for a wife. He had three sons with her, but one day Hera arranged to make him go crazy and kill his wife and children. She drove him crazy either because she was just plain mean, or because she arranged for him to receive an oracle ordering him into service, and he was so mad at having to leave his new family that he went nuts and killed them. Regardless, he was filled with guilt and went to the oracle at Delphi to find out what he could do for penance. The priestess there told him to go to Eurystheus, king of Mycenae, and do whatever he demanded.

The Twelve Labors of Heracles: Work smarter, not harder

Eurystheus was thrilled to have a big strong slave, although he was a little scared of Heracles, too. He told Heracles that he had to do ten seemingly impossible tasks, which Heracles was glad to do as penance for killing his family. The ten turned into twelve because Eurystheus disqualified Heracles on two of them. These tasks were performed in a certain order, so they're numbered here in their correct sequence:

1. The *Nemean Lion* was impervious to weapons; Heracles choked it to death.

2. The *Lernian Hydra* had nine heads, and grew two new ones whenever one was cut off. Heracles seared each neck as he removed the heads, and then buried the last, immortal one under a rock. He poisoned his arrows by dipping them the Hydra's poisonous blood. Unfortunately for Heracles, his charioteer (in those days, the charioteer was a near and dear friend) Iolaus, had helped him kill the Hydra, and Eurystheus said that didn't count.

3. The *Cerynitian stag* had horns of gold and was sacred to Artemis. It took Heracles a year to catch it and bring it back alive.

4. Heracles trapped the great boar on Mount Erymanthus in the snow.

5. The Augean stables hadn't been cleaned in years. Heracles diverted the courses of two nearby rivers through the stables and cleaned them in a single day. This feat was accomplished by a great amount of digging and by giving the rivers a gift to buy their cooperation. But Heracles had asked Augeas (the owner of the Augean stables, of course) for payment for completing this task, and Eurystheus said it didn't count as one of the labors.

6. He flushed out the Stymphalian birds with bronze castanets he received from Athena and shot them with arrows.

7. He caught King Minos's bull in Crete and brought it back to Mycenae in a boat.

8. He slayed King Diomedes of Thrace and stole his man-eating mares.

9. Ordered to bring back the girdle (belt, really) of Hippolyta, a fearsome warrior and queen of the Amazons, Heracles simply asked her if she would give him the belt as a present. She said yes. Typically, Heracles then killed her because of a misunderstanding: Hera, always hateful,

made the Amazons think he was threatening Hippolyta so they would attack him, and he assumed, instead, that she had told them to do it. Heracles always was a "shoot first and ask questions later" kind of guy.

10. He brought back the cattle of *Geryon,* a three-bodied monster on a western island. On the way there, he set up the *Pillars of Hercules* at the end of the Mediterranean: Gibraltar and Ceuta. This would have been his last labor, but Eurystheus disqualified the second and fifth tasks, so he set out to have Heracles do two more.

11. The Golden Apples of the Hesperides proved to be a problem. Heracles went to Atlas and agreed to hold up the sky while Atlas went to get the apples for him. (When Zeus conquered the Titans, he punished Atlas by making him hold the sky on his back forever.) Atlas got the apples, but told Heracles he had to keep holding the earth. Heracles was at least smarter than Atlas; he agreed but asked him to take back the sky for a minute while he put a pad on his head. Of course as soon as Atlas took the sky back, Heracles was outta there!

12. For his last labor, Heracles went to the underworld and retrieved Hades's three-headed dog Cerberus. Eurystheus then decided he didn't want the dog and had Heracles carry it back.

Finally, Heracles was a free man again.

The sneaky centaur and the tragic mix-up

Heracles loved the ladies (he once slept with 50 sisters in 50 days!), and this proclivity was his downfall. He had married again to a woman named Deianira. He got a *centaur,* someone with the body of a horse and a human upper body, named Nessus to ferry his bride across a river. (Heracles was trying to save ferry-fare and swam across himself.) Nessus tried to rape her once they were on the other side. She screamed and Heracles shot the centaur across the river. As Nessus was dying, he told Heracles's wife Deianira to save some of his blood and the semen he had spilled, mix them together, and use it as a charm if her husband ever fell in love with another woman.

Love hurts: Downfall and resurrection

One day, Heracles conquered a king named Eurytus. He'd had it in for this guy since right after finishing his twelve labors and thought he was going to get to marry Eurytus' daughter Iole — he'd won her in an archery contest — but her brother refused to permit it, fearing that Heracles would go crazy and kill her like he had his first wife. So Heracles went to war with Eurytus, killed him and his sons, and took Iole captive.

He sent his herald home to ask Deianira to send him a nice robe to wear to make his sacrifices. The herald told Deianira about Iole, and Deianira thought this was an opportune moment for bringing out her love charm. She smeared it on the robe and sent it off.

As soon as Heracles put on the robe, he felt like his skin was burning — the poison from the hydra still was in Nessus's blood and was doing its work on him. He tore off the robe, which stuck to him and took his skin with it. But it was too late for him.

Deianira hanged herself when she heard what had happened. Heracles built a funeral pyre, got on top, and told his companions to light it. As the fire burned, a clap of thunder was heard and Heracles went up to live with the gods. Hera finally reconciled with him and gave him her daughter Hebe as a wife.

A Home-Grown Hero: Theseus

Athens claimed Theseus for its own because he supposedly helped make Athens into the democratic city-state it eventually became and because he embodied may of the qualities they thought were important about their city — cleverness, skill in negotiation, courage, justice, and protection of the oppressed. They saw Theseus as a strong, fair ruler presiding over a democracy. His story is a good example of a myth that collected lots of events and consolidated them into one neat package. Although it probably took years and many leaders to turn Athens into a great power, it was very simple and satisfying to credit Theseus with everything. Theseus also illustrates how being an irresponsible jerk did not disqualify someone from hero status — he hurt Ariadne and his dad on the same trip, but that didn't hurt his fame.

Theseus was the son of Aegeus, king of Athens, and a woman in a small town in southern Greece, who evidently wasn't married to him. Aegeus returned to Athens before his son was born. But before he left, he hid a sword and a pair of shoes under a stone and told Theseus's mother that when the boy was strong enough to roll away the stone and find the things beneath it, he could come to Athens and claim Aegeus as his father.

Theseus grew up big and strong, and one day his Mom told him about the stone. He tried and tried to lift the stone, which was really too heavy for anyone, even a strapping young hero, to lift. Finally, though, he devised a rope-and-pulley arrangement, and retrieved his dad's old shoes and sword. Evidently, Aegeus didn't want to see his son unless the kid had a brain in his head! His mother tried to get him to take a boat to Athens, but Theseus thought walking overland would give him more opportunity for heroics, and he set off on foot.

Greece was a scary place, full of outlaws and bandits. Theseus ran into several criminals and gave them each a taste of their own medicine. Here are a few of the scoundrels that he used to make his own adventure flicks:

- ✔ Sinis had been fastening people to two pine trees bent to the ground and letting the trees go. He died that same way at Theseus's hands.

- ✔ The bandit Sciron had been making people kneel to wash his feet and then kicking them over a cliff; Theseus kicked him over.

- ✔ Procrustes put his victims on an iron bed. Then he either stretched them or cut them down to fit on it. After he met Theseus, Procrustes himself was the last one to lie on that bed.

News of Theseus's deeds preceded him to Athens, and when he arrived he received a hero's welcome. King Aegeus, unaware that this was his son, invited him to a banquet planning to poison him, fearing that the people would make Theseus king. Medea (see the section "Jason the Jerk" later in this chapter) happened to be at Aegeus's court; she handed Theseus the cup, but at the same moment Theseus drew his sword so that Aegeus would know who he was. (Or Aegeus happened to look right then at the sword hanging at Theseus's side.) Regardless, Aegeus saw the sword, threw the poison on the ground, and proclaimed Theseus his son and heir. Medea ran away to Asia.

More adventure: The Minotaur and the dating game

Aegeus had been having trouble with King Minos of Crete, who had invaded Athens a few years back and demanded a yearly tribute of seven girls and seven boys. These kids were thrown into the Labyrinth for the Minotaur to devour.

Theseus had arrived in Athens just in time for the yearly tribute ship to sail. He offered to be one of the young men, seeing this as a great heroic opportunity to kill the Minotaur and end Athens's subordination to Crete.

Introducing bachelor number one

When the young Athenians arrived in Crete, their hosts marched them into the Labyrinth. Minos's daughter Ariadne saw Theseus as he walked by and fell in love with him. She went to the wise Daedalus, somewhat of a hero in his own right, and asked him to help her get Theseus out of the Labyrinth (see the previous section for more about this). Daedalus told her to give Theseus a ball of string. He could fasten one end of it to the Labyrinth's door and unwind it as he went. (Scuba divers who dive in caves or sunken wrecks use this same technique today.)

Should've chosen bachelor number two

Ariadne met with Theseus and promised to help him escape if he promised to take her to Athens and marry her. Of course, he said yes, and she gave him the ball of string. He tied it to the door and then ventured into the Labyrinth in search of the Minotaur. He found the monster sleeping and killed it with his bare hands. Theseus and his fellow Athenians then fled the Labyrinth, picked up Ariadne, jumped into their ship, and set sail back for Athens.

On the way home they stopped at the island of Naxos, where Theseus left Ariadne, although why he did isn't exactly clear. Some sources say a storm carried his ship away and he was heartbroken, but other say he abandoned her, and the wine god Dionysus married her instead. As the ship approached Athens, Theseus forgot another promise he had made: His father had asked him to hoist a white sail if he was safe instead of the black one that the tribute boat generally used. Theseus forgot and left the black sail up. Aegeus saw the black sail approaching, and, filled with grief over his son's death, jumped off a cliff into the sea. Interestingly enough, the sea that surrounds Athens is called the Aegean Sea in honor of Aegeus.

Centralized management: Theseus the "good" king

Theseus was now king of Athens. He decided that he would prefer a people's government where all citizens were equal. So, he turned Athens into a commonwealth, where all the little villages in the territory of Attica became part of the Athenian state, all this with Theseus himself as commander-in-chief, of course. Athens prospered under his leadership, and he was a good friend to his contemporaries such as Oedipus and Heracles.

He attacked the Amazons and married their queen, Hippolyta. They had a son named Hippolytus. The Amazons invaded Athens to rescue Hippolyta and Theseus defeated them; no other enemy tried to take Athens for the rest of his life. Now that's a real man!

Isn't Hippolyta the woman Heracles killed? Yes. So how could Theseus marry her? Well, he could; because she wasn't dead when Theseus met her. Myths are like that — stories don't fit together perfectly. Some sources, however, say that Theseus married a woman named Antiope, who may have been Hippolyta's sister.

A marriage with a cause

Theseus, like all heroes, had more than his share of love interests. He kidnapped Helen of Troy when she was still a child; her brothers Castor and Pollux retrieved her before any damage was done.

Later, he married Ariadne's sister Phaedra; this marriage was a political union to firm up relations between Athens and Crete. According to Apollodorus, the Amazon Theseus had earlier been married to (Antiope or Hippolyta) showed up at their wedding threatening to kill everyone; the guests quickly shut the door in her face and then killed her. Apollodorus also mentions another version of her death in which Theseus killed her in battle. In any case, Theseus had a new Cretan wife.

Phaedra fell in love with Theseus's son Hippolytus. Hippolytus had absolutely no interest in women and was disgusted at the thought of getting together with his stepmother. Phaedra, consumed with shame, killed herself but left a note for Theseus claiming that Hippolytus had tried to rape her.

Theseus banished his son, who wrecked his chariot and was mortally wounded. The goddess Artemis now told Theseus that Phaedra had lied in her note, and so he forgave Hippolytus before the boy died.

Unsolved mystery: Cliff's descent

A few years later Theseus was visiting his friend Lycomedes, and his host threw him off a cliff because he was jealous of his fame and achievements and feared the people would like him better, or perhaps as a favor to another king, Menestheus. (Plutarch suggests that Theseus may have accidentally slipped and fallen.) The Athenian people built a magnificent tomb for him and made it a sanctuary for the poor.

Jason the Jerk

Jason is most famous for leading the Argonauts on the quest for the Golden Fleece. It's one of Western civilization's quintessential adventure stories. He also was a lousy husband and father. His wife, Medea, was a witch, and she became a model for the evil witches who appear in later fairy tales.

The third-century poet Apollonius of Rhodes wrote a long poem telling about the quest for the Golden Fleece. Pindar and Ovid also told the story. The fifth-century playwright Euripides wrote a play all about Jason and Medea, called (appropriately) *Medea* — it's heart-rending.

The 14K gold rescue: The Golden Fleece

So what was this Golden Fleece? Well, long ago, a Greek king was going to sacrifice his son Phrixus to save his people from a famine. But when the boy was on the altar about to be killed, Hermes sent a ram with a fleece of pure gold to pick he and his sister up and carry them to safety. The boy's sister, Helle, fell off the ram over the strait between Europe and Asia and drowned. That strait now bears her name: the Hellespont. Phrixus landed in the country of Colchis in modern Turkey, where he was taken in by its king, Aetes. Phrixus then rather ungratefully sacrificed the ram to Zeus and gave the ram's golden fleece to King Aetes.

Now back to Greece. Phrixus's uncle was a king in Greece (this king's name isn't important), but a guy named Pelias had usurped his kingdom. The ousted king's son was Jason, which makes Pelias Jason's uncle, and it makes Jason the rightful heir to the throne that Pelias unjustly was occupying. An oracle had told Pelias that he would die at the hands of a kinsman wearing one shoe, so he was pretty shocked when his nephew Jason walked in one day wearing only one shoe — it looked like Jason would be the one to kill him. (Jason had lost the other shoe helping a goddess cross a stream.) Jason said he had come to claim the throne. Pelias told him that he would give up the kingdom if Jason would go to Colchis (remember, Colchis is in Turkey) and bring back the Golden Fleece.

Lifestyles of the heroic and famous: The Argo and the Argonauts

Jason summoned all the most famous heroes of Greece:

- ✔ Heracles
- ✔ Castor
- ✔ Pollux
- ✔ Orpheus
- ✔ Achilles's father Peleus
- ✔ Atalanta
- ✔ A few other folks standing around with nothing better to do

They all set sail in a ship called the *Argo* and called themselves the *Argonauts.* The goddess Hera helped them along the way. They had many adventures on the way to Colchis, and Jason repeatedly lost his nerve and had to be encouraged by his shipmates. Heracles ditched the company when his boy-friend Hylas drowned. The Argonauts fought the *Harpies,* disgusting woman-birds who spoiled their food and left behind a foul stench. They just barely got their boat through the *Symplegades,* two rocks that repeatedly banged together; they timed the opening by letting a dove fly through first, and then rowed as fast as they could. They sailed past the Amazons and Prometheus chained to his rock. Finally they arrived in Colchis, land of the Golden Fleece.

Medea the Witch: Self-starter, proactive, works late as needed

Hera knew that Jason would need help getting the Fleece, so she had Aphrodite's son Eros make King Aetes's daughter Medea fall in love with the hero. Medea was a sorceress.

Jason and his buddies introduced themselves to the king, who welcomed them and gave them dinner. Then Jason stated his business — he wanted the Golden Fleece. Aetes didn't want to hand it over, so he told Jason that he could have it if he completed an impossible task: Yoke two fire-breathing bulls with hooves of bronze, plow a field, plant it with dragon teeth, and fight off the army of men that would immediately grow from the teeth. Jason said he'd give it a try.

Late-night meetings and invincible ointment

Medea visited Jason that night and gave him an ointment to smear on his body and weapons to make them invincible. She told him that if the dragon-teeth soldiers attacked, he should throw a stone into their midst and they would then fight each other instead of him. Jason promised to take her to Greece and be faithful to her forever, and she stole back to the palace.

Yep, she's helpful all right

The next day Jason presented himself before Aetes and all the spectators who had come to watch. He harnessed the giant bulls and plowed the field, casting the dragon teeth into the furrows as he went. By the time he finished plowing and sowing, the dragon-teeth soldiers were already up and ready to attack him. He tossed a stone into their midst, and they cut each other to pieces, just as Medea had said they would.

King Aetes was not pleased. He started thinking of other ways to get rid of Jason, but Medea ran to the Argonauts again and told them that they needed to take the Fleece and run before her father got to them.

Apparently blood is not thicker than water . . .

A giant snake guarded the Golden Fleece. Medea put the snake to sleep with a magical charm, and Jason easily pulled the Fleece out of the tree where it hung. Then they dashed back to the Argo and rowed away as fast as they could. Medea's brother came after them, but she killed him, cut up his body, and tossed the pieces into the sea. Aetes stopped to collect the body parts, and Jason and Media got away.

Behind every hero is a great witch

Back home in Greece, the Argonauts disbanded and Jason and Medea took the Golden Fleece to Pelias. They discovered that Pelias had forced Jason's father to kill himself, and his mother had also died. Jason asked Medea to help him get revenge.

Oh, she's a sweetheart all right

Medea told Pelias's daughters that she could make him young again, and illustrated her technique: She cut an old ram into pieces, boiled it in her cauldron, uttered the magic words, and a baby lamb jumped out. Convinced, the daughters cut up their dad and cooked him. Then they looked for Medea to say the spell, but she was gone and their father stayed dead. Jason had his revenge.

Jason trades up for a more royal model

Jason and Medea moved to Corinth and had two sons. They lived on happily this way for some years in Corinth. But one day Jason announced that he was going to marry the daughter of King Creon of Corinth. Marrying the Corinthian woman was a political move — he wanted royal children, and Medea's sons had no rights and weren't suitable heirs. The Corinthian king, nervous about Medea's magical powers and her two sons, ordered her to leave the country with them. Jason now told her that she was too wild and dangerous for him, and it was her own fault that she had to leave. However, great guy that he was, he had generously asked the king to exile her instead of killing her. He was going to make sure she had plenty of money for her journey to wherever.

Hell hath no fury . . .

Medea tore into him, pointing out the many times she had saved him, but he refused to acknowledge that she had done anything to help him, claiming that the gods had been on his side. Medea was angry now. So Medea killed his new bride by anointing a beautiful robe with poison and having her sons deliver it to her rival. When she put it on, her flesh melted away and she dropped dead.

Then Medea made the most dreadful decision a mother can make. She knew that her boys would be defenseless without their father, and couldn't bear to see them become slaves. So she killed them herself. Jason came looking for her, outraged that she had killed his bride. He found his sons dead and Medea flying away in a chariot pulled by dragons. He cursed her as she left.

Chapter 7

The *Iliad*, the End of the Trojan War, and the *Odyssey*

In This Chapter

▶ Examining the Trojan War and its cast of characters

▶ Fighting the Trojans in Homer's *Iliad*

▶ Mourning Achilles and infiltrating Troy with a horse

▶ Exploring the world with Odysseus

The Trojan War and the adventures of Odysseus were the most exciting stories of the ancient world — the beautiful Helen stolen from her husband, the mighty heroes Achilles and Patroclus, the Trojan Horse, wily Odysseus and his encounters with monsters, witches, and seductresses. These stories mostly come from Homer's *Iliad* and *Odyssey*, with several other authors filling in the gaps. Almost all ancient people, educated or not, knew and loved these tales.

The ancient Greeks didn't have a holy book that told them what to believe. But they did have Homer's *Iliad* and *Odyssey*, two long poems about the Trojan War. These books were not religious — though lots of gods, prayers, and sacrifices are found in them — but that didn't matter. Just as Christians, Jews, and Muslims use their *Bible, Torah, Talmud,* and *Q'uran (Koran),* the Greeks used Homer's poetry to tell them who they were. If an ancient Greek person in the fifth or fourth century BCE had one book in the house, that book was probably one of Homer's poems. (Actually, the "book" hadn't been invented, so what they would have had was a bunch of rolled-up pieces of papyrus in a leather or wooden bucket.)

Homer's poems deal with the Trojan War. The *Iliad* talks about things that happened during the war itself, and the *Odyssey* talks about how the hero Odysseus spent ten years trying to get home after the war was over.

Poems of Epic Proportions

Epic poems traditionally were transmitted orally first, then written in verse. They were metrical because they were meant to be spoken or sung to music. And, more important, epic poems told of great deeds of the past. Listed below are some the specific factors that make up epic poems:

- **Meter (dactylic hexameter):** The *Iliad* and *Odyssey* are poems in Greek. They are not, in fact, in any form of the Greek language that anyone spoke. Instead, they're in an artificial poetic dialect that folks could understand that was quite different from the spoken language. Greek poetry doesn't rhyme (or, at least, it shouldn't rhyme), but it is *metrical,* which means that it has rhythm based on some syllables being longer than others. The particular meter of epic poetry is *dactylic hexameter,* meaning that each line of poetry is divided into six feet and each foot consists of either two long syllables, or one long and two short syllables.

- **Stock phrases (epithets — expansive, digressive, repetitive), stock scenes, set speeches, set pieces:** Certain words, phrases, lines, and entire chunks of lines became *formulaic,* or featuring convenient bits of language that fit well into the meter. The most noticeable of the formulas are the *noun-epithet* combinations; the poet never merely says "Achilles," but, instead, always adds an epithet to his name: Swift-footed Achilles, Godlike Achilles, or Achilles-Son of Peleus. Likewise Hector is Godlike sometimes and Man-Slaying at others. These epithets helped the poet drop characters' backgrounds into particular points of the poem, while maintaining the poem's meter.

- **Similes:** In Homeric poetry, the poet frequently describes some action by means of a simile wrapped in ring-composition. What does that mean? The simile is a "Just like . . . " passage that conjures up an image (usually from the world of nature) to illustrate how, say, Diomedes rushed into battle.

- **Invocations:** At the beginning of an epic poem, the poet invokes the Muse to inspire him. Often, he asks the Muse to sing the song herself. So, the *Iliad* begins with the words, "Sing, Goddess, of the wrath of Achilles."

Setting the Stage: Events Leading to the Trojan War

The *Iliad* starts nine years into the Trojan War, which took place in Troy. Troy is in the northwest corner of what is now the Republic of Turkey right on the Hellespont. Many things had to happen first to get this big war under way.

The judgment of Paris

Three generations of misery and bloodshed started because a wedding planner failed to invite an important goddess.

Peleus, a mortal man, fell in love with the sea nymph Thetis, daughter of Zeus. Peleus had been on a number of adventures, accompanying Meleager on the hunt for the Calydonian boar and sailing with Jason and the Argonauts. He had been married before, but that went sour when he accidentally killed his father-in-law. When he saw Thetis, he tried to kidnap her and she fought him off with a snake, but eventually he won her over and Zeus consented to their marriage.

The wedding was a big affair; all the famous mortals and gods and goddesses came to Phthia in Greece. But Thetis (or whoever composed the guest list) had decided not to invite Eris, the goddess of strife, hoping to avoid conflict. Of course that didn't work. Eris, insulted, snuck into the wedding reception and tossed a golden apple onto the dance floor. On the apple were the words, "To the Fairest."

The golden apple was a party-killer. Who was the fairest, the most beautiful? The competition was stiff between:

- Athena, Zeus's daughter and a real daddy's girl
- Hera, Zeus's wife and Queen of the Gods
- Aphrodite, the Goddess of Love

They asked Zeus to award the prize, but he was no fool and passed the decision off to a young man named Paris. Paris was the son of Priam, king of Troy.

Why did Paris get this dubious honor? Well, Zeus knew it would cause trouble, but he also knew that Troy was fated to be destroyed. Years earlier, the Trojan king Laomedon got into trouble with Apollo and Poseidon. They had agreed to build walls for Troy, but when the job was done, Laomedon refused to pay them. So Troy was doomed. Zeus chose Paris to judge between the three goddesses to get the ball rolling. In fact, when Paris was born, his mother had a dream that she'd given birth to a torch that was going to set the entire city on fire — the torch was, obviously enough, her baby Paris. The parents tried to get rid of their baby by leaving him in the wilderness, but little Paris survived for five days, so Priam gave in and took him back.

Each goddess tried to bribe Paris. Some of the goodies:

- Athena offered him victory in war
- Hera offered him power over nations
- Aphrodite offered him the most beautiful woman in the world

Paris accepted Aphrodite's offer only to discover that the most beautiful woman in the world was already married. She was Helen, daughter of the mortal woman Leda and Zeus (who visited Leda in the form of a swan — Helen was actually born out of an egg!). She was married to Menelaus, king of Sparta, and Paris had travel from Troy, in Asia Minor, to Sparta, in southern Greece, to kidnap her to collect his prize.

The kidnapping of Helen

Paris already had a wife named Oenone (pronounced "Oy-no-nee"), who warned him not to go through with the kidnapping, but he didn't listen. He sailed off to Sparta to be a guest at the palace of Menelaus. While there, he either

- Forcibly carried Helen off to Troy, or
- Seduced her, and they went off to Troy together

Now, one of Zeus's specific roles is "Protector of Hospitality" *(Zeus Xenios)*, and kidnapping your host's wife was certainly against the rules. So, if Troy hadn't been fated to be destroyed before, it definitely was now!

When Menelaus discovered that his wife had been kidnapped, he went running to his big brother Agamemnon, king of Mycenae. Agamemnon agreed to get an expedition together and sail to Troy to wage war and get Helen back.

Because of this vast expedition to get her back, Helen is known as "the face that launched a thousand ships," a phrase that comes from a poem written by the English poet Christopher Marlowe in the late 1500s. Where did those ships sail? Check out Figure 7-1.

Agamemnon had one advantage as he planned his invasion. When Helen's father, Tyndareus, had been planning her wedding, just about every bachelor in Greece had made him an offer. This situation looked as though it was going to be trouble, because whomever Tyndareus chose for his daughter, he ran the risk of gaining one son-in-law and a thousand bitter enemies. But clever Odysseus suggested that all the suitors promise the following:

- Not to kill the lucky fellow.
- To help get Helen back if she should be kidnapped. In retrospect, this effort to avoid trouble led directly to a 10-year-long war that sent many souls of heroes flying down to Hades, so perhaps it wasn't such a good idea after all.

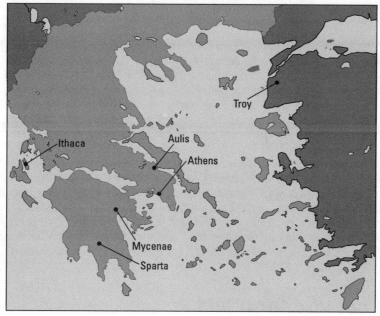

Figure 7-1:
The area of the Mediter-ranean around the time of the Trojan War.

Unfortunately, now that Helen actually had been kidnapped, these guys were not particularly enthusiastic about helping Menelaus! Odysseus, for example, pretended to be insane when the recruiter arrived to collect him; he hitched an ox and an ass to his plow and sowed his fields with salt. The recruiter stuck his baby son in front of the plow, Odysseus stopped short of plowing the kid, and had to admit that he was sane and could go to war.

The marriage of Peleus and Thetis worked out long enough for the two of them to have a son, Achilles.

Achilles's mother Thetis had tried to get her son off the hook, too. When Achilles was 9 years old, she heard from the prophet Calchas that Troy would not be captured without him, so she tried to prevent the whole mess by hiding him. She sent Achilles to the palace of Lycomedes, where he spent several years dressed as and acting like a girl — though he did father a son with the king's daughter.

The Greeks sent Odysseus to Lycomedes's house to find Achilles. Odysseus evidently couldn't tell the real girls from Achilles-in-drag by looking, so he played a trick. One version of the story (the one in Ovid's *Metamorphoses*) says that Odysseus plunked down a basket full of pretty clothes mixed with armor and weapons. The girls all ran to check out the clothes, but Achilles was interested in the armor — busted!

The sacrifice of Iphigenia

Even when he did get his army together, Agamemnon's problems were far from over. As the Greeks got ready to board their ships the winds began to blow, preventing the ships from sailing east across the Aegean Sea to Troy. Agamemnon consulted the prophet Calchas, who said that these were winds sent by Artemis, who liked Troy and who didn't like Agamemnon. The king could get the winds to stop, but only by offering his own daughter, Iphigenia, as a sacrifice to Artemis.

Agamemnon sent a message to his wife, Clytemnestra, saying that he had arranged for Iphigenia to marry Achilles. Mother and daughter packed up and traveled to Aulis, expecting a wedding. When they arrived, Agamemnon killed the girl on an altar, just like a sacrificial animal. The winds died down, and he was free to sail. With this horrible crime, the Trojan War was on. Clytemnestra harbored a grudge against her husband forever after; see Chapter 8, "Greek Tragedy: The Days of Their Lives," for Agamemnon's punishment.

Cast of characters

The important thing to remember about the Trojan War was that the two sides were the Greeks and the Trojans.

Greeks

The Greek heroes came from all over the Greek world — representatives from Mycenae, Sparta, Pylos, Crete, Thessaly, and a hundred other places. Homer lists them all, at great length, in Book 2 of the *Iliad* in the part known as the "Catalogue of Ships;" the list is so long that even Homer seems daunted as he starts it and calls on the Muse a couple of times during the course of the telling.

- **Agamemnon:** King of Mycenae, the leader of the Greeks.
- **Menelaus:** The plaintiff in the dispute, King of Sparta, husband of Helen. Menelaus is portrayed as something of a wimp (like his Trojan counterpart, Paris).
- **Achilles:** The "Best of the Achaeans."
- **Patroclus:** Achilles's best friend.
- **Phoenix:** The old man who more-or-less raised Achilles, because Peleus evidently was too busy being King of Phthia.
- **Odysseus:** From Ithaca. The smartest of the Achaeans.

- ✔ **Ajax** (his Greek name is Aias): Big and dumb, but means well.

- ✔ **Diomedes:** An all-around hero. During the *Iliad*, because Achilles is sulking most of the time (the details can be found later in the chapter), Homer uses Diomedes as a generic example of a great warrior.

- ✔ **Nestor:** The "Gerenian Horseman." No one knows what *Gerenian* means, not even ancient writers who wrote about the *Iliad*. Nestor is too old to fight, but is full of advice and likes to tell long-winded stories about how cool he used to be.

Trojans

The Trojans, too, were not all from Troy; many heroes came from other cities in Asia Minor. But for all of this geographic diversity, all of the heroes are really Greek, on both sides of the conflict: they all speak the same language, have the same customs and values, and worship the same gods.

- ✔ **Priam:** King of Troy, an old man.

- ✔ **Paris (also known as Alexandros, or Alexander):** Priam's son. Kidnapper of Helen. Paris is something of a wimp.

- ✔ **Hector:** Priam's other son. Definitely *not* a wuss. Everyone knows that only Hector can save Troy, but because everyone also knows that Troy is doomed, we know that Hector is doomed.

- ✔ **Andromache:** Hector's wife.

- ✔ **Aeneas:** A sort of Trojan Diomedes. Not very interesting, but there's nothing wrong with him. For more on him, see Chapter 11.

- ✔ **Sarpedon:** One of the many illegitimate sons of Zeus.

The Trojan War, Nine Years Later: The *Iliad*

Homer's poem, the *Iliad* (named for *Ilium*, another name for Troy), takes place during the ninth year of the Trojan War. The poem itself deals with events that happen over a short span of time — just a couple of weeks — during the war. The poem's reputation comes, in part, from the way it brings together events and themes from the war as a whole, while focusing on the quarrel between Achilles and Agamemnon, and the resulting tragedy of Hector.

Two guys for every girl

The Greeks had spent the previous years sacking neighboring cities for loot, captives, and entertainment. During one of these raids, Achilles led the Greeks to victory over the city of Chryse, where they took many of the women in town captive and divided them amongst themselves as war prizes.

When the *Iliad* opens, the Greeks are camped out on the beach a mile or so from the city, and the Trojans are safe behind their walls. An old man named Chryses from the city of Chryse, a priest of Apollo, arrives at the Greek camp to try to buy back his daughter, Chryseis. (These names, by the way, aren't really names; they just mean "man from Chryse" and "daughter of Chryses." They're not important as individuals, but as parts of the story.)

Agamemnon had Chryseis, and he didn't want to give her back. Agamemnon told the old man to get lost, and threatened him if he ever came back. Bad move — it *never* pays to get snappy with a priest of Apollo. Apollo sent a plague among the Greeks.

Trouble in the boys' locker room

After a bunch of Greeks died, they asked the prophet Calchas to explain what was going on. Calchas said that the only way to appease Apollo was to give the girl back. Agamemnon refused, and he and Achilles got into an argument. Finally Agamemnon agreed to give Chryseis back to her father to save the army but insisted on taking Achilles's war-prize, a woman named Briseis, as a replacement. Achilles stormed off in a huff and refused to fight anymore.

This conflict is where the wrath of Achilles gets its fuel and starts doing a good burn for the rest of the poem.

Leave my stuff alone!

Why was Achilles so mad? It had to do with his honor. All the heroes wanted to collect as much honor as they could, by fighting well or by giving good advice. Prizes (gold, silver, horses, captive women, and so on) were the visible symbols of that honor. See Chapter 6 for details about heroes and the heroic code. So when Agamemnon took Achilles's woman, he diminished Achilles's honor to enhance his own. To make matters worse, Achilles's mother had told him that he was fated to have a short life, so he was in a hurry to collect as much honor as possible.

Achilles takes his toys and stays home

Achilles prayed to his mother, Thetis, and asked her to convince Zeus to let the Trojans get the better of the fighting for a while, humiliating Agamemnon and highlighting Achilles' value to the Greek side. Thetis knew that this would only cause trouble, but she agreed and convinced Zeus. While Achilles sulked, the Trojans and Greeks fought a savage battle between the beach and the city, which ended with the Greeks definitely on the defensive.

The old switcheroo

The Greeks continued to lose, and Achilles's best friend Patroclus pitied their (former) allies. He suggested a plan that would help the Greeks, without requiring Achilles to give in and fight: Patroclus would put on Achilles's armor, and show himself to the Trojans; they would panic, and the Greeks would beat them back. That was the plan, anyway.

But Patroclus got too excited and actually entered the fighting. He had a great day, killing Trojans by the dozens. But finally, he faced the Trojan leader Hector. They threw spears at each other. Patroclus's spear missed, but Hector's didn't. Patroclus died, and Hector stripped the armor off his body.

Now I'm really mad

When Achilles found out that Patroclus was slain in battle, he lost his mind. All he could think of was revenge and killing Hector. He had Patroclus's body brought back to his tent and arranged to get some cool new armor.

Achilles goes bad like old milk in the refrigerator

In the early parts of the *Iliad,* Achilles was generally a nice guy. Even the Trojans admitted this. But now with Patroclus dead, Achilles stops being a nice guy. In this sense, the *Iliad* is a tragedy — Achilles clings to his sense of honor but loses his good character. When he came back into the fighting, he killed everyone in sight. At one point, he met a Trojan boy, whom he had already captured and ransomed back once. The boy pleaded for his life, but Achilles laughed in his face and killed him. He even attacked the river Scamander, and nearly won! Finally he came face to face with Hector.

Hector, who was a picture of courage and good sense up until this point, turned and ran. Achilles chased him all they way around the city until finally Hector stopped and fought. It was no contest, especially because the gods were all on Achilles's side. He killed Hector and dragged the dead body around Patroclus' tomb behind his chariot — 33 times!

Okay — I feel better now

With Hector dead and his corpse dishonored, Achilles started to calm down and return to being a nice guy. He held athletic contests for the Greeks, in honor of Patroclus, and handed out prizes very, very fairly. Even old Nestor, who can't compete with the younger guys, got a prize for being old and wise. Finally the old king Priam, Hector's father, came to Achilles's tent to ask for the body of his son. Achilles and Priam wept together — Priam for his son and his city, and Achilles for his own father and his friend Patroclus — and Achilles gave the body back. The *Iliad* ends with the burning funeral pyre of Hector the Trojan and a funeral banquet.

The End of the Trojan War

Some of the best Trojan War stories aren't in Homer's *Iliad*. The death of Achilles, the conflicts that result, and the tale of the Trojan Horse both come from other sources.

A hero falls: The death of Achilles

With Hector dead, Troy's fate was sealed. The fighting continued. Shortly after the events described in the *Iliad*, Achilles himself was killed. Paris shot him with an arrow — there's irony in that, because Paris had the reputation of being the wimpiest guy fighting at Troy, and an arrow was considered a cowardly weapon. But that was that for Achilles. His mother's prophecy was right, though: He lived a short but very glorious life.

I'll see your bronze helmet and raise you a shield

Achilles was dead, so who would get his fabulous armor? Odysseus and Ajax both wanted it. In one story, Odysseus and Ajax play dice or checkers for it. Another version has them competing in athletic competitions with the Trojans serving as impartial judges!

Odysseus won the armor, and it was too much for poor Ajax. He went crazy and decided to kill all the Greeks. But he couldn't even manage that and succeeded only in killing a bunch of cows by mistake. This last humiliating failure drove him to suicide. The Greeks didn't allow his body to be burned on the funeral pyre because of his shameful death, and they buried him instead.

The bow of Philoctetes and the death of Paris

Philoctetes was a warrior who had been with the Greeks as they sailed to Troy. When they stopped on the island of Tenedos, a snake bit Philoctetes on the foot, which began to stink terribly. So crafty Odysseus dumped the poor guy on the island of Lemnos. There poor Philoctetes stayed, with his stinky, sore foot never healing. All he had to eat were birds that he shot with his fabulous bow, which had once belonged to Heracles.

The Greeks at Troy now had another prophecy: They would never capture Troy unless they were in possession of the bow of Philoctetes. So Odysseus and Diomedes kidnapped him or did a terrific job of eating crow, and he rejoined the fight. In Sophocles's tragedy, the *Philoctetes*, Odysseus and Neoptolemus, Achilles' son, try to trick Philoctetes into coming back to Troy. Their plot doesn't work, but Heracles turns up at the last minute and orders Philoctetes to return to Troy. Back at Troy, he used his bow to shoot and kill Paris.

A horse, of course!: The Trojan horse

With Patroclus, Hector, Achilles, Paris, Ajax all dead, both sides were running out of heroes. It was time to end the war. Odysseus (of course) had the plan that finally won the Trojan War. During the night, he had the Greeks build a giant, hollow, wooden horse. (You can see a recreated version of it in Figure 7-2.) A selected band of soldiers hid inside the horse, while the rest of the Greek army got on their ships and sailed around behind a nearby island out of sight. They left the horse in front of the gates of Troy.

Figure 7-2:
Turkish authorities built a wooden horse for people to stand in front of and take pictures.

© David Forman, Eye Ubiquitous/CORBIS

When the Trojans woke up the next morning, the Greek army was gone, but this huge horse was sitting in front of the gate. A Greek "deserter" turned up and told a story about how the Greeks had received omens telling them to leave Troy alone, and how, before they all sailed back across the Aegean Sea, they had left this big horse as a going-away present.

Needless to say, some of the Trojans were skeptical of this story. One of them, a man named Laocoön (rhymes with "saw a shoe on") suggested that the horse might in fact be filled with Greek soldiers waiting for the Trojans to bring the horse into the city. The Trojans tested this theory by producing Helen and having her call out the names of some of the Greeks, imitating their wives' voices (Helen had all kinds of magical powers). Inside the horse, Odysseus had to work really hard to keep his guys quiet while this was going on.

Someone else threw a spear, which stuck in the side of the horse. Then the goddess Athena, who hated Troy and loved Odysseus, sent a giant snake out of the sea to eat Laocoön and his sons, which is shown in Figure 7-3. The Trojans took this as a sign that Laocoön's skepticism was not pleasing to the gods. That was true enough, but the conclusion they drew wasn't so smart. They decided to drag the horse inside the city, go to bed, and worry about it the next day.

Figure 7-3:
Laocoön
and his sons
being eaten
by snakes.

© Araldo de Luca/CORBIS

Well, there goes Troy . . .

After dark, three big things happened in sequence that put the Greeks ahead of the game:

1. The Greek army sailed their ships back to the beach and marched to the walls of Troy.

2. Odysseus and his guys came out of the horse and opened the city's gates.

3. They burned the whole place down, killed the men, and enslaved the women.

The defeat of Troy was ugly. King Priam took refuge at an altar, which should have protected him, but the Greeks killed him (he was decapitated by Achilles's son Neoptolemus — or Pyrrhus) as he clung to the altar. The Greeks also took baby Astyanax, Hector's son, and threw him to his death from the city walls. Finally, most of the Greeks (but not the crafty Odysseus!) forgot to offer sacrifices to thank the gods for all their help. All of this would come back to haunt them.

A Hero Makes His Way Home after the Trojan War: Homer's Odyssey

All of the Greeks had a hard time getting home from Troy. Menelaus got blown all over the ocean and ended up in Egypt. He had to wrestle with Proteus, the Old Man of the Sea, to find out how to get home to Sparta. Agamemnon wasn't so lucky. He got home right away, but was immediately killed by his wife, Clytemnestra. See Chapter 8 for the gory details.

But the most famous homecoming is that of Odysseus, who has his own epic poem, the *Odyssey*. The *Odyssey* is the ultimate adventure story, full of sex, violence, deceit, and monsters. It poses an interesting question, too, of who is more monstrous, the outlandish creatures Odysseus meets on his way home or the human suitors who settle in at his home in Ithaca, waiting to get his wife Penelope.

Don't wait up, honey

When Odysseus left for Troy, he left behind his home on the island of Ithaca, his wife Penelope, and his baby son Telemachus. When the *Odyssey* opens, the war has been over for ten years, but Odysseus still isn't home.

Penelope was having a hard time. She was a wealthy, beautiful woman, forty years old or so — a very desirable catch. But was she available? Lots of men from Ithaca and neighboring islands assumed she was — Odysseus had to be dead by now. All these guys came to Ithaca and camped out in Odysseus's house. They are the suitors, definitely the bad guys of the *Odyssey*.

Penelope kept promising to pick a suitor to marry, but never did. At one point she told all the hopeful fellows that she was busy weaving a fancy sheet that would be used as a shroud when Odysseus's old father, Laertes, finally died, and she would choose a new husband when she was done. Every day, Penelope made a big production of weaving, but every night she undid her day's work. She managed to keep this up for two years before one of her slave-girls told on her and the suitors forced her to finish the job.

Why didn't Penelope just tell the suitors to get lost? Two reasons:

- ✔ It adds to the suspense of the poem to have Penelope under constant pressure to hook up with some new beau — Odysseus better hurry if he wants what's his.

- ✔ If Penelope didn't keep toying with the suitors, they could go to her dad and have *him* arrange a new marriage for her; by leading them on, she could keep stringing them along and wasting more time. Penelope could keep some control over her life.

Telemachus at this point was about twenty years old. He watched these suitors eat up all the family's wealth, which was supposed to be his inheritance. But what could he do, one young man against seventy suitors?

What a long, strange trip it's been!

Odysseus and his men had an exciting trip once they had left Troy. The first thing they did was to sail to the land of the Cicones and start a war with them. This adventure didn't go well, and they only barely escaped with their lives. (Odysseus makes a lot of stupid mistakes in the early part of his journey, but he learns from them all, and that experience helps him deal with the evil suitors once he gets home.) The lesson of the Cicones: Don't start fighting until you're sure you can win.

From the Cicones, they went to the Land of the Lotus-Eaters. These folks did nothing but eat *lotus,* which was some kind of drug that makes them mellow and lazy. Some of Odysseus's men got stoned on the lotus, and he had to drag them back to the ship.

Odysseus meets the Cyclops

Odysseus's encounter with the Cyclops named Polyphemus was his most famous adventure. Odysseus landed on an island and told his men that he wanted to see what kind of men lived here — maybe they would give him presents! On the island, they found a giant cave filled with giant stuff, let themselves right in, and waited for the cave's owner to come home. When he did, they saw that he was a monstrously huge man with a single eye. He brought his sheep into the cave with him, then rolled a huge stone over its entrance — a primitive form of locking the door.

Then he addressed his uninvited guests: "Who are you, and where are you from? Are you pirates?" (This was a question Odysseus got asked by just about everyone he met. Evidently being a pirate was just another job, which no one felt the need to hide.) Odysseus told him that his name was "Nobody" and suggested that his "host" give him a present, which is what Zeus liked to see when strangers meet.

The Cyclops said that his name was Polyphemus, and he didn't care one little whit about what Zeus wanted. *His* daddy was Poseidon! But, as a nice present for his puny new acquaintance, he promised to eat Odysseus last. Then he grabbed two of Odysseus's men, slammed them on the ground and ate them raw. He slept all night and ate two more men for breakfast. Then he went out with his sheep and rolled the stone back over the entrance of the cave, trapping the men inside.

Odysseus spent the day concocting a plan. He found a long piece of wood, sharpened one end into a point, and hardened it in the fire. Polyphemus came home that night and ate two more men, but this time Odysseus gave him some wine — lots of wine, enough to put him into a drunken stupor. Then he and his guys got their spike, heated it in the fire, and stuck it right into Polyphemus's one eye. The blind Cyclops tried to catch his attackers but couldn't. He cried out to the other Cyclopes on the island, but when they asked who was attacking him, all he could say was the name Odysseus had told him: Nobody. So no one came to help him! That Odysseus is a sly fox!

Now Odysseus got the sheep and tied them together in groups of three, side by side. At dawn, the men clung underneath the sheep as they walked out of the cave. Polyphemus felt the sheep's backs to make sure no one was riding them, but he didn't think to feel their bellies, so the men escaped. They ran to their ship and set sail. As they floated away, Odysseus screamed a last insult at the Cyclops. Polyphemus, enraged, grabbed a huge rock and threw it in the direction of the ship. It nearly crushed the boat, and churned up huge waves. Odysseus shouted his name to Polyphemus as they escaped for good — a mistake, because that gave Poseidon reason to hate him.

The winds of futility

Next they came to the Aeolian Islands, home of King Aeolus, lord of the winds. As a gift, he gave Odysseus a bag containing all the winds but the one that would blow him home. Odysseus's silly men, though, thought the bag must be full of treasure. So when their boss fell asleep, they opened it up. All the winds came out at once and they found themselves in a terrible storm. They eventually blew back to Aeolus's shore, but he was too angry to help them again.

Show me who's boss, baby: Circe and the underworld

Next they landed on the island of the witch Circe. She turned all Odysseus's men into swine (pigs, that is). Hermes showed up and gave Odysseus a special herb that prevented the same thing from happening to him and told him how to get his men back — he had to threaten to stab Circe with his sword unless she freed his guys. Circe kind of liked that treatment — when she saw what a real man Odysseus was, she immediately fell in love with him. He and his men spent a pleasant year living with her in her fancy house.

It was Circe who told them what they had to do next: They had to visit the underworld and ask the dead prophet Teiresias (see Chapter 8) how to get home. Dead people liked blood, and when they got to the underworld, Odysseus killed a sheep and filled a pool with its blood. All the ghosts came running up to get some, but Odysseus held them off with his sword until Teiresias showed up. Teiresias drank the blood and then told them that Odysseus would certainly get home, and at all costs they should avoid doing harm to the cattle of the sun. A bunch of other dead people then came up to say "Hi," so many that everyone got weirded out and ran back to the ship.

Sirens (and not the ones on police cars!)

The island of the Sirens was the next obstacle. The *Sirens* were women who sang beautifully and lured men to their deaths on the rocks surrounding the island. Odysseus blocked his men's ears with wax, but he wanted to hear this famous song himself. So he got the men to tie him to the mast, and made them promise not to untie him no matter what he said. When he heard the singing, he begged and pleaded to be released so he could go to the Sirens, but the men couldn't hear him, so they all got safely away.

The lovely and talented Scylla and Charybdis

The passage between Scylla and Charybdis was next. (Some people say this was the Straits of Messina between Sicily and Italy.) Scylla was a six-headed monster, and if they went too close to her, she would snatch up six men and eat them. But Charybdis was a whirlpool, and if they went close to that the entire ship would go down. So Odysseus chose Scylla; as they passed she reached down and grabbed six men, much to the dismay of everyone, but the boat got through safely.

Tired, hungry, and demoralized, the men stopped at the Island of the Sun, where Apollo kept the famous cattle of the sun, which Teiresias had warned them not to harm. The men didn't care about any warning, though, and they killed and ate the sacred beasts while Odysseus was off by himself. As soon as they left that island, Apollo destroyed the boat and all the men died except Odysseus. He clung to the wreckage and washed up on Calypso's island, where he spent several years as her love-slave. Finally the gods interceded, Calypso released him, he built a raft, and washed up on the shore of the Phaeacia.

Oh my achey breaky heart

So where was Odysseus? He was sitting on a beach crying. He had been abducted by the goddess Calypso and had been living with her for years, a prisoner of love. Athena, his sponsor goddess, decided that enough was enough, and asked Zeus for permission to bring her buddy home. Zeus agreed, but noted that it wouldn't be easy, because the god Poseidon was really, really angry with Odysseus for hurting his son the Cyclops.

But Athena got the ball rolling. She visited Telemachus and suggested that he go on a trip to look for news of his father. This would do two things:

- Make a man out of him.
- Keep him away from the suitors, who had been plotting to kill him because he was heir to Odysseus's stuff and didn't want them getting their hands on it.

Then she sent the god Hermes to tell Calypso that she could no longer keep her pet. Calypso wasn't happy about that, but agreed to help Odysseus build a raft.

Raft-wrecked on Phaeacia Island

Odysseus sailed off on his raft, toward home. Everything was going well until Poseidon noticed him and tried to kill him with a huge storm. It almost worked; the raft was smashed to bits, but Odysseus managed to swim to shore, on an island called Phaeacia.

As he lay naked on the beach, the teenaged daughter of the local king found him, thought he was cute, and brought him home with her — this sort of thing happened to Odysseus all the time. In the palace of the king, Odysseus told the whole story of his travels, from when he left Troy after the Trojan War until he came to the island of Calypso.

Heading home: Heads are going to roll

After hearing this exciting tale, the Phaiacian king gave Odysseus a new boat and a bunch of parting gifts. He and his Phaiacian crew sailed away to Ithaca. He was asleep when they arrived, so the crew put him and his belongings on the beach and departed without waking him. He woke up in Ithaca disoriented.

A young man came up to speak to him, really Athena in disguise. She told him he was in Ithaca and explained that his house was full of suitors plaguing his wife and son. She promised to help him root them out, and they concocted a plan.

The old beggar disguise

Odysseus, disguised as a beggar, went to stay with his old faithful swineherd, and Athena got Telemachus to come meet him there. Odysseus changed back into himself and introduced himself to his son, who, after all, hadn't seen him for twenty years.

The next day Odysseus, again disguised as a beggar, went to his house. On his way through town, no one penetrated his disguise. No human, that is, but his old, old dog, Argus, sick and abandoned and lying on a pile of dung, covered with ticks, saw his master and recognized him. Argus had been waiting for 20 years to see Odysseus one last time. When he saw him, the dog wagged his tail and died.

He found the suitors sitting around, bloated after a big meal. They all made fun of him. Now Penelope showed up. She didn't know who the beggar was, but wanted to talk to him. First she complained to the suitors that they hadn't been giving her expensive gifts like they should have, and they jumped to comply and shower her with gold and jewelry. Then she summoned the beggar to talk to her. Odysseus still didn't reveal his identity, but told her that he had seen her husband alive recently. Penelope wept to hear that. She let the beggar sleep in the house that night.

The only person in the house who sees through Odysseus's divine disguise is Eurycleia, who, while washing his feet, noticed a distinctive scar. Odysseus urged her to remain quiet, and she kept his secret safe.

The bow of Odysseus: Only real men need apply

The next morning, still unaware that Odysseus was home, Penelope brought down Odysseus's old bow, and challenged the suitors: if one of them could string it and shoot an arrow straight through 12 rings in a row, she would take him as her husband. Telemachus set up the rings and encouraged the suitors to try. All of them gave it a shot, but no one was strong enough to string the bow.

Now beggar-Odysseus asked for a chance. The suitors complained, but Telemachus insisted that he be allowed to try. Quick as a wink, Odysseus strung the bow and sent an arrow straight through all 12 rings. Telemachus and his helpers ran to bring in more arrows, and Odysseus shot all the suitors but two. These two begged for mercy; Odysseus killed one with his sword but spared the other one because he was a musician.

The old servants rejoiced to have their master back. They ran to tell Penelope that her husband was home. Penelope, who was no fool, wanted to test this strange man one more time to make sure that he really was Odysseus. She told Odysseus, "Great! Let's move our bed to a better spot, and hop in it!" Odysseus saw through the trick: "No one can move that bed, because it is built on a tree-stump, rooted in the ground." That fact, which no one but Penelope and Odysseus knew, convinced Penelope that her husband was home at last.

Trouble still stirred among the relatives of the suitors, but Athena stepped in, told them that their kids had asked for everything they got, and told Odysseus how to make one last journey to appease Poseidon. With that, the long odyssey was completed.

Chapter 8

Greek Tragedy:
The Days of Their Lives

*O*ne of the best ways to find out about Greek myths is to look at Greek tragedy. These are plays written in the fifth century BCE that were performed at public expense in the city of Athens. Most Greek tragedies deal with mythological subjects, especially a couple of really dysfunctional legendary families and the events and characters of the Trojan War. Only a handful of these plays actually survive today, a tiny fraction of the Greek tragedies that existed in the fifth century. But even though the surviving sample is so small, these tragedies tell us a lot about Greek myths, especially how different versions of a single myth could exist side by side.

What's On Today?

People always talk about plays they've seen, and some of them even become professionals at doing so. The first "professional discusser-of-plays" in the West was the philosopher Aristotle (in antiquity, philosophers didn't just do what we call *philosophy,* but they also investigated astronomy, physics, medicine, and any other fields of knowledge they felt drawn to). Aristotle wrote, among dozens of other works, a book about poetry called the *Poetics,* which dealt with all kinds of poetry — epic, comedy, tragedy, and dithyramb. However, the part of the work that survives today deals mostly with tragedy. Aristotle was a clear-thinking, methodical guy, who approached his topics carefully. The way he decided to talk about tragedy has determined, to a large extent, how people have talked about tragedy (and drama, in general) ever since.

Aristotle defined different aspects of tragedy and said that they're all important to the success of a play, including:

- **Music:** All dramatic performances were accompanied by music.
- **Spectacle:** The set and the costumes.
- **Plot:** What happens.
- **Diction:** How things are said.
- **Character:** Who says what and how.

Aristotle's *Poetics* is a prescriptive work, meaning that it tells how the poet *should* do things — based, of course, on what Aristotle thinks is best. But Aristotle was a smart guy, and his opinion carried weight in his own day, and carries some weight still.

Greek drama involved three actors and a chorus. All actors and chorus members were men, even when there were female roles in the play. The actors and the chorus all wore costumes and masks. Plays were accompanied by music — probably a flute-player and a drummer at least — but today no one knows what that music may have sounded like.

A temple on some days, a theater on others

In Athens, tragedies and comedies were performed in the Theater of Dionysus. This was a typical Greek theater with a semicircular stage at the bottom and level upon level of seats fanning up from the stage. Visitors to the Acropolis, the hill in the center of Athens, can actually look down into the Theater of Dionysus, which is cut into the side of the hill. (Actually, the theater that's there now is the new-and-improved theater built by the Romans, but no matter.) This theater was more than just a theater. It was a temple to the god Dionysus. In fact, Dionysus didn't have any other temple in Athens, only this theater, which kept audiences on their best behavior, because causing trouble in the theater was an act of sacrilege, subject to harsh punishments. One time, two spectators got into a shoving match over a seat, and the guy who started it was convicted of sacrilege, had all his property confiscated, and was exiled from the city!

Dionysus: You gotta fight — for your right — to party!

Dionysus was the god of wine, of occasionally going crazy, and of theater. These three go together, actually, because each has to do with setting aside normal reality, if only for a little while. Twice a year, the city of Athens honored Dionysus (and had a good time in the process) by celebrating "dramatic festivals," big citywide parties centered on the performance of plays. The two big ones in Athens were the City Dionysia, a huge springtime extravaganza in honor of Dionysus, and the cozier mid-winter Lanaea, a smaller affair in honor of Demeter.

And the winner is . . .

At both the Dionysia and the Lanaea, plays appeared in the context of a competition. After all the tragedies had been performed, a panel of judges awarded prizes — for best trilogy, best costumes, best actors — very much like the Academy Awards. Winning the "best trilogy" award could do great things for a playwright's career.

Theatrical welfare or theatrically well fared?

All Athenians (excluding slaves), resident aliens, and foreign visitors were welcome to watch the plays for the price of a ticket. In fact, the Athenians thought that these plays were so important that in the fourth century BCE, the Athenian democracy put in place a *theoric fund,* a public fund (such as the American Social Security Administration) charged with subsidizing theater tickets for any Athenian too poor to buy one.

Send in the Clowns (Not!): Tragedy 101

What all tragedies have in common that makes them tragedies is almost impossible to say. Most tragedies involved someone dying, or at least suffering, but by no means do all of them. Most tragedies are serious, but by no means are all of them. Euripides's tragedy, *Helen,* actually is funny, no one gets killed, and it has a happy ending. Aristotle — author of the first "Tragedy Made E-Z" book — says that the best tragedies (in his opinion) have certain things in common, but he doesn't say that every tragedy had to have certain things in common.

What made a tragedy a tragedy? Mythology may be one answer. Of the surviving tragedies, all but one have plots based on mythology. The one exception is Aeschylus's *Persians,* which is about the battle of Salamis during the Persian Wars at the beginning of the fifth century. You may even be able to say that the victory over the Persians was so important, and so unlikely, that it became "instant mythology." Anyway, except for *Persians,* all tragedies have mythological plots, which certainly distinguishes them from comedy, which invariably dealt with the day-to-day world of Athens.

In tragedy, the chorus generally represented the "normal folks," who spent the play observing the main characters and making comments on their behavior. Tragedies appeared in *trilogies,* groups of three plays. A poet would write a trilogy of three plays to be performed together, one after another.

Sometimes the three plays would tell a continuous story in three parts (the one trilogy whose three plays all exist today, Aeschylus's *Oresteia,* does this). In other cases, the three plays would tell three unrelated stories.

Myths and mythological recycling

What were these Greek tragedies about? Tragic stuff, of course, but not just any tragic stuff. Tragedies tended to be about mythological characters and events. The Trojan War provided plenty of plots for the tragedians to work with, of course, but so did other myths. They also worked with the two mythological royal families, the House of Cadmus from Thebes and the House of Atreus from Mycenae. In many tragedies, one character or another makes the observation: "Once a family is cursed, it will be miserable forever." The stories of these two extended families certainly provide evidence to support that assertion.

This pool of myths provided plenty of material, but not so much that tragedians didn't repeat stories. After all, they had to come up with 20 or so plays every year, and they kept that pace for almost a century! A few stories come down to present-day in versions from more than one tragedian. The story of Electra, for example, exists in plays by Aeschylus, Sophocles, and Euripides. All three poets started with the same myth, but each presented a slightly different version of it. Evidently, the Athenian people didn't mind.

The "tragic flaw" is tragically flawed

Now is a good time to mention a couple of extremely widespread misconceptions about Greek tragedy. Many people think that the point of tragedies, such as *Oedipus Tyrannos,* is that Oedipus has this *tragic flaw,* which is *hubris,* a Greek word meaning pride, and because of his pride he suffers a terrible disaster, right? Wrong!

A mistake made in ignorance . . .

So where does this notion of tragic flaw come from? It comes from a mistake people made when reading the philosopher Aristotle in the original Greek. Aristotle says in *Poetics* that in the best plays, the tragedy arises from a *hamartia.* To Aristotle, this Greek word meant a "mistake made in ignorance, as opposed to something intentional." If I were fixing my roof, and accidentally dropped a plank, and it killed someone, that would be a hamartia. Someone died, but it wasn't a crime, because I didn't mean to do it.

Turns into a genuine sin . . .

What happened, however, was that people in the nineteenth century read Aristotle in Greek after having read the New Testament in Greek. In the New Testament (written 500 years after Aristotle), *hamartia* means sin. So they thought that Aristotle was saying that the best tragedies depend on some sin, or as they came to call it, *tragic flaw*. Adding to the confusion, this way of thinking — the New Testament way, that is — about tragedy works pretty well when applied to Shakespeare's tragedies — Hamlet gets into trouble because he is indecisive, King Lear is vain, Macbeth is henpecked, and so on.

But the Greeks didn't read it that way

But that isn't the way Greek tragedy works. And what is more tragic, someone who "gets what he deserves" or someone who does his best but suffers anyway?

The big three

Aeschylus, Sophocles, and Euripides were the Big Three tragedians. They lived and wrote in the fifth century BCE, Aeschylus first, Sophocles second (overlapping a bit with Aeschylus), and Euripides third. Many, many others wrote tragedies, of course. Number Four on the list of Great Tragedians probably was Agathon. None of his works survives, but he is well known from other sources, most notably from his appearance in Plato's *Symposium*. The versatile Ion of Chios, also wrote tragedies and many other kinds of poetry, including (perhaps) comedy (which would make him the only poet known to have worked in comedy and tragedy). After the end of the fifth century, no more great tragedians came along, and the Athenians increasingly contented themselves with restaging the old classics.

Aeschylus

Aeschylus was first; his career began around 499 BCE and lasted until his death in 456 BCE. He was a pioneer. Before Aeschylus, Greek drama featured only two actors, which kind of limited the excitement. Aeschylus had the idea to add a third actor. With three characters onstage, they could have real tragedy because the third person could act as a foil to the other two. For instance, two lovers and a bad guy; or a killer, a victim, and a witness; or an imposter, a nonimposter, and the guy who has to tell them apart. Aeschylus's plays won first prize at least 13 times. Aeschylus's most famous plays are *Agamemnon, Seven Against Thebes,* and *Prometheus Bound* — more about them later.

Sophocles

Sophocles was next. His career overlapped that of Aeschylus and (later) with that of the younger Euripides. His first plays competed against Aeschylus in 468 BCE, and his last plays appeared in 406 BCE — that's a career of 62 years! He wrote over 120 plays — making him the most prolific tragedian — and won first prize at 20 festivals. His most famous plays are *Oedipus Tyrannus* (often called *Oedipus Rex* or *Oedipus the King*) and *Antigone*. Sophocles' plays are powerful, partly because he wrote in very straightforward, economical language, unlike the more high-falutin' diction of Aeschylus.

Euripides

The third biggie was Euripides. His first public performance was in 455 BCE, the year after Aeschylus died. He died in 407 or 406 BCE, just before Sophocles died. Euripides wrote 90 plays, as far as anyone knows, but didn't win nearly as often as Aeschylus or Sophocles did. Euripides was certainly the most innovative of the three. He liked to take well-known plots and give them a twist — so in his play *Electra,* the heroine, Agamemnon's daughter Electra, comes across as a snotty, spoiled brat, and remains one throughout the play. He liked to make jokes and include witty, subtle references to other plays in his works.

Meet the Parents: The House of Cadmus

The First Family of Greek Tragedy was the House of Cadmus, the royal family of Thebes. Thebes was a real city in central Greece with a real history just like any city. But Thebes also had a mythological history that was much, much more bizarre and disturbing than most.

Two famous cities were named Thebes in the ancient world. One was in central Greece and one was in Egypt. The Greek Thebes was "Seven-Gated Thebes." The Egyptian city was "Thebes of the Hundred Gates." Egypt was the Texas of the ancient world with everything there being bigger.

Weird beginnings

Lust and a cow started it all. Agenor, son of the god Poseidon and the goddess Lybia, was a king of Phoenicia (modern Lebanon). He had a beautiful daughter named Europa. Zeus fell in love with this girl (see Chapter 4 for more details), and when Zeus's wife Hera found out, she turned the girl into a cow. Then, to add injury to insult, she sent stinging horseflies to drive the girl/cow crazy and cause her to run off. Agenor sent his son Cadmus to look for his missing daughter. Cadmus made his way from Asia Minor to the continent to the west (which came to be called Europe after his wandering bovine sister).

Cows are okay, I guess

Cadmus never found Europa. After a while, he went to the oracle at Delphi to ask Apollo what to do. Apollo's priestess told him to forget about his sister but to follow *another* cow and start a city wherever it settled down to rest. Cadmus left Delphi and came to Boeotia (an area in central Greece). There he met a guy named Pelagon, who had a big herd of cows. One of them wandered off, and Cadmus followed it.

The cow stopped to rest, and Cadmus had the spot for his new city! Conveniently enough, there was a spring of water nearby. Inconveniently, the spring of water was sacred to the god Ares, who had put a dragon there to guard it. Cadmus killed the dragon, and then sacrificed his cow to the goddess Athena. Athena suggested that he plant the dragon's teeth to see what would happen. When Cadmus did this, the teeth immediately sprouted and grew into armed men, called *Spartoi* or "Sown men" (after the fact that he had sown the seeds).

Dragon teeth: Alternative population census method

Cadmus started throwing rocks into the middle of the group. Each Spartos assumed that another Spartos was throwing rocks at him, and they all started fighting each other. When the dust settled, all but five of them were dead, and they were too tired to cause anyone any trouble. And Cadmus now had a population for his new city (small, but you have to start somewhere).

A successful family

Cadmus was forced to serve Ares for eight years (a period called, in Greek myth, an *eternal year*) to make up for killing his dragon. But afterward, Athena arranged for him to be king of the new city of Thebes. Zeus even found him a wife, the daughter of Ares and Aphrodite, a goddess named Harmonia. (Get it? "War" and "Love" had a kid named "Harmony.")

Cadmus and Harmonia had a bunch of kids. They were Semele, Agave, Polydorus, Ino, and Illyrius.

You can see this genealogy in Figure 8-1. Cadmus's daughter Agave married Echion, and they had a child Pentheus. When Cadmus left Thebes, either his son, Polydorus, or his grandson, Pentheus, succeeded him as king. This part of the myth is confused. Illyrius was born last, after Cadmus and Harmonia had moved to Illyria (to the north of Greece), where Zeus eventually turned them into serpents in their old age.

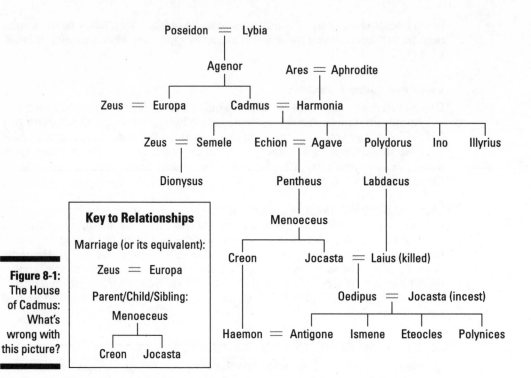

Figure 8-1:
The House
of Cadmus:
What's
wrong with
this picture?

The Oedipus saga

Polydorus's son Labdacus became king of Thebes, and after him, his son Laius. Laius finally settled down and married Jocasta, who was the daughter of Menoeceus, who was Pentheus's son. So Laius and Jocasta were third cousins, but in light of what happens later, a marriage between cousins is no big deal! Jocasta also had a brother, Creon.

Oh, there's always an oracle somewhere

After Laius married his cousin Jocasta, he received an oracle from Apollo that went something like this: "Apollo regrets to inform you that you will have a son who will kill you." Now, the Number One rule with oracles from Apollo is *they always come true, no matter what!*

No matter, when a baby boy was born to these two, they hobbled him by piercing his heels and tying his feet together, and then placed him on a mountainside so the wild animals could eat him. No such luck (of course). A shepherd found the baby, picked him up, passed him along to another shepherd, who dropped him off with the king and queen of Corinth, who were looking to adopt a son. They named him "Oedipus," because of his swollen feet. They also neglected to tell him that he was adopted, which turned out to be a mistake.

The other side of the oracle

When Oedipus was a young man, he learned from an oracle that he was fated to kill his own father and marry his mother. In an effort to avoid this fate, Oedipus decided to leave his adoptive parents, the King and Queen of Corinth, and hit the road. As he walked, he came to a place where three roads come together near Delphi. Just then a wagon came rolling along with obviously some important person, and the attendants hit him with a club to get him out of their way. In a rage, Oedipus attacked the traveling party and killed everyone, including the old guy in the wagon. No biggie, he thought (travel was rough back then).

The riddle of the sphinx

Walking along, Oedipus came to the outskirts of the city of Thebes. There he discovered that a monster had moved into the neighborhood. The monster was a *sphinx,* a creature with a woman's head, a lion's body, a snake for a tail, and wings. This particular sphinx was asking everyone a riddle and killing anyone who failed to answer it. In fact, the king had recently left to ask Apollo's oracle at Delphi what the answer was, but he had been murdered somewhere on the road, leaving Thebes with no ruler. See Figure 8-2.

Figure 8-2:
Oedipus and
the sphinx.

Oedipus decided to have a shot at the riddle, which was this: What creature walks on four legs in the morning, two at midday, and three legs in the evening? Oedipus knew that the answer wasn't a magical monster, but a human being, because humans crawl as infants, walk upright as adults, and use a cane in old age.

The sphinx, foiled, killed herself, and the people of Thebes chose Oedipus to be their *tyrannos*. This term comes into English as "tyrant," but for the Greeks it simply meant a sole ruler chosen by the people, as opposed to a king, who got to rule by right of birth.

You sure do look familiar . . .

The new ruler was expected to marry the widow of the former king. This was Jocasta, Oedipus's mother. Oedipus and Jocasta got married and had four children:

- Eteocles
- Polynices
- Antigone
- Ismene

After many years, the people of Thebes began to suffer from a plague. Oedipus sent the queen's brother, Creon, to Delphi to ask Apollo what should be done.

The blockbuster release of Oedipus Tyrannos

Creon went to Delphi to ask Apollo what should be done (see preceding section). This is the point in the story where the most famous Greek tragedy of all time begins: Sophocles's *Oedipus Tyrannus* (often published in English as *Oedipus Rex*). The actual events of the play are easy to summarize. Creon reported to Oedipus that, according to Apollo, the plague would not go away until the people of Thebes found the murderer of their old king, Laius, and brought him to justice. Oedipus promised to do just that and began an investigation. One disturbing fact after another came to light. Everyone told Oedipus to back off, to stop asking questions, but he had promised to save the city. Eventually the whole story came out.

Jocasta hanged herself in shame, and Oedipus blinded himself — his reasoning was that if he simply killed himself he would have to face his father and mother/wife in the underworld, which would be awkward to say the least. His daughters, Antigone and Ismene, led him out of the city, never to return.

Creon became temporary ruler of Thebes until the sons of Oedipus and Jocasta could figure out which one would rule the city. The two young men, Eteocles and Polynices, first agreed to share power; each was to rule every other year. It probably didn't surprise anyone when this agreement fell apart. Eteocles threw his brother out, and Polynices went off to Argos to find some allies who would help him seize power in Thebes.

Sophocles is on a roll: *Oedipus at Colonus*

This work returns to poor old Oedipus, who was last seen wandering, homeless and blind, guided by his daughter Antigone. The end of his life is the subject of Sophocles's tragedy *Oedipus at Colonus,* another one of Sophocles' blockbuster tragedies. Both Eteocles (in Thebes) and Polynices (not in Thebes, but wishing he were there) got an oracle: whoever possessed the body of Oedipus would be blessed forever. Oedipus was special because of the extraordinary curse on him and his extraordinary suffering (none of which he deserved). Oedipus got wind of this and didn't want to become a pawn in a power struggle between his sons. So he made his way to Athens. Theseus was king of Athens, and welcomed Oedipus with open arms. When Oedipus knew that he had found someone who respected him for his remarkable life, he decided that his life was complete. He went into a grove of trees in a suburb of Athens called Colonus. There was a flash of light, and no one ever saw Oedipus again.

Many people think that the point of *Oedipus Tyrranus* is that Oedipus had a tragic flaw — hubris, or excessive pride — and that because of his flaw, he suffered a disaster. Not so. The point of this play is that *Oedipus did everything right!* Apollo told him to find the murderer, and he did! In fact, Oedipus is the only person in the play, including the prophet Tiresias, who seems to take the gods seriously. He has to save the city. And he does save the city!

It ain't over 'til it's over: *Seven Against Thebes*

After the death of Oedipus, Athens became blessed, and Thebes went on being cursed. Polynices collected an army, featuring six other champions (making, with him, seven heroes, one for each gate of Thebes). They attacked the city. These events are the subject of Aeschylus's play *Seven Against Thebes.* The war ended with seven instances of single combat, one in each gate. The two brothers, Eteocles and Polynices, faced each other, and managed to kill each other simultaneously. So that power struggle was over, and Creon was once again temporary ruler of Thebes.

A bitter legacy: *Antigone*

Picking up where *Seven Against Thebes* left off, Sophocles gets back into the action with his play *Antigone.* Antigone, Oedipus's daughter, was back in Thebes now that dad was gone. She was also engaged to be married to Creon's son, Haemon. After the war, Creon passed a law commanding that all the soldiers who died protecting Thebes would have proper burials, but all those who died attacking it would be left to rot. Antigone found this intolerable — why should she honor one brother, but dishonor another? Wasn't family more important than politics, even if one's family has had its share of problems?

So Antigone snuck out of the city and buried Polynices (burial was really important, because the soul of an unburied corpse couldn't go down to the underworld). Creon found out and ordered that Antigone be "killed." Actually, he didn't order that she be killed, because that would be killing his blood-relative, a big no-no. He ordered that she be locked in a cave with one day's supply of food, using the old "She was fine when I left her" trick.

Haemon, Antigone's fiancé, found out and went to rescue her. At the last minute, Creon had a change of heart and went to let Antigone out. Too late! She had hanged herself. Haemon had found her dead, and when his dad showed up, Haemon killed himself, too. Creon's wife killed herself when she heard all of this bad news, and Creon was left all alone.

Guess Who's Coming to Dinner: The House of Atreus

The other big, extended, screwed-up mythological family that provided lots of fodder for tragedians was the House of Atreus. Unlike the House of Cadmus, which was mostly unlucky, the House of Atreus was filled with despicable characters, starting with the patriarch, Tantalus.

Tantalus was king of Sipylus in Asia Minor. He was so wealthy he could invite the gods for dinner, but messed up by serving them his son, Pelops, for dinner. This was evidently his ill-advised experiment to see if the gods were *really* omniscient; they were. They weren't fooled, and arranged for Tantalus to have a particularly nasty punishment in the underworld (see Chapter 12, "Ovid's *Metamorphoses*: Don't Go Changin'"). Afterward, they reconstituted poor Pelops. Or, actually, they mostly reconstituted him. The goddess Demeter, who was worried about her daughter, had accidentally eaten Pelops's shoulder. But the gods made him a new shoulder out of ivory.

The charioteer's bitter curse

Pelops got over being made into stew and moved to Greece. He decided to marry Hippodameia, daughter of Oenomaus, King of Pisa (not the one in Italy, but an area in southern Greece). Oenomaus had declared that anyone who wanted to marry Hippodameia had to carry her off in a chariot, with himself in pursuit and get away with her. Losers would be killed. Pelops succeeded — he bribed Myrtilus, Oenomaus's charioteer, to loosen the lynchpin on Oenomaus's chariot (the pin that held the horses to the chariot). Dad went crashing to the ground, and Pelops got away with the girl.

Pelops then threw Myrtilus into the sea either to hide the shameful way he had won the contest or because Myrtilus had the hots for Hippodameia himself. Just before he disappeared beneath the waves, Myrtilus cursed Pelops and his whole family. This murder polluted Pelops, but the god Hephaestus cleansed him. He also gave Pelops a scepter, symbolic of power throughout southern Greece — hence the name for the southern peninsula of Greece, the Peloponnese.

But *I* wanted the kingdom!

Pelops and Hippodameia had many sons, who grew up and went their separate ways, setting up their own kingdoms in different parts of the Peloponnese. But who would be top dog when Pelops died?

Pelops had an illegitimate son, Chrysippus, born before he knew Hippodameis. His legitimate sons Atreus and Thyestes killed him by throwing him down a well to protect their claims to the throne and to please their mother (who was understandably resentful of her hubby's bastard son). Pelops found out and cursed those two — the family was now doubly cursed! See Figure 8-3.

Atreus was married to Aerope, but she was in love with Thyestes. One day, when Atreus was getting ready to make a sacrifice to Artemis, a beautiful golden lamb wandered by. Atreus grabbed the lamb and stuck it in a box, but forgot to complete his sacrifice to Artemis (big mistake!). Aerope stole the lamb, and gave it to Thyestes.

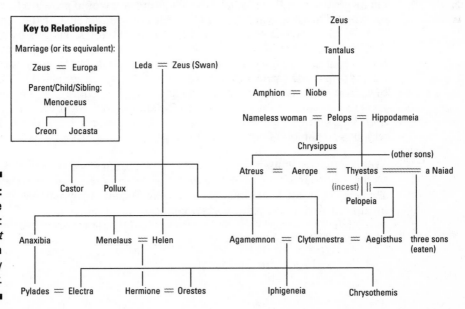

Figure 8-3: The House of Atreus: Where *not* to have a holiday dinner.

Shortly thereafter, the people of Mycenae got an oracle telling them to arrange for one of the sons of Pelops to be their king. Atreus and Thyestes showed up to try to nab this prized position. Atreus (who didn't realize that his wife had stolen his lamb) suggested that whoever owned a beautiful golden lamb should be king of Mycenae. Thyestes, of course, immediately agreed — this ready agreement surely surprised Atreus, but probably not as much as Thyestes's producing a box, opening it, and showing off the Golden Fleece.

Zeus, however, did not like Thyestes's trick, so he gave Atreus some advice: Pretend to be happy with things, but ask Thyestes to agree to hand over the throne of Mycenae on the day the sun goes backwards. Thyestes (who should have known better) agreed; the sun promptly went backward in the sky; and Atreus was king of Mycenae after all.

It's a recipe I got from my grandfather

Atreus wasn't done, however. He still wanted payback for his brother's adultery with Aerope. He pretended to want to let bygones be bygones, and invited Thyestes over for dinner. For a main course, Atreus killed Thyestes's three sons, cut off their hands and feet, and made them into a stew. After Thyestes had eaten heartily, Atreus showed him the head and hands, and presumably said, "Ha!" or whatever would be appropriate under those circumstances. Thyestes now realized he had just eaten his sons for dinner.

Apollo told Thyestes how to get revenge. All he had to do was have sex with his own daughter, Pelopia, and the resulting son would grow up to take care of things. Thyestes committed incest with his daughter, and sure enough, she had a son, Aegisthus. Pelopia tried to get rid of baby Aegisthus by exposing him, but some shepherds found the baby and arranged for a goat to nurse him — that may be the origin of the name Aegisthus, because *aiges* is the term for goats in Greek. Atreus found out about this baby, and raised him as his own. Now Thyestes was king of Mycenae (and the people of Mycenae were probably having doubts about their decision to invite a son of Pelops to be their king). Sophocles wrote a tragedy called *Thyestes,* but it doesn't survive, which is a shame.

Atreus's two sons, Agamemnon and Menelaus, survived. When they grew up, Menelaus became king of Sparta and Agamemnon returned to Mycenae, killed Thyestes (but not Aegisthus, his son), and became king himself. The two brothers married two sisters: Agamemnon got Clytemnestra, and Menelaus got Helen. This would be a sweet story — two brides for two brothers — but of course it isn't sweet at all.

But the fun doesn't stop there

Agamemnon was the leader of the Greek war against Troy, a role that, for complicated reasons, led him to sacrifice his own daughter, Iphigenia. (See Chapter 7.)

While Agamemnon was fighting for a decade at Troy, Clytemnestra's resentment over her dead daughter festered. Aegisthus — who, as Thyestes's son, had lots and lots of reasons to hate a son of Atreus, especially one who had killed his dad — egged her on.

The spoils of war: Agamemnon

When Agamemnon returned from Troy, victorious, they were waiting for him. Aeschylus's most famous play, *Agamemnon*, tells the story of the king's return. In the play, Agamemnon is not a sympathetic character — among other things, he shows up with a new girlfriend, Cassandra, a Trojan captive, and the first thing he tells his wife is, "Look after her, would you, honey?"

Clytemnestra and Aegisthus killed Agamemnon, but not his son, Orestes, or his remaining daughter, Electra. Orestes eventually came home and, with the help of his sister Electra, killed Aegisthus and his mother. This story is the subject of *three* surviving tragedies:

✔ Aeschylus's *Choephoroi* (or *Libation Bearers*)

✔ Sophocles's *Electra*

✔ Euripides's *Electra*

Pursued by the Furies

Orestes was in big trouble, because killing one's own mother was deeply taboo. The Furies, ancient female goddesses, existed just to punish people who did stuff like that, and they were on Orestes in a flash. This was a little unfair, because the god Apollo had specifically told Orestes to take his revenge.

Euripides's play *Orestes* tells this story, as does Aeschylus's *Eumenides*. In Aeschylus's play, Orestes eventually makes his way to Athens with the Furies hounding him at every step. There the goddess Athena arranges a trial with Apollo representing the defendant (Orestes), and the Furies acting as the prosecution. The jury of Athenians was deadlocked, so Athena decided for Orestes. Her reasoning? Mothers are less important than fathers, so Orestes was right to kill his mom as revenge for his dad. Her justification? She herself had a father, but no mother (see Chapter 5 for more about her bloodlines), so mothers are clearly less important.

Orestes, off the hook, eventually married Hermione, daughter of Menelaus and Helen, the "face that launched a thousand ships" and the cause of the Trojan War. Hermione was Orestes's first cousin, sure, but if her mother was any indication, she was probably a real looker. Electra married Pylades, another first cousin. First cousins are too close to marry, really, but with this family it was probably just as well.

Part III
The Cultural Spoils of an Empire: Roman Mythology

The 5th Wave   By Rich Tennant

MEDUSA'S BEAUTIFUL BUT TERRIFYING GAZE COULD TURN A PERSON TO STONE.

Oh shoot – looked too hard at my dessert! Well, there goes a perfectly good Kahlua soufflé.

In this part . . .

The Romans were into borrowing gods and goddesses — it all went along with their empire-building mentality. With their mix-and-match pantheon, they managed to come up with an elaborate and very flexible system of beliefs and rituals — they had something for everyone.

Chapter 9

Will the Real Roman Mythology Please Stand Up?

· ·

In This Chapter

▶ Conquering the world

▶ Creating a "history" that was acceptable

▶ Being too pragmatic to worry much about religion, though very superstitious

▶ Adopting religions as they came, including Egyptian religion and Christianity

· ·

*R*ome borrowed almost all its myths from Greece and other sources. The Romans had their own homegrown gods, of course, and liked to tell stories as much as anyone, but as Rome expanded, the Romans embraced the gods and heroes of the people they conquered. Before long, the line between "Roman" mythology and "foreign" mythology became blurred and later erased altogether.

But even when the Roman gods look an awful lot like Greek gods or when a Roman myth seems like a rip-off of a myth from Persia or Egypt, those gods and myths are still Roman — important for Romans, true for Romans, and with a distinctive Roman flavor. So, Virgil's *Aeneid* (see Chapter 11) — which tells the story of the earliest origins of Rome, and how it became great — describes how a Trojan prince, an African queen, Greek gods, and an Italian prophetess all served the needs of the world-conquerors . . . the Romans!

This chapter explains why Roman mythology is such a slippery subject. It has to do with how Rome worked, how Romans worked with each other, and how they dealt with the non-Roman people who came to be a part of the Roman empire.

The Powers That Were: Before the Empire

At the height of Rome's power, about 1 million people lived in the city of Rome and over 50 million in the empire as a whole. They spoke hundreds of languages, and worshipped a vast array of deities. Rome kept them together with a tremendously efficient Latin-speaking central administration, but also let the people observe their own customs as much as possible.

But Rome wasn't always a great city, and didn't always control a great empire. Back in the eighth and seventh centuries BCE, Rome was a modest town in Italy—nothing more. In the earliest times, Romans worshipped gods that were shapeless (so there are no surviving statues of them), closely associated with the earth (so there are no big temples to them), and without distinct personalities (so there is no great body of mythology about their adventures, love affairs, wars, and so on).

It wasn't until the Romans started coming into contact with Greeks (who had many settlements in Italy) and some other Italian peoples (especially the Etruscans, see below), that Roman gods started to look human, and the Romans started to tell myths about them.

So, in the early days, Roman religion and mythology looked a lot like the religion and mythology of the other people of Italy. A quick look at those people, the Etruscans and other Italians, will help make some sense of what the Romans believed.

Home-Grown Gods: The Original Italians

Rome was a city in Italy, but not all Italians were Romans (at least, not at first). It took many centuries for Rome to dominate the whole Italian peninsula. Before that happened, and even after it had happened, the various non-Roman Italians had their own gods and their own myths. Some of these were very similar to the gods and myths of the Romans; others weren't.

Some of the other groups who shared Italy with the Romans were the following:

- Oscans
- Umbrians
- Sabines
- Etruscans
- Vestini
- Marsi

All the people of Italy shared a basic set of deities. However, each group had slightly different names for them and slightly different rituals associated with them. But each group had its own special gods, too.

Variations on Jupiter

Jupiter was common all over Italy, going by the name Jupiter, Juve, Juveis, Juvei, and so on. So was Mars (who was otherwise known as Mamars), Hercules (who also went by Hercle, Hercele, Herekleis), Juno, Hera, and Venus. Some Italians worshipped Fortuna, said to be the first-born daughter of Jupiter. In the area around Iguvium, they especially worshipped a Trinity of gods:

- Jupiter-of-the-Oak-Tree
- Mars-of-the-Oak-Tree
- Vofionus-of-the-Oak-Tree.

Gotta have a grain goddess

The goddess of grain, who was Ceres to the Romans, shows up with many, many different names all over Italy: Ammai, Diumpais, Pernai, Fluusai, Anafriss, and Maatuis. Grain is very important, and perhaps each ethnic group needed to have a special relationship with the goddess who gave them their daily bread. See Figure 9-1 to see a statue of Ceres.

Figure 9-1:
A statue
of Ceres.

Etruscans — we love babies!

Of all the nations that inhabited Italy while Rome was getting its act together, the Etruscans probably had the most highly developed culture and the richest body of myths. The Etruscans were closely related to the Greeks if their language (what is known of it), their art, and the remains of their buildings and pottery are any indication. Unfortunately, the Etruscans didn't leave a lot of written documents behind and what they did leave got destroyed when they were conquered by the Romans and became Romans themselves. So scholars don't have much to read and, as a result, don't really know the Etruscan language that well.

What did the Etruscans leave behind? Tombs and mirrors. These can tell more than you may expect. Etruscan tombs were little rooms, with beautiful paintings on the walls. Inside each tomb was a stone sarcophagus, often with decorations carved on it. The mirrors are bronze hand-mirrors, of the sort you might use to brush your hair. The front of these mirrors was smooth and polished, but the back often had scenes from Etruscan mythology on them. Favorite topics included scenes from the Trojan War and women holding babies.

This baby thing gives us the idea that the Etruscans (at least the women, who probably used the mirrors) really had a nice domestic existence and were more interested in family life than battle scenes. Even the Trojan War mirrors focus on feminine topics — mothers and babies and a little illicit sex for spice. Several mirrors show Uni (the Etruscan name for Hera) breast-feeding the full grown Hercle (Heracles) — in one picture, Heracles has a full beard, suggesting that it was really high time he be weaned! Another shows Minerva/Athena, Mercury/Hermes, and a bunch of other gods, all holding babies. Even myths that are kind of creepy become sweet and sentimental when they show up on Etruscan mirrors: one of them shows Pasiphaë, the queen of Crete, holding the baby Minotaur on her lap. (For more on the Minotaur, see Chapter 6.)

The carvings on *sarcophagi* (coffins) were not as light-hearted. Many of these seem to draw on myths popular with the Greeks as well, particularly the myths of the House of Atreus and the House of Cadmus (see Chapter 8). One sarcophagus shows Eteocles and Polynices, the two sons of Oedipus, fighting each other at Thebes. Another shows Pelops killing Oenomaus. (For more on these myths, see Chapter 8.)

Making Way for Rome with a Very Big "R"

Rome was supposedly founded around 753 BCE Rome started off as a single city ruled by kings. After about 250 years of that, it became a republic, ruled by a Senate elected from the aristocracy. This "Republican" period lasted from 509 to 31 BCE. As a republic, it grew from being just one city in Italy to controlling all of Italy, Sicily, Sardinia, and Greece. So — and this is a little strange — the Romans controlled an empire long before they were ruled by an emperor: a Roman empire before the Roman Empire!

But it did become an Empire, ruled by an Emperor (though the Romans still pretended that it was a republic). The Emperors expanded the Empire until it covered most of Europe, the Middle East, and North Africa. See Figure 9-2. The Roman Empire lasted until (approximately) 476 CE, when the last Roman emperor in the west was deposed, though it had lost a lot of power in the previous centuries when the empire was divided into different parts.

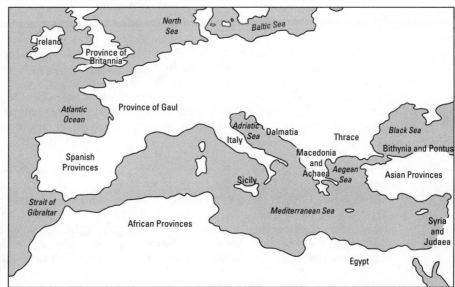

Figure 9-2: The Roman Empire at its height.

Roman mythology doesn't make much sense without an understanding of how big the Roman Empire was and how many different groups of people were part of it. And that doesn't make any sense without an understanding of how the Romans got to control such a big empire.

Building the empire: Spoils of war

One reason that the Roman empire expanded to include so many people was that Roman politicians always needed money — lots and lots of money. Ambitious politicians held a series of offices, ending with the office of *consul,* which was like a president, only there were two of them. This political career was expensive, but a good politician could make up all his debts if he advanced far enough to be appointed governor of a province.

If he was lucky, there would be a war and he could amass huge amounts of booty, returning a rich man, able to pay off his debts (if there were no war, he could still tax the people of the province, which worked, too). So it was in the best interest of every governor of every Roman province to fight a war. When they won wars, they added to the empire. Thus, the Roman Empire grew, Roman civilization followed Roman greed across the world, and new mythologies and new religions entered the imaginations of Romans.

Sure, they're Romans, too

"Rome" is, in one way, the opposite of "Greece." "Ancient Greece" describes a huge number of people, living all over the Mediterranean, in different, independent cities, with different kinds of governments all doing their own thing; what held them together were a shared language and a shared mythology. "Ancient Rome" is one city, with relatively few Romans living in it. But those folks got themselves in a position of power over lots of other people. A lot of the world became part of the Roman Empire, but didn't really become Roman — they kept speaking Greek or Hebrew or Gallic or whatever, and kept their own mythologies.

The result was that Roman religion became a hodge-podge of different customs. The Romans liked Greek mythology — they generally thought the Greeks were the last word in sophistication and culture — so they adopted the Greek gods as their own. But the native Italians who lived on the peninsula before the Romans took over had their own religions, and the Romans went ahead and took them on, too. They thought the Egyptian deities were pretty cool, so they incorporated some of the myths of Isis and Osiris. And so on.

The founding-of-Rome myths: Rome is the world!

The story of Romulus and Remus and the seven kings of Rome helped explain that and let the Romans feel no guilt about grinding indigenous peoples into the mud.

Consider Rome's age-old animosity against Carthage in North Africa. Sure, the politicians could argue that the people of Sicily had wanted the Romans in charge of them instead of the Carthaginians and come up with economic arguments why Sicily should be Roman. But it was more satisfying for everyone to know that Carthage had been Rome's enemy for centuries, and it was Carthage's own fault because their queen had cursed the Romans. They used the story of Aeneas and his affair with Dido to excuse the fact that they had conquered part of North Africa and kept it.

How It All Got So Darn Mixed Up

Roman religion, and therefore Roman mythology, was a long, drawn-out process of bringing together the gods, stories, and rituals of various cultures, and making them Roman. People who study religion or mythology for a living call this *syncretism.*

A Roman might nod to his Lares and Penates (original Roman gods) in the morning, pray to Isis (an Egyptian goddess) at lunchtime, attend a feast in honor of Heracles (a Greek hero), in the afternoon, have his future told by a *haruspex* (a priest who had learned the Etruscan art of liver-based fortune telling) later in the day, and ended the day attending a meeting of the cult of Mithras (a Persian deity whose followers met in caves).

By doing all of this, this Roman wasn't betraying his culture; he was being a good Roman! After all, what was the point of conquering the world if you don't have cool new gods, and cool new stories to show for it?

Why the Greek pantheon?

Chapter 10 is all about the Roman Pantheon of gods, but it isn't any secret that the big-time Roman gods were more or less the same as Greek gods, just with different names. How did Greek gods come to Rome? They followed the Romans home, and the Romans decided to keep them!

The story goes like this: Livius Andronicus was a Greek who lived from approximately 284 to 207 BCE. He lived in the city of Tarentum, which was a city settled by Greeks in southern Italy. In 272 BCE, the Romans conquered Tarentum, and Livius became a slave to a Roman. This Roman brought his new slave to Rome, and sometime later set him free.

Livius Andronicus's name was probably, originally, Andronikos, a Greek name. When he was freed from slavery, or *manumitted,* he took the name of his former master, who was one of the Livii, a very old Roman family. So he became Livius Andronicus.

After he was freed, he set himself up in business as a schoolteacher. But he also wrote literature. His biggest work was a translation of Homer's *Odyssey* into Latin, a work called the *Odyssia.* He had to work hard to bring that Greek epic into Latin. The existing Roman gods didn't always fit neatly with the Greek ones. So he made some substitutions. For example, the Greek Muse (daughter of Zeus who inspires poets) he replaced with the Roman Camena (a goddess of a fountain). He replaced Moira (the Greek goddess Fate), with Morta (the Latin goddess Death), and so on.

By making changes like that and lots of other changes, Livius Andronicus made his *Odyssia* more than a cheap copy of the *Odyssey*. He made it into a real Latin epic poem just for Romans. And by populating the story of Odysseus with Roman gods — Jupiter, Venus, Juno, and the others — he tied those gods together closely with the Greek gods. The idea caught on, and Roman mythology suddenly became much more "Greek" than it had been before.

Imported deities from other shores

Rome got some of its gods from other sources. A big empire has lots of influences in it. Governors in the provinces and the armies that accompanied them got to experience different cultures and often foreign wives; and plenty of provincial folks emigrated to the big metropolis of Rome, bringing their foreign ideas with them. Romans were always the sort to take up new fashions, so they had no problem incorporating some foreign beliefs into their daily rituals.

Egypt

The Egyptian goddess Isis was a particularly popular goddess in Rome. People identified her as Demeter, Selena (Roman goddess of the moon), and Hera. She fused with other mother goddesses, and was worshiped as Diana on the Greek island of Crete. Romans equated Osiris with Dionysus and Horus with Apollo.

The King of the Egyptian gods was Amon, and the Greeks had long ago decided that Amon must be the same as Zeus, so they worshipped him, when they were in Egypt, as Zeus-Amon. After Alexander the Great conquered Egypt, the rulers of Egypt were all Greeks — a bunch of kings all named Ptolemy, and a long line of queens all named Cleopatra — and Egyptian religion became more Greeky (or *Hellanized* to use the technical term for "becoming more Greeky").

The last Cleopatra was the famous one, the one played by Elizabeth Taylor in the epic movie of the same name. After her, Egypt became a province of Rome, and Roman stuff got mixed in with the Greek stuff that was mixed in with the Egyptian stuff. (This happened whenever Romans moved into foreign countries — they encountered new deities and incorporated them into their mythologies.) So where once there was a temple to plain-old Amon, by the first century CE there was one to Jupiter-Zeus-Amon!

When Christianity came to Rome and then to Egypt, things got even more complicated. Many folks who visit Egypt are surprised to see paintings that look like Mary and the Baby Jesus, but are actually Isis and Baby Horus. The two mother-and-divine-son stories were so similar that they influenced each other, and this shows up in art.

Persia

Before Rome became the huge empire that it was, a large portion of the world was under the control of the Persian Empire. This empire started in Iran, but spread through war and conquest until it stretched from India to the Aegean Sea from southern Russia to Ethiopia. Persians ruled Egypt for several hundred years, and also ruled many Greek cities in what is now Turkey. So Persia was a big deal.

Alexander the Great, a Macedonian Greek, conquered the Persian Empire, but didn't put an end to Persian culture. He just replaced Persian bureaucrats with Macedonian bureaucrats, and things went on as they always had. Later, Romans replaced those Macedonian bureaucrats with Roman ones, but Persian culture still remained lively and was a rich part of much of the Roman Empire.

The Persians had two religions, which may or may not have overlapped:

- ✔ The Eastern Persians, the ones in Iran, were Zoroastrian. Their big god was Zarathustra.
- ✔ The big god of the Western Persians was Ahuramazda.

The Greeks and Romans came in contact with these religions, and thought they were interesting.

Plutarch — who was Greek by birth, but a Roman citizen — wrote a book about Isis and Osiris, two Egyptian gods, but included in it a bunch of stuff about Persian mythology. He talks about how *Zoroastrianism* was started by a priest named Zoroaster, five hundred years before the Trojan War, who said that there were two gods fighting to control the world. One was good, either Zarathustra or Oromased, and the other was bad, Ahriman. The "umpire" in this context for control of the world was Mithra.

Mithra, even though he was Persian, was super popular with Romans, so much so that he became, essentially, a Roman god, under the name Mithras (see Chapter 10 for more on him).

The most famous part of Persian religion today is the office of the Magi. Many people familiar with the Christian mythos know the Magi as the Three Wise Men from the East who followed a star to visit the baby Jesus. *Magi* were Persian priests who specialized in interpreting dreams, reciting tales of the birth of the gods, and educating young rulers. These last two jobs of theirs would explain their trip to see little Jesus.

The Middle East

Romans were in charge of Palestine in the first century CE. The Jews were a part of the Roman Empire, just like just about everyone else in that part of the world. There were many Jews in Rome, too, who enjoyed a reputation for learning and piety but also a reputation for being a little strange.

For one thing, Jews were monotheists. They acknowledged only one god and weren't about to worship Jupiter, or Isis, or Ahuramazda, or anyone else. They certainly weren't about to worship Julius Caesar or Augustus. This was very strange and unsettling to Romans. Would Jupiter get mad if a bunch of people in Rome refused to worship him?

As is too often the case, Romans were suspicious of people with different beliefs, and a lot of Roman literature complains about the Jews. The poet Horace was particularly given to inserting anti-Semitic comments in his *Satires*.

This tension and many other political tensions made for a complicated situation in the Middle East (what else is new?). The Romans did their best to deal with it. They allowed Jewish kings to rule over Palestine — King Herod the Great is the famous one — while providing Roman military governors to keep the taxes coming in and keep the peace. That's the position that Pontius Pilate, who oversaw the Jesus of Nazareth incident, held in Jerusalem.

The problems between Jews and Romans came to a head in the 70s CE when the people of Palestine revolted and the Romans destroyed a lot of Jerusalem. Many Jews left the Middle East then, and that was the beginning of the *diaspora,* the spreading of the Jewish people around the world.

Down on the Farm: Roman Religion

Religion was a central part of Roman life during both the Republic and the Empire, and that included public affairs. Romans were incredibly superstitious. They weren't religious in the way modern people think of religion— Roman religion was not about "faith"—but they were extremely careful to observe rituals and rules. The rituals of Roman religion served to ensure good weather, the city's luck, its military success, the fertility of its farms, of its livestock, and of the Romans themselves. The rituals performed by the priests had to be done *perfectly* or it would bring bad luck to the city. The people responsible for performing these rituals were priests, and Roman religion required so many priests that just about any Roman man (or woman!) with a few connections and some ambition could get to be one.

We all serve somebody

Because there was no law against the joining of church and state, it was entirely possible for a man to hold both an important political office and an important priesthood. In fact, some of the more important priestships were elected, and conferred political power—the office of Pontifex Maximus, the chief priest of Jupiter, was like that. Being a priest was not necessarily a profession; people often held priesthoods in addition to another profession, like being a notary in addition to having a full-time job.

There were 15 major priests in Rome. They were called *flamines,* which is the plural; each one was a *flamen.* There were 12 minor flamines, each one responsible for duties toward a specific god — Ceres, Flora, and Volcanus are 3 that we know of. There were three major flamines:

- ✔ Flamen Dialis
- ✔ Flamen Martialis
- ✔ Flamen Quirinalis

They served (respectively) the gods Jupiter, Mars, and Quirinus. Unlike other, less important priests, these major flamines were selected by other priests from a limited list of aristocratic families — they weren't elected. Most of the flamines had a really good deal. The job was for life, and the flamen got a nice house at public expense, with only limited duties toward the gods.

Animal omens and astrology

One of the most important jobs the priests did was predicting the future. They did this in a bunch of ways. First of all, any aspect of the weather could indicate that something good or bad was going to happen. The behavior of a sacrificial bull during its execution was significant; it was important that the bull nod its head (bulls do "nod" their heads up and down, but they had to do it on the altar for the best effect) to "consent" to the sacrifice.

Priests also consulted the heavens for news from the gods. Astrology was a big business in Rome, despite periodic attempts to drive out the more fraudulent astrologers. A certain amount of astrology was expected of non-priests as well: The two men who had been elected consul — the office was like being President of the Republic, but there were two of them — were supposed to stay up all night before their inauguration looking at the sky to see if there were any omens.

Even the flights of birds could indicate the favor or displeasure of the gods, to those who knew how to interpret them. What kind of bird, which direction it flew, what it was carrying in its beak, and where it came to rest could all indicate the will of the gods.

The art of liver-gazing

One gift that the Etruscans passed along to the Romans was the craft of *haruspicy,* which is the business of looking at the liver of a sacrificed animal and using it to tell the future. How did the Etruscans learn this useful skill? A myth tells the tale!

One day a farmer in Etruria, where the Etruscans lived, was plowing his field when a little guy popped out of the ground. This was Tages, the "old-baby." He looked like a baby, but had the wisdom of an old man. Tages taught the farmer how to use livers to tell the future. When he was sure that the farmer could do it, he popped back into the ground and was never seen again.

Once the Romans learned how to do this entertaining trick, they never looked back and no major ritual was complete without some determined liver-gazing.

Chapter 10

Begged, Borrowed, and Stolen: Roman Religion

. . . .

In This Chapter

▶ Comparing Greek and Roman deities

▶ Meeting really Roman deities and spirits

▶ Encountering the feminine side of Roman religion

. . . .

Many scholars often dismiss Roman mythology, claiming that the Romans just borrowed their pantheon from the Greeks and didn't contribute anything original to their body of religion. But that is simply not true.

Yes, many Roman deities are also Greek ones. But not only did the Romans have their own approach to the Greek deities, they had a huge body of gods and spirits that were all their own. Romans were very superstitious and loved rituals (very much like the modern Roman Catholic Church). They also weren't jealous of other gods or particular about which gods their neighbors chose to worship. Roman religion was a free-for-all of ritual, private devotion, public observation, and festivals, and personal choice. Unoriginal? Hardly.

The Greek-Roman Pantheon

During the Republican period (509–31 BCE), Greece became the last word in culture and sophistication, and fashionable Romans imported Greek deities and made them their own. A lot of them arrived in a Roman version of the *Odyssey* (see Chapter 7). Roman names were substituted for Greek names, with the end result being a whole new version of the old familiar Greek immortals. (We discuss this more thoroughly in Chapter 9.)

Once they had adopted the Greek pantheon, the Romans built temples to the various deities, held festivals for them at appropriate times, and even came up with a certain number of stories about them — see Chapter 12 for some of those.

The Roman deities and their Greek equivalents can be found in Table 10-1. Most of these gods started out as Italian originals but over time became more and more like their Greek counterparts (because the Romans spent more and more time reading Greek literature and associating with Greek people). So by the second century BCE, the Greek and Roman gods came to be very, very similar.

Table 10-1	Roman and Greek Deity Equivalents	
Roman	*Greek*	*Function*
Jupiter (or Jove)	Zeus	King of the gods
Juno	Hera	Goddess of marriage
Neptune	Poseidon	God of the sea
Saturn	Cronos (maybe)	King of the Titans
Gaea	Gaia	Goddess of earth
Venus	Aphrodite	Goddess of love
Pluto (Dis Pater)	Hades	God of the underworld
Vulcan	Hephaestus	God of the forge
Ceres	Demeter	Goddess of the harvest
Apollo	Apollo	God of music
Minerva	Athena	Goddess of wisdom
Diana	Artemis	Goddess of the hunt
Mercury	Hermes	Messenger of the gods
Bacchus	Dionysus	God of wine
Proserpine	Persephone	Queen of the underworld
Cupid	Eros	God of love
Mars	Ares	God of war

The Roman gods have given their names to a huge number of English words. *Cereal* comes from Ceres. *Jovial,* meaning jolly, comes from Jupiter, who was also called Jove. *Venereal,* having to do with sex, comes from Venus. Someone with a *mercurial* temperament has frequently changing moods, after Mercury, who was always coming and going. The heavy metal used to make nuclear weapons is called *plutonium,* because it comes straight from hell, where Pluto is king. A military court is a *court martial,* or a "court of Mars." Primavera, the goddess of spring, shown in Figure 10-1, gives her name now to pasta with lots of vegetables.

Figure 10-1: Sandro Botticelli's *Primavera.*

© Bettman/CORBIS

Roman astronomy

The nine planets in the solar system take their names from Roman gods: Mercury, Venus, Earth, Mars, Jupiter, Saturn, Uranus, Neptune, and Pluto. Scientists speculate that a tenth planet may exist out there. Because no one can see it, but it makes Pluto move in funny ways, they have dubbed this ghostly planet Persephone, after Pluto's mysterious wife.

The moons of planets are often named after the gods' children. Mars had two children, Phobus and Deimus, which are the names of the planet Mars's two small, lumpy moons. Jupiter had a bunch of kids, but he is better known for having a bunch of lovers, so his planet's moons are named for them. Two of the biggest moons of Jupiter are Europa, named for one of the god's girlfriends, and Ganymede, named for one of his boyfriends.

It's all Roman to me

The names of the months come from Roman mythology (or history) as well.

- ✔ January was named after Janus, the two-faced god of coming and going.

- ✔ February was named after a Latin ceremony for the forgiveness of sins.

- ✔ March was named after Mars.

- ✔ April might have been named for Aphrodite, or possibly took its name from the verb *aperire,* "to open," because many flowers open in April.

- ✔ May was named for Maia, mother of Mercury.

- ✔ June took its name from Juno.

- ✔ July got its name from Julius Caesar, who liked the idea of having a month with his name on it.

- ✔ August came from Caesar's successor Augustus, who also wanted a month named after him.

- ✔ September means "seventh month." Before Julius Caesar and Augustus got involved in month-naming, September was the seventh month; now it's the ninth. October through December suffered the same fate.

- ✔ October means "eighth month."

- ✔ November means "ninth month."

- ✔ December means "tenth month."

The names of the months have remained constant for about 2,000 years, which is a pretty good track record.

Special Roman Gods

The Romans and native Italians hadn't lacked for deities before they imported the Greek pantheon, and they kept worshipping their own spirits even while they built temples to Jupiter and Ceres and all the others. These spirits were everywhere, influencing all spheres of existence, from cooking at home to Roman citizenship.

Sharing spirits at home and in public

A Roman couldn't turn around without coming face to face with a god. Spirits were everywhere: *Lares* watched over the home and the crossroads, Di Penates lived in cupboards, and the two-faced god Janus guarded doors and gates. And no Roman could get rid of a nagging father just by having the old man die — ancestors lurked around the house in the form of exquisitely detailed masks called *imagines*.

Original Italian gods — numena

Modern scholars call the original Italian and Roman gods *numena,* a word that means divinity. The numena weren't much like the Greek deities and in fact were more like spiritual forces — they didn't have personalities or genders or any other *anthropomorphic* (that is, looking like humans) attributes. Because they didn't have bodies, they couldn't have sex, eat dinner, go visiting, or play games, so the Romans didn't have many stories to tell about them.

But even without good stories, these numena were forces that took care of everything — yes, *everything*. Numena were guarding the crossroads and the boundaries of the city, entities that watched over rain, wind, and households, and forces that created good or bad luck.

Household gods — Lares

The *Lares* (singular *Lar*) were numena who guarded places, groups, activities, or nations. They had no form, shape, gender, or number, and the Romans didn't really come up with stories about them the way the Greeks did with their gods and goddesses. A family would have its own private Lar and the whole nation shared the public Lares of Rome. Some of the more important Lares hung around crossroads, and special clubs held rituals to keep them happy.

Many houses had little shrines to their *Lar Familiaris* (the Lar of the Family). These shrines included little statues or paintings of young men in short tunics carrying a drinking horn and a bowl, or of two young men with a dog. In Roman households, if food fell on the floor during dinner, it was customary to burn it in front of the shrine to the Lar Familiaris.

The Lares might have been ghosts of dead ancestors. One inscription (a bit of writing carved in stone) that survives from ancient Rome records a present given to a Lar Familiaris and refers to the Lar as an ancestor's ghost. At a Roman festival, *the Compitalia,* Roman families hung up little puppets representing all the members of the family and all the slaves. The idea was that if the Lar wanted to take someone to the land of the dead, it might get confused and take the puppet instead.

Spirits in the closet — Di Penates

The *Di Penates* (Gods of the Indoors) also were numena; they were the gods of the storage cupboards within the home. Romans worshipped them at home along with Vesta and the Lar Familiaris (see the previous section). The Roman state had its own Di Penates, who were supposed to help keep the nation financially solvent. Like the Lares, the Di Penates were depicted as young men. Some people think that the Di Penates are the same as Castor and Pollux, who were twin sons of Zeus and Leda, thus Helen of Troy's brothers.

The most famous appearance of Lares and Di Penates in mythology is in Virgil's *Aenead*. The mythological founder of Rome, Aeneas, was a Trojan who survived the Trojan War, sailed to Italy, and set up shop there (see Chapter 7). In Virgil's poem, when Aeneas was fleeing from the burning city of Troy, he manages to carry his old father, his son, and the statues of his Lares and Di Penates, but he didn't manage to keep track of his wife! No doubt where his priorities were.

Makes a better door than a window: The two-faced Janus

Janus was the two-faced god of doors and gates (which look both directions). Because any enterprise has to "go out the door" to get started, Janus was the god of beginnings as well. That's why the first month of the year, January, is named after him.

Looking back to a time when all Roman armies started out on campaigns by going through the city's gates, there was a special gate in the Roman forum, the gate of Janus Geminius. If Romans were involved in a war anywhere in the world, the gate stood open (to welcome the army back home). Only in times of complete peace was the gate of Janus closed. This happened once in 235 BCE; three times at the end of the first century BCE, when Augustus was emperor; and a few more times under later emperors. But mostly, Janus's gate stood open, as the Romans fought perpetually to expand their empire and defend its borders.

Imagines — Masks of the Ancestors

Romans didn't have many original myths about their own gods, but they made up for it with endless discussion of their own ancestors. It was perfectly common for a Roman man to know what his ancestors had been doing 400 years earlier! They even knew what they looked like, thanks to *imagines* (the source of the English word "images").

If a Roman did something noteworthy — earned some military award or got elected to political office — he would be entitled to have an *imago* made. This was a mask of his face. His family would keep it in a special cabinet shaped like a tiny temple. Inside the temple, they would include a written document that described everything about the ancestor, like how he moved, distinguishing gestures and marks on his body, height and build, and anything else that could help someone imitate him.

The reason for all this detailed description was that when the person died, an actor would wear the mask at his funeral and march in the funeral parade, imitating him so perfectly that observers would swear he was still alive. And that wouldn't be the last time he would appear in a funeral. Once he died and became an official "Ancestor," an actor wearing his mask and imitating him would walk in all subsequent family funerals. An old Roman family would have a cabinet full of imagines, alongside their cabinet full of Di Penates and their Lar. A Roman funeral procession must have been quite a spectacle, with all those ancestors marching alongside the newly dead person.

Gods of ideals and mysterious gods

Some gods of the Romans embodied ideals. Some were really more "ideas" themselves than actual deities. For example, several of the most important spirits personified human qualities such as faith (Fides), honor (Honos), and hope (Spes). The most interesting of the "gods of ideals" was the one who embodied the idea of Roman citizenship: Quirinus. And the origins of some gods are a complete mystery today. Saturn, famous for his fabulous holiday, the Saturnalia, is one.

The Roman citizen: Quirinus

Quirinus was one of the most important original Italian gods. Although no one could say exactly what he was, they knew that he was the embodiment of the Roman citizen. The Romans appointed a special priest in his honor and they held a festival called the *Quirinalia* every year.

Quirinus originally was either Latin or Sabine, and his home was on the Quirinal Hill in Rome. The Quirinal Hill was fused into Romulus's new city (Rome, that is), and Quirinus and Romulus somehow merged into the same entity. According to stories, after Romulus got the city of Rome going and died, he appeared to one of his soldiers in a dream and announced that he was now a god named Quirinus. Because he was supposedly now identical with the mythical founder of Rome, it was natural for him to embody the idea of the city and citizen.

Ho-ho-ho, Merry . . . Saturnalia?

The merriest festival of the Roman year was the Saturnalia, on the 17th of December. On this happy day, slaves had dinner with their masters, people lit candles, and everyone exchanged presents. A king of the festival was crowned the *Saturnalicius Princeps,* whose job was to preside over the parties and feasts. The Roman poet Catullus calls this the "happiest day of the year."

But who was this Saturn in whose honor the Romans permitted themselves be so merry? No one really knows. Some scholars see Saturn as the Roman equivalent to the Greek Cronus, but that Greek god was far from merry. (Although the word *saturnine* means dour or melancholy, Saturn must have had some reputation for being a serious sourpuss, maybe from Cronos.) Others see him coming from the Etruscan god Satre, about whom nothing is known. Still others see Saturn associated with Satus, some sort of deity having to do with planting and growing grain.

Whatever his origins, Saturn had his own temple in one corner of the Roman forum, and a delightful festival December 17. In fact, the festival went on for six or seven days after the 17th.

If this holiday sounds a lot like Christmas, that's no accident. Because no ancient Christian knew just when in the year Jesus of Nazareth was born (just as no one knows today), the celebration of his birth came to coincide more or less with the traditional Roman mid-winter festival.

A God for Every Taste

As most people know, Rome had a big army. Almost every man in the Republic, and later the Empire, spent some time marching up and down the landscape, putting down uprisings or just conquering new land. Rome also had its fair share of merchants. A big, prosperous empire is a huge temptation to anyone involved in trade, and merchants were everywhere. And anyone who has seen the beautiful gardens throughout Italy knows that the Italians have a great affinity for plants; so did the ancient Romans.

The Romans had gods for all tastes and walks of life. Soldiers liked the Persian god Mithras, while traders appreciated Hercules Invictus (especially the all-you-can-eat buffet in his temple.) And everyone knows a garden needs statuary, and that's where Priapus came in.

Mithras, patrolling good and evil

Mithras came to Rome from Persia, where he was known as Mithra. In the dominant religion of Persia, Good and Evil were in a constant battle for control of the world. Mithra was the referee in this battle; he also was the god of legal contracts and of cattle stealing. So he covered a wide range of things, and all were important.

A god for the working man

The cult of Mithras seems to have been brought to Italy by pirates (or "unofficial sea-going merchants," depending on where you stood on the issue) from Cilicia, which was the province of Rome around the Black Sea. Once Mithras got to Rome, he became associated with the Sun God, and members of his cult seem to have regarded him — at least when they were participating in his rituals — as almost the One-and-Only God. His title was *Deus Sol Invictus Mithras,* or "Invincible Sun God Mithras."

Ordinary folks became members of Mithras's cult, especially soldiers and minor government bureaucrats. That suggests the cult was comfy and down-to-earth, but one unfortunate side effect is that those people didn't write many books, so they didn't leave much of a record about what actually went on in this popular cult.

Competition for Christianity

The Cult of Mithras was especially popular among Romans in the second and third centuries CE — at the same time the cult of Jesus of Nazareth was gaining popularity and evolving into Christianity. And, in fact, many striking similarities exist between Mithraism and early Christianity.

The Cult of Mithras was divided into *cells;* members of the cult belonged to a certain cell, and the cell often served as a focal point of their social lives, much like the role that a modern church, synagogue, or mosque plays as a social center.

Each cell met in a *cave,* which was in many ways the opposite of temples erected to the more traditional Greek and Roman gods. Temples were heavily decorated on the outside with no room inside to do anything. People stood around temples on the outside and sacrificed to the gods; the gods lived in the temples. Caves of Mithras were plain on the outside but had plenty of room inside for the members to practice their worship.

Each cell had a complicated hierarchy of leadership, and members of the cult assuming different leadership positions, similar to deacons or presbyters in a Christian church. One of the lay offices was the *Nymphus,* a Latin term that seems to mean "male bride." A strange term, perhaps, but the letters of Paul that are part of the Christian *New Testament* are full of Bride and Groom imagery describing the church.

Many Mithras caves are preserved today because Christian churches were built on the same spot — another connection between the two faiths. A good one to visit is under the Church of San Clemente in Rome. Another, under the church of Santa Prisca in Rome, has an inscription saying that Mithras "saved us all with the shed blood," which sounds much like the language of Christian rites. In the case of Mithras, however, the blood probably wasn't his own, but rather the blood of a cow he killed with his bare hands. You can see a representation of this in Figure 10-2.

Figure 10-2:
Mithras killing the bull and saving the world with the bull's blood.

The all-you-can-eat buffet chef: Hercules

The Romans knew Heracles, the Greek hero who turned into a Greek god, as Hercules (or "Heracles," if you weren't "really" Roman, but just Italian). The Romans accepted him as their own, and loved him as much as the Greeks did.

He started life as a mortal, worked hard helping folks out, suffered more than his fair share, died as a result of betrayal, but became a god — see Chapter 6 for the full story. His was an encouraging story, probably because of the happy ending to his biography. The Romans worshipped him as "Hercules Invictus" ("Unconquered Hercules").

Hercules's cult was popular with Romans from all walks of life but especially among merchants. Merchants, like Hercules, worked all the time and their jobs forced them to travel. Because members of the cult of Hercules Invictus were supposed to *tithe* — to give one tenth of their profits to the god — his cult was very wealthy.

He had a sanctuary in Rome called the *Ara Maxima,* the "Greatest Altar," which was the site of daily sacrifices in his honor (daily, because they could afford it!). No women or dogs were allowed at his sanctuary, but men were welcome, and they came in droves. One reason, perhaps, for such a good turnout was a particular rule of his cult: All meat from the sacrifices to Hercules had to be eaten the same day. The Ara Maxima must have been like a daily, free, all-you-can-eat steak buffet for cult members. So, once again, Hercules the Unconquered helped his fellow man get through the working day!

Ancient dirty jokes: Priapus

What's not to like about the god of fertility, sexual humor, and farming? Nothing, according to the Romans! Priapus was the god with a sense of humor.

He was a very ancient Italian god. A Greek writer in Italy named Xenarchus wrote a play about him in the fourth century BCE, and he became more and more popular in the third century, spreading all through Italy.

He appeared as a male god with enormous genitals, so it was natural for him to be associated with both sex and fertility, and with the most important kind of fertility, the fertility of the farm. It was rare for a male god to be responsible for things growing out of the earth — that was normally for female divinities like Demeter or Ceres or the Bona Dea. But Priapus took on the job with a smile.

Many Romans kept a statue of Priapus in their garden, and his job was to keep intruders out. He was supposed to accomplish this by threatening intruders with his huge genitals.

A whole genre of poetry, called *Priapeia,* consists of short, funny poems in which Priapus issues threats to garden intruders, with lots of really nasty humor. Often, much of the humor of these poems is at the expense of the god himself. For example, in a poem by Horace, Priapus says that he started out as a fig tree. Someone cut this tree down and made it into a Priapus garden statue, who is now speaking; he reflects that he was lucky, because he could have ended up as a stool instead. In these poems, Priapus often reflects on what a minor god he is, but he doesn't seem to mind.

Keeping It Real: The Goddesses

Some of Rome's most important deities were female. Vesta, goddess of the hearth, kept everyone's household functioning; her priestesses, the Vestal Virgins, held Rome's luck in their bodies. The Magna Mater, or big mother goddess, was responsible for making things grow every spring. Bona Dea, the good goddess, was an extremely ancient Italian deity of fertility and the earth, who also oversaw the progress of growing things, from plants to unborn babies. Although manly gods like Mithras were popular with particular groups, these goddesses belonged to everyone in Rome.

Although Roman women were disadvantaged compared to men, as has indeed been the case with women in most of the world for centuries, they still participated in the maintenance of the city to quite a large degree. Many women took an active interest in politics, they were important to keeping the family running, and they could be religious professionals.

Vesta and the virgins

Vesta was goddess of the hearth. Or rather, she was the hearth. She was one of the most ancient of Roman spirits and was extremely important within the home and the family. Each family worshipped Vesta along with its other household gods, the Lares and Di Penates.

Vesta also had an extremely important public cult, served by a group of special priestesses and supervised by the *Pontifex Maximus,* the chief priest in Rome. Her priestesses were called the *Vestal Virgins.* There were always six of them, and they had to be virgins — no exceptions, no excuses. See Figure 10-3 to check one out.

Figure 10-3:
A Vestal
Virgin:
guardian of
Rome's luck
and keeper
of its last
wills and
testaments.

© Araldo de Luca/CORBIS

A virgin for life (or until retirement)

Rome's luck depended on the Vestal Virgins' remaining chaste, so no funny business for them. If someone accused a Vestal Virgin of breaking her vows, she was tried before a special court. If the court found her guilty, her punishment was ugly — she would be thrown into a hole in the ground, the hole would be sealed up, and she would be left to die.

The Vestal Virgins were inducted into the priesthood as young girls, and stayed there for about 30 years. They were allowed to marry after retirement, but usually didn't — it was considered bad luck. Vestal Virgins were by no means sequestered. They could go out in public and have friends, and were popular guests at dinner parties — they had kind of a celebrity status in Rome.

They don't do windows but they do secretarial work

The Vestal Virgins had many important jobs. They made sure that the perpetual fire on the Public Hearth never went out. They were also in charge of public records. All wills, birth certificates, certificates of citizenship, documents recording the freeing of slaves, and death certificates came to the Temple of Vesta, and the Vestal Virgins collected them, catalogued them, and filed them away for safekeeping and easy retrieval. Any Roman citizen could file a will with them, and many people did — for poor folks, it was one of their few chances to feel important.

Magna Mater — the Big Mama

The Magna Mater, or Great Mother, came to Rome from Anatolia, in what is now Turkey. She also went by the name of Cybele (and in some Persian account, Agdistis). She had cults all over the Mediterranean world, but the Romans welcomed her with open arms. She had a temple of the Palatine Hill in Rome, and all of the priests at the temple had to be from the east (so Big Mamma would feel at home).

The Magna Mater enjoyed festivals every spring, because she was at least partly responsible for making things grow — a job that she shared with Ceres and some other female gods. One of her festivals involved cutting down a pine-tree and putting it in her temple, which may be the ritual ancestor of the Christmas tree.

Ancient sex change

Magna Mater, however, wasn't all sweetness and sprouting plants. The one myth associated with her is the story of Attis. Different versions of this story abound; none of them is pretty.

The poet Catullus wrote a poem recounting the most famous Roman version of this myth. He described Attis as a young Roman man who got involved with the cult of Cybele. In a religious frenzy, he sailed off to an island and immediately cut off his own genitals. Later, he regretted this, and wondered out loud what he would say to the guys at the gym.

Followers of the Magna Mater also revered Attis, but they didn't worship him as a god.

From Persia with love

The Persian version says Agdistis (another name for Cybele/Magna Mater) was originally androgynous, but the gods castrated him. Agdistis's cut-off genitals grew into an almond tree. Another god, Nana, ate the almonds, which made her pregnant and she gave birth to a son, Attis. Agdistis (now completely a woman after the castration) fell in love with Attis, but to make sure that he didn't cheat on her, she castrated him. So he (for lack of anything better to do) became a devoted servant of Agdistis.

Bona Dea, the Good Goddess

The Bona Dea was the Good Goddess — she didn't have a name, or rather, her name was secret and not supposed to be uttered. Everyone referred to her by her title. She was not specifically Roman, but was an Italian goddess, who was in charge of the earth and all the good things that come from the earth. She was also the patron goddess of chastity and fertility in women (evidently, chastity and fertility each in its proper place).

The priestesses of the Good Goddess sometimes gave her the names Fauna ("Critter"), Maia (just a name), or Ops ("Wealth"). But the priestesses knew that these weren't her real names.

A ladies club: The snaky lady

Pictures of the Good Goddess show her with a wreath of vines around her head, a jar of wine beside her, and a holy snake nearby. The Good Goddess had a temple on the Aventine Hill in Rome, and the temple was inhabited by a bunch of holy snakes. The temple had a garden with lots of healing plants growing in it.

Men were not allowed to enter her temple, because she was a goddess just for women.

Lady's Night — Oh what a night!

A special annual festival was held in December in honor of the Bona Dea (the festival was called "the Bona Dea"). The point of the festival was to put the Good Goddess to sleep for the year. If this was not done correctly, she might not sleep well, and all growth would be cursed until the next year.

The festival was held in the house of one of the two Consuls of Rome (the office of Consul was like that of President — two Consuls ruled at the same time), but the Consul himself wasn't present. Only women could come. The Consul's wife and the Vestal Virgins presided over the festival. At the festival, the women of Rome said the secret name of the Good Goddess, and it was very, very bad luck for any man to hear it. All the women drank wine, but called it "milk" — this was part of the secret all-woman nature of the festival, because according to Rome's most ancient laws, a husband could legally kill his wife if he caught her drinking wine (the law was long out of date, but it must still have been fun for the women to drink lots of wine with no men around to disapprove).

In 61 BCE, a Roman man named Publius Clodius Pulcher snuck in to the festival of the Bona Dea, dressed as a woman. When this was discovered, the Roman women panicked, fearing that all childbirth that year would be cursed. Clodius was brought to trial and was prosecuted by the famous orator Cicero, but managed to escape conviction by bribing the jury.

Chapter 11

Virgil's *Aeneid* and The Founding of Rome

*O*ne of the jobs of mythology is to justify or validate a current state of affairs. So the people of the Greek city of Thebes had a myth in which the original inhabitants of the city sprang right out of the ground — this validated the city, because they could say, "We've always lived here." Likewise, the story of Christopher Columbus (which is mythology and history at the same time), according to which he "discovered America," validates the European control of the continent, even though there were lots of folks already living here. Myths like this are called *foundation* myths.

Rome had two foundation stories, the one of the twins Romulus and Remus, who were raised by a wolf, and the story of Aeneas the Trojan, told in the *Aeneid*. It also had a story of how its government came about, which involved a virtuous woman who got raped. All of these stories helped the Roman people explain to themselves and everyone else how they came to be in control of the entire Mediterranean.

Why the Romans Needed Another Myth: Down with Carthage!

Discovering more about Rome's foundation myths, you first need to know a little bit about Carthage. Carthage was a city in North Africa, in what is now Tunisia. People from Carthage were called *Carthaginians*.

Sicily, more important than you may think

On a map, Italy and Carthage are directly across the Mediterranean from each other, with only one thing in between them: Sicily!

Unlike its present-day status as a charming backwater, Sicily was an important place for most of recorded history. Located at the center of the Mediterranean, and rich in natural resources, it was a favorite place for empires to conquer. The Romans used it as their breadbasket, growing grain there the same way the United States grows grain in its heartland.

In 264 BCE, the Romans and Carthaginians bumped into each other in Sicily. Sicily's population was mostly of Greek origin; Greek people had come from Grecian cities, looking for more room and land to live and farm on, and they had settled the island. At this point, however, Sicily had no centralized government and didn't belong to Rome, Greece, or anyone else. Sicilian cities controlled the regions surrounding them and vied with one another for a greater share of the island. Some of the cities in Sicily were big and powerful, and Syracuse was the most powerful of all.

Syracuse was so rich and powerful because it was a center of trade. The people who did most of the trading there were the people of Carthage, who were skilled navigators and avid entrepreneurs. The people of Syracuse and of Carthage saw nothing wrong with controlling the whole island of Sicily, which was fertile and grew a lot of food.

Romans to the rescue and the first Punic War

Some of the other people on Sicily had other ideas, though. The folks in the city of Messina, on the northeastern tip of Sicily, preferred not to have Syracuse or Carthage tell them what to do, so they invited the Romans to come protect them.

At this point, Rome was not a great empire. It was just a city of moderate size whose people had a reputation for getting things done. The Romans agreed to help out Messina, and they found themselves in a war with Syracuse and Carthage. Yikes!

Because the Carthaginians were originally Phoenicians from what is now Lebanon, and because the Roman word for Phoenicians is *Punici* in Latin, this war became known as the First Punic War. It lasted from 264 until 146 BCE — a really long time!

Syracuse and Carthage had big navies, and the Romans didn't have any navy at all. This was a problem if they were going to have a war in Sicily, which was, after all, an island. So the Romans built a navy, learned how to use it, and eventually defeated their enemies to gain control over Sicily. See Figure 11-1 for a cool example of a Roman warship.

Figure 11-1:
A Roman
warship.

© Archivo Icongrafico/CORBIS

The Trojan War started it all

But what does the First Punic War (see the preceding section) have to do with mythology? Well, a good foundation myth can help justify this conquest of Sicily and make lasting enmity between Rome and Carthage perfectly sensible.

The Romans already had myths about their own origins — Romulus, Remus, and so on — which were good and useful. But it sure would be convenient to have a foundation-myth that helped justify Roman control over the Greek cities of Sicily.

Now, the Romans were great engineers. They solved whatever problems they found. So when they found themselves at war with folks who fought in ships, they built themselves a navy. When they needed a new foundation myth, it was no big problem for Roman "mythological engineers" to go to work building one.

Gnaeus Naevius was a Roman who actually fought in the First Punic War. While the war was still going on but after he had retired from military activity, he wrote an epic poem, the *Punic War*. This poem was the first major piece of Roman literature — as far as anyone can tell — to tell the story of Aeneas. Aeneas was a Trojan, who escaped from the city of Troy when the Greeks captured it. In Naevius's poem, Aeneas sails away from Troy and comes to Carthage, where he falls in love with the queen, Dido. He eventually leaves her to start his own country, which would one day become Rome. Dido kills herself, but not before putting a curse on Aeneas: Forever and forever, the curse went, there would be hatred between Aeneas's people and Carthage.

So that's why Rome hates Carthage

This Punic War story had been around for a long time (see preceding section) — the Greeks knew about it in the 400s BCE — but no Roman had made a big deal about it before. Naevius did make a big deal about it — just as Virgil would make a big deal about it a couple of centuries later, writing another epic poem about the same events (see the following section) — and Naevius's point was political:

- ✔ Naevius wrote an epic poem, and everyone knew that epic poetry was *important,* and that the stuff in epic poetry was *mythology,* and therefore was *true*. So merely by writing his story as an epic poem, Naevius made sure that it would be taken seriously.

- ✔ Aeneas was Trojan, and anyone reading Homer's epic poems can see that the Trojans were really Greeks; they spoke Greek, worshipped the Greek gods, and did all the same things that the Greeks did.

By claiming that Rome was *really* started by a Trojan, Naevius was claiming that Romans were actually Greeks, or at least that Romans and Greeks were close cousins. So, as Rome was fighting a war for control of Sicily (which was full of Greeks), Naevius's poem helped make the claim that Rome had more business in Sicily than the Carthaginians did, because Romans and Greeks were related.

Naevius's poem provided a mythological excuse for Romans to fight Carthaginians — Dido cursed Aeneas, so it was inevitable that they fight. Because Rome was fighting not only Carthage but also the Greek city of Syracuse, Naevius's poem justified that was well — the descendants of the Trojan Aeneas were just getting some revenge on the descendants of the Greeks who had destroyed Troy.

There! A nice new mythological history, designed to help Romans feel good about this century-long war!

Emperor Augustus and Virgil's PR Machine: The Aeneid

When Augustus made himself into an emperor in the first century BCE — ending the period of the Roman Republic and instituting the Imperial period, he thought he could use some more history. So around 30 BCE, he hinted to the poet Virgil that he wouldn't mind too much if someone were to write a long epic poem talking about how he, Augustus, had personally saved Rome from a century of civil war. Virgil got out his *Iliad* and *Odyssey* (see Chapter 7) and read them along with Naevius's *Punic War* (see preceding section) and came up with the perfect hero: Aeneas. (See following section, "Duty calls," for why Virgil liked him.) Virgil started writing his great epic poem, the *Aeneid,* in 29 BCE and kept right on writing until he died on September 20, 19 BCE. He actually asked (in his will) that the poem be burned, because there were a couple of bits that didn't perfectly satisfy him. However, Augustus, pictured in Figure 11-2, knew a good thing when he saw it and had the poem published.

Figure 11-2:
In addition to making Virgil write an epic in the Greek style for him, Augustus had a sculptor make him look like the Greek god Apollo.

© Araldo de Luca/CORBIS

The *Aeneid* told the story of Aeneas but was also loaded with "prophecies" about how Aeneas's job as founder of Rome would eventually be brought to fulfillment with Caesar Augustus. The poem was a big propaganda piece intending to lead its readers to see Augustus as a Savior sent by the Gods to fulfill an inevitable history. But that doesn't mean that the *Aeneid* is "only" propaganda. Anything worth reading has lots of different meanings that are all "true" at the same time. So the *Aeneid* is propaganda, but also mythological history, and a fine work of art in its own right.

Duty calls: Aeneas is just the guy

Why was Aeneas so perfect for Virgil's purposes? He was a Trojan who escaped from the city of Troy when the Greeks captured it, which are events described in Homer's *Iliad* (see Chapter 7). Other stories about him said that he had sailed to Italy and set up shop there. His mother was the goddess Venus; before he was born, she had foreseen that he would rule over the Trojans and found an everlasting dynasty. He hadn't done anything particularly heinous in the *Iliad,* and best of all — for the Romans — he hadn't died during the war.

Escape from Troy

At the end of the Trojan War, the Greeks destroyed the city of Troy and killed all the Trojan men. (They had other plans for the women.) Aeneas managed to escape, carrying his aged father Anchises on his back and his son Ascanius in his arms. He also brought along his images of his household gods, the Lares and Di Penates (see Chapter 10).

The reason Anchises was too frail to walk is that long ago he had spent the night with the goddess Venus, and the ancients knew that sex with a goddess would enfeeble a mortal man forever (but was worth it, nevertheless). That's how Venus came to be the mother of Aeneas.

Duty calling is a big theme in Virgil's *Aeneid.* This picture of Aeneas, carrying everything but the kitchen sink (or his wife) out of Troy sums up this hero: He was dutiful. Odysseus was crafty and Achilles was brave (see Chapter 7), but Aeneas did what he was supposed to. Another theme is the anger of the goddess Juno, who hated Aeneas and hated the fact that he would eventually found Rome. In fact, the title of the *Aeneid* could just as well be *Duty versus Anger.*

That's easy to say now!

Virgil's *Aeneid* was written between 29 and 19 BCE, but the events in it were supposed to have happened a thousand years earlier. In the poem, various prophets tell Aeneas what "will happen" in the history of his people. Obviously, even though Virgil's characters are prophets, Virgil himself didn't have to be a prophet, because the events in the prophecies had already happened. This is the easiest kind of "prophecy" to write: prophecy after the fact!

A Mediterranean cruise

Aeneas and company got into a boat and sailed away. He had a lot of adventures on the trip, and in fact the first half of the *Aeneid* has a lot in common with Homer's *Odyssey* (see Chapter 7) — Aeneas even sailed past the island of the Cyclopes, close enough to see the big critters (but he didn't stop).

At his father's suggestion, the Trojan fugitives made a stop in Epirus, where Helenus was king. Helenus was another Trojan survivor. He was the son of Priam, king of Troy. Like his sister Cassandra (see Chapter 8), Helenus had the gift of prophecy, and he did a little fortune telling for Aeneas and his buddies. See the "The prophecy comes true" section later in this chapter to find out what he said. Aeneas and his guys would have liked to stay with Helenus in Epirus, but duty called, and so they had to sail off.

My Carthaginian queen

After leaving their pit stop in Epirus (see the preceding section), they sailed on. Duty and anger played a big part in what happened next.

As they sailed along, Aeneas and his Trojans were tossed by a terrible storm, sent by Juno to smash them to bits. But Jupiter, Juno's husband (see Chapter 10 for more about Juno and Jupiter), noticed what was going on and set her straight: no killing Aeneas would be allowed, because he was just doing his job, which was to sail around until he founded Rome.

Aeneas's ship washed up on shore in Carthage, modern Tunisia. There he met Dido, the Carthaginian queen.

Dido was a Phoenician, born in the city of Tyre in modern Lebanon. She had fled her homeland after her husband had been murdered and settled down at the site of Carthage. She was just completing construction of her new city when Aeneas and his men arrived.

You're cute — let's move in together

Dido welcomed Aeneas and his men, and (predictably) fell in love with Aeneas. He returned her affection. One day they went out hunting and got caught in a storm. They hid in a cave together, and made love as long as the storm raged. From then on, they lived together like a married couple and Aeneas acted as king of Carthage. Dido started to hope that he would marry her.

But the gods had other plans. Tired of Aeneas's dalliance, they had the god Mercury send him a message reminding him that he was supposed to go to Italy to found a new Troy. Aeneas, ever dutiful, decided it was time to leave Carthage and continue his journey. He had no plans to take Dido with him, even if she had wanted to go.

Our "hero" was a real snake about it, though. He tried to slip away without even letting Dido know he was leaving. This didn't work (she was the queen of the city, after all, and someone was bound to tell her). So she confronted him at the harbor.

Dido's curse: Why Carthage and Rome didn't get along

Dido was really, really angry, but Aeneas could only hem and haw and say that the gods had told him to leave. So she built a giant funeral pyre, claiming it was a magical rite to bring Aeneas back. Once the pyre was built, Dido went to bed. She tossed and turned all night, and rose in the morning to discover that Aeneas and his buddies had already set sail — they hadn't even said goodbye.

Furious, Dido cursed Aeneas and prayed for everlasting hostility between Carthage and her faithless lover's descendants, the future Romans. Then she climbed on top of the pyre and stabbed herself with Aeneas's sword.

And as Virgil "predicted," Rome and Carthage never did get along very well. The Romans used the story of Dido's prayer for enmity as justification for going to war against Carthage in the days of Hannibal (218–201 BCE).

Aeneas lands in Italy

After deserting Dido (see the preceding section), Aeneas finally landed at Cumae in Italy (which later became a beach resort popular among wealthy Romans), where he encountered a priestess of Apollo called the *sibyl* (see Chapter 4). She took him on a quick tour of the underworld, where he met his dad. His father told him that he was going to found a great race and showed him the souls of future Romans, just waiting to be born.

Aeneas also ran into the ghost of Dido. He tried again to explain himself and make excuses, but she wouldn't listen and went off to be with the ghost of her Phoenician husband.

The prophecy comes true

Aeneas sailed off again, and landed in the kingdom of Latium in Italy. They sailed up the Tiber River, and then pulled their ship over to the shore. Exhausted, they decided to have lunch. After they had eaten all of their food, they were still so hungry that they ate the pita bread that they were using for plates. Ascanius, Aeneas's young son, said, "You guys are eating your tables!"

It was the prophecy that Helenus had told them way back when they were in Epirus. (See the earlier "A Mediterranean cruise.") Like most prophets, Helenus's prophecies were often difficult to figure out until whatever they foretold had already happened (when it was sometimes too late).

Helenus told Aeneas that when he was really tired, he would find a spot by a river where a huge pig would be laying nursing 30 piglets. He could rest there. And he shouldn't worry about eating the tables because Apollo would make everything okay.

So there they were, by a river, eating their tables. But what about that giant white pig with 30 piglets?

That giant white pig represented the city that Aeneas's people would start. No, it wasn't Rome, but Aeneas's son, Ascanius, did found a place called "Alba Longa" (*alba* is "white" in Latin, hence the color of the pig). Ascanius was the first king of Alba Longa. The 30 piglets were the 30 tribes of Italians who were all "Latins" and who would later join together in the Latin League, which Rome eventually conquered. So Aeneas's city Alba Longa would be "mommy" to all the Latin people.

A bride and a war

To pull this off, though, Aeneas had to make some local connections. So he looked up the local king, a man named Latinus. Latinus promised him that he could marry his daughter Lavinia — an oracle had said that she would marry a foreign prince, and Aeneas looked good.

Unfortunately, Latinus was hedging his bets; he had already promised Lavinia to Turnus, the leader of another Italian tribe called the Rutulians. Turnus was insulted and went to war against Aeneas and Latinus. The armies fought, and eventually Aeneas came face to face with Turnus, and killed him in single combat.

Nope, he didn't found Rome

One surprising thing about the *Aeneid* is that Aeneas didn't actually come to a city called Rome or even start a city called Rome. In fact, because of Dido's curse, Aeneas didn't get to found any city at all. All he did was get his people to the Tiber River in Italy.

But Aeneas did get to see the spot where Rome would eventually be. One of his allies in the war against Turnus (see preceding section) was Evander, a Greek guy who was king of a city called Pallanteum. Evander showed Aeneas around Pallanteum, which was built on one hill, with six other hills nearby.

Those seven hills would, one day, be the seven hills of Rome: the Palatine Hill (the site of Evander's city of Pallanteum), the Capitoline Hill, the Viminal Hill, the Esquiline Hill, the Aventine Hill, Quirinal Hill, and the Caelian Hill.

Romulus and Remus and the Founding of Rome

The name "Rome" comes from the name of the city's legendary founder, Romulus. He was one tough customer.

The Greeks saw a pun on the name "Rome," because *rhoma* means "strength" in Greek. The Romans probably didn't mind this joke.

Our uncle didn't love us

Procas was king of Alba Longa, the city founded by Aeneas's son Ascanius. See the earlier "The prophecy comes true" section for the inside story about that. He had two sons: Numitor and Amulius. Numitor was older, but Amulius seized the throne for himself and (for good measure) had Numitor's sons killed. Amulius also forced Numitor's daughter, Rhea Silvia, to become a Vestal Virgin (see Chapter 10) to make sure that Numitor's immediate family wouldn't produce any more male heirs.

Amulius's plan must have seemed rock-solid, but things have a way of happening in mythology. Rhea Silvia was seduced by the god Mars and got pregnant.

When her uncle, the king (and jerk!) Amulius, noticed that she was pregnant, he chained her up and, when she gave birth to twin sons, Amulius ordered that they be placed on the banks of the Tiber River, where they would (he assumed) surely die.

Infanticide happened very, very often in ancient (and more modern) times. People had babies they didn't think they could raise or unmarried women had babies without fathers. Rather than bankrupt the entire family or disgrace themselves, they simply abandoned the newborns they didn't want out in the street or on a hillside or riverbank. They didn't think of it as murder — there was always the chance that someone would pick up the child and raise it.

As it happened, Romulus and Remus didn't die. A mother wolf found them (or perhaps a prostitute — the words are the same in Latin) and nursed them herself. Figure 11-3 shows the famous sculpture of Romulus and Remus with the she-wolf.

Eventually a shepherd named Faustulus found the babies and adopted them. They grew up and devoted themselves to a life of crime.

Figure 11-3:
Romulus,
Remus, and
she-wolf.

© Bettmann/CORBIS

On one sheep-stealing expedition, Remus was captured and brought before his uncle, King Amulius. Faustulus decided this was a fine moment to tell Romulus the story of his birth. Romulus got angry, stormed the castle, murdered his uncle, rescued his brother, and made his grandfather Numitor king of Alba Longa.

Romulus rhymes with Rome

Feeling refreshed and inspired after the death of their late uncle (see the preceding section), Romulus and Remus thought it would be cool to found their own city where the wolf had rescued them. But they couldn't agree on where it should go. Romulus said he had received a sign from the gods and started marking a boundary on the Palatine Hill (see the earlier section "Nope, he didn't found Rome") — he did this by digging a ditch, or *pomerium*. Remus jumped over the ditch to show how little he thought of it. Romulus got really mad, killed Remus, and founded the city all by himself. He named it "Rome," after himself.

Now I need some Romans: The rape of the Sabine women

Alone after killing his brother and marking off his territory (see the preceding section), Romulus had a city, but no one lived in it. So he made it known that anyone needing a place of refuge — criminals, runaway slaves — could find it in Rome. Soon he had a nice motley collection of thieves, murderers, and other unsavory types.

This was a start, but a population of men couldn't keep a city going for long. They needed some women to make the Roman people self-sustaining. So he sent a message to the people in the surrounding areas, the Sabine tribes, inviting everyone to a big track meet and picnic — he told them to bring along the whole family. The Sabines showed up. But just as the party was getting fun, Romulus gave a signal and his men grabbed all the Sabine women and ran away with them.

Too late, we're already assimilated and acculturated

Considering the unsavory types of men that were living there at the time, this behavior toward the Sabine women perhaps isn't so surprising (see the preceding section). The Sabines were pretty upset about this, but they took their own sweet time retaliating. After a few months, the Sabine king Titus Tatius got his army together and marched on Rome. The Romans started fighting with them, but after a little while, the women intervened. A bunch of them had Roman babies and husbands by now, and they didn't see any point in continuing hostilities.

So the Sabines and the Romans made peace and their two peoples united. Titus Tatius and Romulus ruled together for a short time. After Tatius died, Romulus ruled alone for another 33 years, the first king of Rome.

The gods take Romulus

After Romulus died, he vanished mysteriously. One night a Roman fell asleep, and who should appear in his dream but Romulus! Romulus said that the gods had taken him up to be one of them. His new name was Quirinus. Interestingly, one of the most important local gods, perhaps a Sabine god, was also called Quirinus. They became one and the same — a frequent phenomenon.

The Seven Kings of Rome

Including Romulus and before the dawn of the Republic, Rome had seven legendary kings — seven kings for the city on seven hills (see the earlier "Nope, he didn't found Rome" section). These seven kings were:

✔ Romulus ruled from 753 to 715 BCE.

✔ Numa ruled from 715 to 673 BCE. Numa established Rome's major religious establishments.

✔ Tullus Hostilius ruled from 673 to 642 BCE. He got his name "Hostilius" from his love of war.

- ✔ Ancus Marcius ruled from 642 to 616 BCE. He enlarged Rome.

- ✔ Tarquin the Elder ruled from 616 to 579 BCE. Tarquin the Elder built lots of temples and other edifices, including the Temple of Jupiter and Minerva on the Capitol.

- ✔ Servius Tullius ruled from 579 to 534 BCE. He created a new Constitution for the city.

- ✔ Tarquin the Proud ruled from 534 to 510 BCE. This Tarquin was into expanding Rome's territory, and he was also a lousy king. He was overthrown after he raped a woman named Lucretia.

The Romans had mixed feelings about these kings. On the one hand, they liked to celebrate their cool early history. On the other hand, once the Republic had been established, "king" came to mean "bad guy who tells everyone what to do, unlike our excellent Senate, which tells everyone what to do." Perhaps these mixed feelings are why the last king, Tarquin, has such a bad reputation — "Oh, the kings started out fine, but that last one was horrible, so we're really lucky to have a Republic."

The last king of Rome, the tyrannical Tarquin the Proud, fell in love with a woman named Lucretia. She was married to someone else and famous for her virtue.

Tarquin went to her house one day when her husband was away at war. She greeted him and entertained him properly. Then he grabbed her, threw her down, and "invited" her to make sweet love with him. She, of course, resisted, but Tarquin informed her that if she didn't consent, he would kill her and one of her slaves and pose their bodies so that it looked like she had committed adultery with the slave.

Lucretia gave in, but as soon as Tarquin had finished up and left, she called in her husband and father. She told them what had happened. They assured her that she had done nothing wrong, but she killed herself anyway — apparently this was meant to serve as an example to Roman women.

Her relatives gathered their swords and spears and went after King Tarquin, who ran away to a nearby city. They decided they didn't want any more kings, so they set up a new Republican form of government. Lucretia's husband was one of the first consuls (like a President, but there were two at a time). And the rape of Lucretia became part of the myth of Rome's foundation.

Chapter 12

Don't Go Changin':
Ovid's *Metamorphoses*

• •

• •

*R*oman mythology has lots of good stories involving romantic relation-ships between gods, mortals, and everything in between. The Romans were excellent story tellers; they were so good, in fact, that their Roman tales of doomed love, mistaken identity, and magical changes are often more famous than the Greek originals.

The Roman author Ovid (43 BCE–17 CE) had great literary success with his famous work *Metamorphoses,* in which told a bunch of tales involving individ-uals who transformed from one shape into another. Ovid drew much of his material from the body of Greek myths, such as the story of Hades's rape of Persephone and lots of stuff about the Trojan War and the hero Ulysses (the Latin name for Odysseus). But not all of his stories were Greek, and even those that were became Roman once Ovid was done with them.

Ovid's *Metamorphoses* begins with the creation of the world (during which chaos transformed into order), then describes how Jupiter sent a flood to kill all humans, except for the virtuous Deucalion and Pyrrha. Ovid then, for many, many chapters, describes the adventures of the gods, with particular emphasis on their love affairs. After the gods come the heroes of the Trojan War, and last (and best) comes the story of how Julius Caesar turned into a star after his death.

Ovid wasn't the only Roman writer to make myths into fun literature. The story of Cupid and Psyche comes from Apuleius, a Roman writer from the second century CE; he told it in a book that was also called *Metamorphoses,* just to keep things confusing. The poet Virgil's poems, his short ones and his great epic, the *Aeneid,* are bursting at the seams with myths, all of them heavily influenced by Greek myths, but all of them having a distinctive Roman twist.

Surprising Transformations and Heroic Hunters

Ovid called his book *Metamorphoses* because it told the stories of magical transformations — for example, in the story of Arachne (below), a young women gets turned into a spider. In some stories, the transformation is a very insignificant part of the plot — for example, the tale of the Calydonian Boar Hunt (also below) is about a hunt for a boar (duh!) but Ovid slips in a transformation at the very end.

Arachne and Minerva

Arachne was a young woman of no particular nobility who was famed far and wide for her skill in weaving. She was so good at it that people thought she must have been taught by the goddess Minerva, whose specialty was weaving. But Arachne claimed that no one had taught her, and actually issued a challenge to the goddess: She said that Minerva could come compete with her, and if she lost, the goddess could do whatever she wanted to her.

Minerva heard this, and went to see about this contest. All the other women around Arachne were terrified, but the girl insisted on going through with the games. So she and Minerva set up their looms and got to work. Minerva wove a tapestry illustrating all the great things gods had done and foolish mortals who had challenged them. Arachne depicted all the failings of the gods, particularly the many human women Jupiter had seduced. Arachne's tapestry was really good — so good that no one could find anything wrong with it. Minerva lost her temper and whacked her on the head with the *shuttle* (a piece of wood used in weaving). Arachne felt humiliated and went and hanged herself.

Now Minerva relented a little; she told Arachne that she could keep living, but she would have to be suspended in the air forever. She sprinkled her with some magic herbs. And with that, Arachne turned into a spider. She lived the rest of her life suspended by a thread and always weaving.

The name Arachne is the origin of the word *arachnid,* the scientific name for spiders.

Hermaphroditus

Venus and Mercury had a son whom they named Hermaphroditus, after both of them (their Greek names, Aphrodite and Hermes). When he was fifteen, a nymph named Salmacis saw him and fell in love. Hermaphroditus would have nothing to do with her, no kisses or hugs or anything else. Salmacis lived in a beautiful pool, with crystal clear waters and surrounded by perfectly green grass. After Hermaphroditus rejected her, she left him by her pool and pretended to go away. Actually, though, she hid in the woods to watch him. He walked up to the pool and dipped his toes in it, and then decided to go for a swim. He stripped naked, much to Salmacis's delight, and jumped in.

Salmacis now jumped in after him and wrapped her arms and legs around his body. He fought her off, refusing to give her what she wanted. So Salmacis cried to the gods, asking that nothing ever separate her from her unwilling lover. The gods apparently liked this idea, and granted her wish in a weird way: They merged Salmacis and Hermaphroditus together, so that their joint body was both male and female. Hermaphroditus was the first hermaphrodite.

Hermaphroditus got his own wish out of this business. When he saw what had happened to him, he called on his mom and dad and asked them to grant him a favor: that any man who bathed in that pool have the same thing happen to him. Venus and Mercury pitied their son and granted his wish, and from then on, according to Ovid and his sources, any man who swam in that pool lost half his masculinity and became half female.

The Calydonian Boar Hunt

One year, King Oeneus of Calydon, while he was giving the annual offerings to all the gods, messed up and forgot to give anything to Diana. She was offended, and to punish the people, she let a giant wild boar loose in the countryside. This boar was as big as a bull, had tusks like an elephant's, and breathed fire. It trampled down the plants in the fields, destroyed the vines, killed flocks of sheep, and was generally a nuisance.

Super heroes to the rescue

A hero named Meleager decided to take care of this problem. He got together a group of other heroes, many of whom appear in their own stories: Jason,

Theseus and Pirithous, Peleus (Achilles's dad), Nestor (who appears as an old man in the *Iliad*), the twins Castor and Pollux, and the woman warrior Atalanta were part of the team. Meleager had the hots for Atalanta. See Chapter 6 for more on those heroes.

Two points for Atalanta

The warriors chased the boar into the forest, where they mostly failed to hurt it with their spears, and it even killed one of them. As it was running away, Atalanta shot it with an arrow, much to the embarrassment of the guys. The hero Ancaeus went after it with an axe, but it gored him in the groin and all his insides fell out. Theseus and Jason both threw spears at it with no success, and then Meleager threw two spears one after the other; the first one missed, but the second stuck in the boar's back. Now everyone ran up and stabbed the beast, both to make sure it was dead and so that they could say they had helped kill it.

Meleager presented Atalanta with the boar's head, tusks, and skin, but two of the men got angry and took them away from her — what could a mere woman have done to deserve that honor? Meleager got angry and stabbed both of them with his sword.

Nothing for Meleager

As (bad) luck would have it, those two men were Meleager's mother's brothers. Now, when he was just born, his mother had learned that he would die when a particular log on the fire burnt up completely. She had snatched it out of the fire and kept it in a safe place, but now she wasn't so sure she wanted her son to live. She wrestled with her conscience for a while, and finally her love for her brothers won out over her love for her son. She threw the wood in the fire and Meleager died as it burnt up. After she had killed her son, Meleager's mom stabbed herself with a sword and died. His sisters wept bitterly at his grave, and finally Diana decided that she had gotten enough revenge. She turned the sisters into birds and stopped tormenting everyone.

Ovid's Lovers

Ovid loved romance. In fact, before he wrote the *Metamorphoses,* he published a book called *The Art of Love,* which was a handbook for the use of upper-class Romans. So it's no surprise that the *Metamorphoses* are full of stories of lovers, in infinite variety.

Pygmalion and Galatea

The sculptor Pygmalion hated women. He would have nothing to do with them.

Well, almost nothing. He did like to look at them and decided to make a sculpture of a perfectly beautiful woman. He worked and worked at it until it was more beautiful than any living woman. In fact, it hardly looked like a statue at all, it was so life-like.

This statue became the focus of Pygmalion's existence. He kissed it and hugged it, dressed it up in pretty clothes, and even brought it little presents. He put it to bed at night, tucked in under blankets like a doll. And he decided that he wanted a woman in his life after all.

Venus got wind of this strange relationship, and was impressed that a mortal had come up with a new and unusual kind of love. On Venus's feast day, Pygmalion went to her temple to ask the goddess to help him find a woman just like his statue. The flames on the altar jumped up when he made his prayer, which looked like a good sign. Then he went back home.

There stood his statue, more enticing than ever. He put his arms around it as usual and kissed its lips. But something different happened this time — the statue started kissing him back! He felt it all over, and the cold stone turned warm and soft as he touched it. He looked into its eyes, and the statue-woman smiled at him. You can witness the representation of this magical moment in Figure 12-1.

Figure 12-1:
Pygmalion's
statue
comes to
life.

© *Christie's Images/CORBIS*

Now that Pygmalion's statue was a woman, she and Pygmalion married. They had a son and named him Paphos, and later Venus's favorite city took that for its name too.

Now that Pygmalion's statue was a woman, she and Pygmalion married. They had a son and named him Paphos, and later Venus's favorite city took that for its name too.

We called this story "Pygmalion and Galatea," but Ovid doesn't give Pygmalion's statue-wife a name. The name Galatea seems to have been added in the Renaissance, but it's a common convention now. If you read a translation of Ovid, you can probably find a reference to Galatea in either the table of contents or the index, even though her name doesn't appear in the text. Another Galatea can be found in Greek myths, a sea-nymph with whom a Cyclops fell in love, but she's not the same as Pygmalion's wife.

Bernard Shaw's play *Pygmalion* is about an English gentleman who transforms a poor street girl into a fine lady, mainly by dressing her up and giving her lessons in elocution to get rid of her outrageous accent. This play was the basis for the movie *My Fair Lady*.

Orpheus and Eurydice

Orpheus was the son of one of the Muses. He was the greatest musician ever to walk the earth. When he played, all things on earth, right down to the rocks and rivers, stopped to listen to him. See Figure 12-2.

Figure 12-2:
Orpheus

© Mimmo Jodice/CORBIS

Orpheus married a woman named Eurydice. Right after their wedding, a snake bit her and she dropped dead. Eurydice went straight to the underworld, but Orpheus didn't want to let her go. He decided that he would go down to the underworld and get her back.

The power of music got him through. The three-headed watchdog Cerberus went to sleep when he played. Sisyphus stopped rolling his stone, Tantalus for a moment wasn't thirsty, and even the Furies wept at the beauty of the song.

Some of Ovid's characters have turned into English words. Sisyphus and Tantalus, mentioned above, both suffered eternal punishments in the afterlife. Sisyphus was sentenced to roll a rock up a hill; every time he got close to the top, it slipped and rolled back down. That kind of hopeless difficult task is called *Sisyphean*. Tantalus served his son to the gods for dinner; his punishment was to be endlessly hungry and thirsty while surrounded by food and water that he could never drink, the origin of the word *tantalize*. And Midas asked the god Bacchus to grant him a wish: that everything he touched turn to gold. Midas wasn't happy with the results, but today the phrase *Midas touch* describes anyone with the knack for making money out of nothing.

Not even the king of the dead could resist Orpheus's music. He told Orpheus he could have Eurydice, but on one condition — she would walk behind him up to the world of the living, and he couldn't look back at her until they were both out of the underworld.

Orpheus started walking back home. He could hear Eurydice walking behind him. It drove him crazy, but he resisted the temptation to look back until he was almost out. Just as he stepped into the daylight, he turned around. Eurydice was right there, but she wasn't all the way out of the underworld yet. As he reached out to touch her, she disappeared. All he heard was her voice saying "Farewell."

Orpheus wandered the earth alone, playing music to himself and the rocks and the trees. One day a band of wine-crazed Maenads, wild women who worshipped the wine god Dionysus (see Chapter 4), found him and ripped him to pieces. They scattered his limbs, but his head floated down a river to the sea, singing as it went; it washed up on the island of Lesbos. Orpheus went to the underworld a second time, where he was reunited with Eurydice forever.

Pyramus and Thisbe

Pyramus was the best-looking young man in town, and Thisbe the most beautiful girl. They happened to live next door to one another; their apartments shared a wall in common. They were in love, but their parents wouldn't let them marry.

The frustrated lovers found a crack in the wall that separated them, and every day they would whisper through it. When they went to bed at night, they kissed the crack in the wall instead of kissing each other.

One day, they decided to sneak out and get together. They planned to meet under a mulberry tree at the Tomb of Ninus after dark. Thisbe got to the tomb first. She waited and waited, but Pyramus didn't come. Suddenly she saw a lion coming to drink from the spring by the tomb and ran away to hide, dropping her cloak as she fled.

The lion had just killed an animal and its mouth was bloody. It pounced on the cloak and tore it a little before heading back home. Sure enough, this is when Pyramus turned up. He saw Thisbe's cloak torn and bloody, and jumped to the conclusion that the lion had killed her. In despair, he pulled out his sword and stabbed himself.

Now Thisbe came back. She found her lover lying on the ground bleeding to death. She gathered him in her arms and said goodbye; he opened his eyes and recognized her before giving up the ghost. Thisbe saw his sword lying on the ground and stabbed herself, too. She died next to Pyramus.

Their parents relented after this, and put their ashes together in one urn. And the blood-red berries on the mulberry tree, whose color had changed from white to red as Pyramus's blood soaked its roots, symbolized their eternal love.

The story of Pyramus and Thisbe must have been one of William Shakespeare's favorite tales. Not only does the play *Romeo and Juliet* borrow much of its plot, in *A Midsummer Night's Dream*, a group of uneducated crafts-men perform a very funny version of it for a royal wedding.

Baucis and Philemon

One day, Jupiter and Mercury disguised themselves as poor travelers and went knocking on doors in Phrygia. This was a test for the local people so that Jupiter and Mercury could see how hospitable they were.

They knocked on doors and asked for food and a place to stay, but no one would take them in. Most people were downright rude and slammed the door in their faces.

Just in time for dinner!

Finally they arrived at the most pathetic excuse for a house in the whole country. They knocked on the door and asked for food, and this time the homeowners let them in. They were an old man and woman named Philemon and Baucis.

Philemon pulled a bench up to the fire and invited his visitors to sit on it, while Baucis bustled about cooking a rather pathetic meal. When it was done, she seated the gods at their broken table and fed them her boiled cabbage and cheap wine. The old couple were delighted to have visitors and talked happily as the meal progressed.

They noticed something strange: though their guests had eaten and drunk a huge amount, the levels of food and wine in the bowl and pitcher remained constant. When they saw this, Baucis and Philemon realized that their visitors must be gods. They apologized for the lousy food and announced that they would now catch, kill, and cook their goose in honor of their guests.

The goose didn't want to be caught, and the old couple chased it for a while, much to the amusement of Jupiter and Mercury. Finally they gave up, exhausted.

Membership has its privileges

Now Jupiter and Mercury rewarded their hosts. They informed them that they were, in fact, gods, and told them that although everyone else in the country was going to die, they wouldn't. Baucis and Philemon looked around and saw that the country all around was now covered with water. Their tiny hut turned into a beautiful white marble temple with a roof of gold.

The Sorcerer's Apprentice

This story doesn't come from Ovid. Lucian, a Greek poet writing during the time of the Roman Empire (120 to 180 CE), wrote this in his work, "The Teller of Lies." In this story, a young man served an apprentice to a magician. Every night, the magician would put a spell on a pestle (a piece of wood used to pound grain into flour). The spell animated the pestle, which went downstairs to bring up a couple of buckets of water for their use. After the pestle brought the water, the magician uttered another spell, and the pestle returned to being just an ordinary pestle. One night, when the magician was out, the apprentice tried to duplicate the trick. He uttered the spell and got the pestle moving without a hitch. But once the pestle had brought enough water, the apprentice was unable to duplicate the spell that made the thing stop. In a

panic, he grabbed a sword and cut the pestle in two. Nice try, but this only made matters worse — now he had *two* walking pestles carrying more water. Just when things were getting completely out of hand, the magician returned, cried out the magic words, and returned the pestle-halves to their ordinary, inanimate state.

This story, from a Roman work of fiction, has become mythological, thanks to a poem by the German poet Goethe (pronounced "gurt-uh"), which inspired a piece of music written in 1897 by the French composer Paul Dukas, which inspired Walt Disney and his diligent animators to cast Mickey Mouse in the role of the "Sorcerer's Apprentice" for a segment in the 1942 film *Fantasia*.

Jupiter told them that he would grant any wish they had. Their request was as humble as their lives had been: They asked if they could be the priests of Jupiter's new temple and if they could die at the same time — they had lived together so long, neither one could bear the thought of living without the other.

Baucis and Philemon lived in the temple for many years. One day, they started reminiscing about the old days when they had lived in a poverty-stricken hovel, but had been very happy. As they talked, they started sprouting leaves and their skin turned to bark. They just had time to say goodbye to one another before they turned completely into trees, one oak and one linden growing out of a single trunk.

Cupid and Psyche

This story comes from Apuleius, not Ovid. It's one of the best-known of Roman myths, explaining how Love and the Soul came to be united.

Too pretty for her own good

Psyche, whose name means "soul," was the most beautiful of three sisters, the daughters of a king. She was so beautiful that people compared her to Venus, goddess of love (see Chapter 10), and even began to give her the tribute they used to give the goddess Venus. This ticked Venus off.

Venus called Cupid, her son, and asked him to shoot Psyche with his arrows and thus make her fall in love with some monster or horrible oaf of a man. He said he would, but the instant he laid eyes on the girl, he got distracted, shot himself, and fell hopelessly in love with her.

Venus didn't know what had gone wrong with her plan. She assumed that because she had sent Cupid off with specific instructions, young Psyche would soon lose her heart to some vile creature. But she didn't . . . she didn't seem to fall in love with anyone at all. And no one fell in love with her. Men came to admire her beauty, but none of them ever thought to propose to her. This frustrated her parents, who were ready to marry her off. Her father went off to the oracle of Apollo (see Chapter 4) to find out what the problem was. Now, Cupid had told Apollo all about his love for Psyche, and Apollo had agreed to help him out. So the oracle gave Psyche's dad some instructions: dress Psyche in mourning clothes and send her to sit alone on a rocky hill. She was to wait until her new husband arrived (the good news). This new husband would be a winged serpent (the bad news).

Psyche's family was devastated; they were sure the dragon would kill her. But Psyche said she would rather die this way than spend her life suffering and alone because Venus was jealous of her. So she dressed in mourning, said goodbye to her family, and sat on the hilltop waiting for the end.

It's Psyche in wonderland

Suddenly she felt the wind pick her up and fly her through the air until she landed on a grassy meadow, where she fell asleep. When she woke up, she saw a beautiful mansion that looked fit for a god. It seemed empty.

Psyche walked into the house and heard voices speaking to her, telling her that this was her house and they were her servants. She couldn't see them, but they waited on her hand and foot. She spent the day alone, and then went to bed to await her husband. Somehow she wasn't dreading him as much as she had the day before.

After she got in bed and blew out the lamp, she felt a man get in with her. She couldn't see him, but he sure didn't feel like a dragon. They made love all night, and Psyche decided that her husband wasn't too bad.

But she never could see him. Every day she spent alone, and every night she slept with her unseen husband. She wondered who he was and what he looked like.

Here comes trouble

One night, he told her that her sisters were coming to the hill where she had disappeared to lay flowers on her grave. He didn't want her to go. But she desperately wanted to see her sisters in person, and begged and pleaded until finally he relented, though he warned her that if she let them persuade her to try to find out who he was, their marriage would be ruined.

The next day, she went out to meet her sisters and invited them to see her new home. They were pretty impressed with all the gold and the fancy food and demanded to know who Psyche's husband was, but all she would tell them was that he was a young man and was out hunting. She gave them presents and sent them back home.

That night, Psyche's invisible husband told her that she couldn't see her sisters anymore. She refused to listen, and complained that since she never could see him, it wasn't fair for her not to see her sisters at least. He relented again, and the next day the sisters came back.

Now, Psyche's sisters had gotten pretty suspicious about her husband. She hadn't answered their questions very consistently and they got the idea that she had never actually seen him. They told her they had heard from Apollo's oracle that her husband really was a dragon, and that even though he was nice now, one day he would turn on her and eat her.

Psyche got scared — what if they were right? So she took her sisters' advice: She got a lamp and knife and hid them by the bed. That night after her husband fell asleep, she picked up the knife and lit the lamp.

And there in her bed lay not a monster, but the handsomest young man she had ever seen. Her hand shook, and some hot oil dropped onto his shoulder. He woke up, looked at her, and immediately disappeared. Psyche ran after him into the night. She couldn't see him, but heard his voice. He said that he was Cupid, and that her lack of trust had ruined their marriage.

Cupid went home to his mother to ask her to fix his burn. When Venus heard how he had gotten it, she left him in pain and went after revenge against Psyche.

Mommy-in-law dearest gets involved

Psyche had been looking all over for her husband. She finally went to Venus herself. Venus scornfully gave her humiliating tasks to do. She dumped a bunch of tiny grains on the ground and told Psyche to sort them by evening; tiny ants came and helped the girl. Next, she sent her to get the golden fleeces from the sheep on the stony riverbank; she waited until they had gone home and then gathered golden wool from the bushes where they had shed it.

Next, Venus sent her to the underworld to ask Persephone, queen of the dead, to lend Venus a little beauty ointment (she said that she was worn out from caring for Cupid and her looks were suffering). Psyche made it all the way to the underworld and Persephone gave her some ointment in a box, but before Psyche brought it back to Venus, she opened it to see if she could use some of it herself. She instantly fell into a deep sleep.

Cupid's burn had finally healed, and he had left the house. He found Psyche asleep, woke her up, and told her that he would work everything out. He went to Zeus and asked him to make Psyche a goddess. Zeus consented, and at an assembly of the gods and goddesses, Cupid and Psyche were officially married — Love and the Soul united.

Part IV

One Big Family Feud: Northern European Mythology

The 5th Wave   By Rich Tennant

"It's the neighbor's son, the son of Surt, Guardian of the fires of Muspell. He wants to know if we have a fire extinguisher."

In this part . . .

Something about the cold weather in northern Europe made people think really heroic thoughts. Most of their myths are about warriors, battles, and monsters, although the Arthurian stories have a fair amount of sex, too. This part covers the Norse deities, a couple of the important heroes of sagas (Beowulf and the Volsungs), and the world famous King Arthur.

Chapter 13

Snow, Ice, and Not Very Nice: Norse Deities

Norse mythology is cold and dark, reflecting its origins in a land of snow and ice. These stories come from the Vikings, the fighting seafaring folk who took northern Europe by storm between the years 780 and 1070. The Vikings were descendants of Germanic people who had lived in the area that is now Germany during the Roman Empire. After Rome's power declined, these folks spread into Denmark, Norway, and Sweden and eventually colonized much of the British Isles, parts of Spain, France, Russia, Iceland, and Greenland. They even settled in North America.

The Germanic ancestors of the Vikings had many myths that told of conflicts between deities and monsters; the gods gradually brought order to the chaos that the monsters and giants constantly strove to create. Scandinavians kept many of these stories, which were suited to their restless ways and life in a harsh climate. The people in Norway, Sweden, and Denmark kept their old religion long after Christianity had established itself throughout continental Europe and the British Isles; the Scandinavians didn't convert until the eleventh century.

The people of the north had a very developed system of poetry, and poets were important members of the community. Most myths were told and retold as oral performances — imagine everyone sitting around the fire on an excessively long winter night, the poet in the center, chanting for hours about the characters everyone knew and loved. It was at least as good as TV.

Oral poems can and do change in the telling. People started telling stories about the Germanic deities before the birth of Christ, and these gradually turned into the Norse gods and goddesses. Most Norse poems weren't written down until sometime around the tenth century, and although the stories started to solidify at that point, there were still many different versions of them. That's why it's impossible to get a completely consistent view of the Norse cosmology.

Norse mythology has several main literary sources. The *Prose Edda* and other works written by the Icelandic Snorri Sturluson (1179-1241) are extremely important sources. The *Poetic Edda,* a collection of poems from Iceland, is the source of a number of Norse myths. The Icelandic sagas such as the *Saga of Volsungs* (see Chapter 14) are also important. There are also actual histories, many of which were written by visitors to northern Europe. All of these sources help build a picture of pre-Christian Scandinavia.

Ashes to Ashes and Dust to Dwarves: Creation of the World

Norse myth is full of fun and interesting stories, but we don't have room for most of them here. So here's a quick version of how the world came about.

In the beginning, there was a stretch of emptiness called *Ginningagap.* North of it was the frozen *Niflheim,* and south of it lay the burning hot *Muspell.* Ginningagap had been icy, but now was warming up. The ice began to melt, and as water dripped down, some of the drops turned into an evil frost giant called Ymir. He was the ancestor of all frost giants.

Ymir fell asleep. While he slept, sweat dripped from his armpit and turned into a man and a woman; sweat from his leg turned into another man. More ice melted, and this water turned into a cow named *Audumla.* Ymir drank her milk, and she licked the salty ice. As she licked, she uncovered a man; his name was Buri.

Buri (somehow) had a son named Bor. Bor married a frost giant named Bestla, and they had three sons: Odin, Vili, and Ve. These three sons hated Ymir, and eventually killed him. So much blood came from his body that it drowned all the frost giants except for one named Bergelmir and his wife. These two escaped the flood in a boat made of a hollow tree trunk.

Odin and his brothers carried Ymir's body to the center of Ginningagap and made the world from his body. They used his flesh for the earth, his unbroken bones for mountains, and his broken bones for rocks. They made an ocean out of his blood and put it around the world in a ring. They put Ymir's skull in the sky, and set a dwarf under each corner; their names were East, West, North, and South. They put sparks and embers in the sky to form the sun, moon, stars, and planets. They threw Ymir's brains in the sky to make clouds.

The gods set aside an area called *Jotunheim* for the giants. They enclosed the nicest area with Ymir's eyebrows, and called it *Midgard;* that's where humans live.

Now the gods made humans: they found two fallen trees and turned them into a man named Ask and a woman named Embla. All people are descended from them.

One of the giants had a daughter named Night. She had a son named Day. Odin put Night and Day in horse-drawn chariots and got them to travel around the world every day. A man then had two children, a son he called Moon and a daughter he called Sun. Odin took these two children and placed them in the sky to guide the chariots of the sun and moon as they travel around the earth every day.

Now the gods noticed that maggots were growing in Ymir's dead flesh. They turned the maggots into dwarves and gave them the caves and caverns to live in.

Last, the gods built *Asgard,* a mighty fortress high over Midgard. The two regions were linked by *Bifrost,* a flaming rainbow bridge. All the *Aesir,* the guardians of humans, crossed the bridge and moved in to Asgard. There were twelve gods, twelve goddesses, and a bunch of other Aesir up there.

Over everything grew the tree *Yggdrasill.* Its three roots burrowed into Asgard, Jotunheim, and Niflheim, and each one had a spring under it. An eagle and a hawk sat in the branches, a squirrel scurried up and down its trunk, deer nibbled at it, and a dragon down below tried to eat it. Yggdrasill always was and is and will be.

The Good, the Bad, and the Mortal: Norse Deities

The Norse deities came in two flavors, the *Vanir* and the *Aesir.* The Vanir were the older fertility gods; they included Freyr, Freya, and Njord. The Aesir were more modern warlike gods, including Odin and Thor. The Norse told a story of a war between the Vanir and the Aesir after the creation; the deities formed a truce and exchanged members with the result that they fused together and were thereafter collectively known as Aesir. Scholars think this story describes a time when two cults struggled against one another and ultimately merged into one.

Before the Vikings started rampaging around Europe, their ancestors, the earlier Germanic tribes, held sway on much of the continent. They had their own collection of mythical figures, many of whom turned into Norse deities when the time came. That's why the names of German and Norse gods seem so similar and why lots of characteristics of the gods and stories get repeated. Many characters are essentially the same with slightly different names. For example, Odin was Wodan in German; his wife Frigg was called Freya.

An odd thing about the Norse deities — they weren't immortal. They could and did die, unlike the Greek immortals who lived up on Mount Olympus (see Chapters 4 and 5). Their interests weren't the same as those of humans; they helped and hurt people as they chose. The deities existed to battle the monsters and the outer darkness, and part of their interest in people was gathering enough warriors to help them fight the last battle.

Norse gods: A rough and tough bunch

If the stories about them are anything to go on, the Norse gods spent most of their time wandering around with each other looking for interesting things to do. They didn't have daily jobs, so if they disappeared for a few days it didn't much matter.

King Odin

Odin was the king of the gods. He was the father of most of them and in some accounts created everything — heaven and earth and humans; this accounts for his nickname, "Allfather." He had a special high seat called Hlidskjalf, from which he can see everything in all the worlds. Only he and his wife Frigg were supposed to sit up there, but occasionally other deities snuck up there when no one was looking. See Figure 13-1 for what Odin looked like.

Odin was immensely wise, but his wisdom didn't come cheaply. He bought a drink from a spring of wisdom at a high price: one of his eyes. This drink made him want more wisdom, so he spent nine days hanging from the tree Yggdrasill, pierced by a spear, to get even wiser; during this experience, he symbolically died and was reborn. Odin apparently was embarrassed by his empty eye socket, because he usually covered it up with a broad-brimmed hat or a deep hood — whenever an old man with a deep hood strides into a saga, it's pretty easy to identify him as Odin.

People who worshipped Odin practiced human sacrifice, which they accomplished by hanging their victims from a tree and piercing them with spears. To gain wisdom, Odin died in the same manner as his sacrificial victims and was reborn. The story of Odin's hanging on Yggdrasill has several elements in common with Christ's crucifixion, but scholars don't think the Norse poets were especially influenced by the Christian story.

Figure 13-1:
One-eyed
Odin.

© Christel Gerstenberg/CORBIS

Odin was god of war and battle, a role that he inherited from the two older Germanic war gods Wodan and Tiwaz. He loved to stir up war among humans. Slain warriors got to go party in his hall, *Valhalla;* they were brought up there by the *Valkyries,* warrior women who chose only the most heroic for this honor.

A cult of warriors called *Berserks* used to go into battle dressed in bear skins. They were out of their minds with battle frenzy and would fight like demons and seem impervious to pain.

Odin was also the god of poetry, perhaps one reason why he appears in so many poems. He was responsible for bringing the magical mead of poetry to Asgard (see the preceding section for more). A giant had stolen this mead and sent his daughter to guard it. Odin burrowed into her cave in the form of a snake and then turned back into his handsome self. He spent three days and nights with her, after which he sucked down all the mead and held it in his mouth. He turned into an eagle, flew back to Asgard, and spit out the mead into a pot, where all the deities could use it.

Loki the trickster

Loki was a strange character. On the one hand, he was a clever trickster, often good for a laugh and handy at getting himself and the gods out of tight spots. On the other, he was malevolent and spiteful, fighting at the head of the giants in the last battle at the end of the world. It's hard to know whether to hate him or not.

Loki was the son of two giants, but grew up as Odin's foster brother. In stories about Loki, it's hard to figure out if he was a god or a giant, because he behaved like both — sometimes he was a happy and helpful member of the gods in Asgard, and sometimes he was most definitely their enemy. He was dynamic and unpredictable, and thus supplied an element of instability to an otherwise boring existence. Lots of Norse myths involve Loki getting himself or all the gods into trouble out of sheer meddlesomeness.

Loki could change shape at will, and often turned into different animals to accomplish his goals — for example, he turned into a flea to steal Freya's necklace from her, and he turned into a salmon to escape the wrath of the gods after he caused Balder's death. Once a giant offered to build a wall around Asgard (see the preceding section for more) if he could have Freya as a wife. Just before the giant finished the job, Loki turned himself into a mare and enticed the giant's stallion away, leaving the giant unable to complete the wall and claim his prize. Loki left Asgard and returned several months later leading an eight-legged foal (a baby horse), the child he had borne with the stallion. (Does that make him bisexual or just weird?) He gave the foal, named Sleipnir, to Odin.

That horse wasn't Loki's only child. Though he had a wife, he occasionally ran off to have flings with a giantess named Angrboda. They had three other children, all of great concern to the other gods:

- ✔ Fenrir, their first son, was a wolf. He grew really big, and the gods decided they would have to chain him up. Tyr played a key role in this job — as you'll see in his description in the section "Tyr" later in the chapter.

- ✔ Jormungand, their second son, was a giant snake. Odin threw him into the ocean surrounding Midgard. He grew so big that he encircled the whole world and bit his own tail. People called him the Midgard Serpent.

- ✔ Hel, their daughter, was alive from the waist up and dead from the waist down. Odin threw her into Niflheim, the underworld. She became goddess of the dead.

All three of these monstrous creatures were waiting for the end of the world, Ragnarok, when they would all be released to wreak havoc.

Thor the thunderous

Thor was the son of Odin and Earth. While Odin stood for violence and war, Thor represented order — he was the god people called on if they wanted stability. He was immensely strong and manly. He carried around a huge hammer, called Mjölnir, which he used to keep the giants in line — no matter how far he flung it, it always returned to his hand (like a boomerang), and he could make it small enough to hide inside his shirt. He had a bushy red beard, a huge appetite, and a quick temper, though he didn't stay angry for long. He was the patron of peasants. Thor was also god of thunder and lightning — the wheels of his chariot made thunder, and lightning came from a whetstone lodged in his skull.

Once the king of the frost giants stole Thor's hammer. He refused to give it back unless he could have Freya for his wife. The gods agreed, but then they tricked the giant. Thor dressed up as a bride and Loki as his bridesmaid, and the two of them went to the giants' hall. The giants invited them to sit down at the table, and Thor proceeded to devour all the food and drink all the mead in a most unbridal manner. Loki claimed that "Freya" hadn't eaten in days, so excited was she about her wedding. Captivated, the giant king called for Thor's hammer so that they could swear their marriage vows on it. Thor instantly grabbed it, ripped off his veil, and killed all the giants at the feast.

Freyr the fertile

Freyr was the god of plenty. He seems to have descended from the ancient Earth Mother who the ancient Danes had worshipped (and had somehow changed sex along the way). He decided when the sun would shine or the rain would fall and thus whether the earth would be fruitful or not.

People turned to Freyr when they wanted some prosperity or progeny themselves. The statue of Freyr in Uppsala, Sweden, had an enormous phallus — clearly people knew what they wanted out of him! His favorite toys, a magical ship and boar, were also long-standing fertility symbols.

Tyr the brave

Tyr was the son of Odin. He was the bravest of the Aesir, the war gods. He got his start as Tiwaz, the Germanic war god, and was actually Odin's precursor, but had lost importance over the years.

Tyr had only one hand. He lost his right one binding the wolf Fenrir, Loki's son. Fenrir had been getting bigger, and the gods were worried that he would kill Odin. They decided to chain him up. The wolf broke the first two chains they put on him, but then they got the dwarves to make another, stronger one. This chain, which looked like a silk ribbon, was named *Gleipnir*.

When Fenrir saw it, he feared it could hold him, so he said he would only let the gods tie him up if one of them would put his hand in the wolf's mouth. Only Tyr was brave enough. He put his right hand in Fenrir's mouth. The gods tied the wolf with Gleipnir, and though Fenrir struggled mightily, he couldn't break his bonds. He bit off Tyr's hand, but he was stuck. The gods tied him to a giant boulder that they sank deep into the earth.

Other gods

There were several other gods in the Norse pantheon. Here are a few of them:

- ✔ Njord governed the sea and the ocean winds, and was the guardian of ships and sailors. Njord was the father of Freyr and Freya.

- ✔ Heimdall was watchman of the gods. No one knows exactly what he was all about, but he was associated with the sea. He was the son of nine maidens (or maybe nine waves). He had a big horn named Gjall whose sound could be heard throughout the nine worlds.

- ✔ Balder the Beautiful was the wisest, sweetest, and most merciful of the gods; once he pronounced a judgment it could not be altered. His death precipitated the conflict that would bring about the end of the world.

Goddesses: Tough, sexy, and equal

Norse women had the same legal rights as men, and they were a fairly tough bunch. Outspoken women appear in many poems. Goddesses, too, have minds of their own, and were equal to the gods. Unfortunately, few poems survive in which goddesses play a large role.

Freya, goddess of love

Freya was goddess of love and of lust. Every male who saw her wanted to have sex with her, and many of them did. She was fabulously beautiful, simply dripping with gold jewelry. When she cried, she wept tears of gold; after a particularly long fit of weeping, the floor would be covered with gold. (This happened fairly often, because she was always being promised in marriage to some horrible creature or other.) She owned a falcon skin, which she used to turn herself into a bird for occasional visits to the underworld. Check out Figure 13-2 to get a look at her.

Her most famous possession was the Necklace of the Brisings. Freya acquired it from the four dwarves who made it; their price was that she spend one night with each of them — she really wanted that necklace, so she agreed. When Loki found out how Freya had gotten it, he told Odin, who ordered Loki to steal the necklace from her. Loki turned into a flea, bit her cheek as she slept so she turned her head, and undid the clasp. Odin refused to give the necklace back until Freya agreed to stir up war among humans.

Surprisingly, Freya was also a war goddess. She went to war riding in a chariot pulled by two cats, and helped Odin divide dead warriors on a battlefield; half went to Valhalla and half to her hall, *Sessrumnir*.

Figure 13-2:
The
beautiful
goddess
Freya.

© Bettmann/CORBIS

Frigg, wife and mother

Frigg was Odin's wife. She was a daughter of Earth and, like Freya, probably evolved from the ancient Earth/mother goddess. Like Odin, she could foresee the fates of humans. Women in labor called on her for help.

Scholars love to see similarities among different myths. With the Norse deities, they say that Frigg and Freya represent two sides of womanhood, Frigg as wife and mother and Freya as mistress and seductress, just like Hera and Aphrodite in Greek myths. Artemis the young virgin was the third component of the Greek trio; she isn't obvious in Norse myths, though the ski goddess Skadi may have once occupied that place.

Hel — half dead

Hel was goddess of the dead. She was a daughter of Loki and the giantess Angrboda. Her appearance was unusual: from the waist up, she was pink and warm, but from the hips down her flesh was green and half-decayed. Hel had her citadel (also called Hel) in Niflheim. Everyone ended up here after they died.

Hel, the citadel of the dead, was not the same as the Christian Hell. You didn't have to be particularly bad to go there, and though it wasn't what you would call "nice," it wasn't a place of everlasting torment, either — though it was kind of cold.

Other goddesses

Some of the other goddesses were:

- ✔ Idun, the guardian of the apples of youth. The deities had to eat these apples to stay young. Loki helped the giants steal them from her, and all the gods aged overnight. But they got them back, once again with Loki's help.

- ✔ Skadi was the goddess of skis and the daughter of the giant Thiazi. She married the sea god Njord, but their marriage broke down because she wanted to live in the frozen mountains and he wanted to live at the fertile seaside.

- ✔ Sif was Thor's wife. Loki cut off her beautiful blonde hair for a (sick) joke, but made it up to her by getting the dwarves to make her hair of gold. They made the gods some other presents, including Thor's hammer, at the same time.

- ✔ The Norns were the goddesses of destiny, who shaped the fates of humans. There were three of them: Urd (Fate, sometimes considered the past), Verdandi (the present), and Skuld (the future). They sometimes appeared as weavers, similar to the Greek Fates (see Chapter 5).

Some other magical beings

The gods and goddesses didn't have a monopoly on magical ability; the Norse cosmos was full of various fantastic creatures. Most of them didn't have a very good relationship with the deities in Asgard, though they did manage a certain amount of peaceful interaction.

Giants

Giants were mostly evil; they were constantly trying to get the better of the gods and goddesses. But at the same time, this didn't prevent the giants from having almost normal (if somewhat tense) interactions with the deities. Thor and Loki spent a couple of days traveling around with giants and visiting with the giants in their hall.

The word "giant" of course implies great size; evidently the gods were (or could be) more-or-less same size, because they had a number of sexual relationships with giants. Giants were forever asking to marry the beautiful goddess Freya, and both Odin and Loki had giant mistresses; in fact, Loki himself might have been a giant. At the end of the world, the line between the giants and the gods is most clearly drawn; then they are most definitely on opposite sides.

Tolkien

J.R.R. Tolkien of *Lord of the Rings* fame took lots of his Middle Earth material straight out of Norse mythology, especially his propensity for naming inanimate objects such as swords — that appears in lots of northern European stories. The names of dwarves who appear in *The Hobbit* (and of Gandalf the wizard) come straight from Snorri Sturluson's *Prose Edda*. The name "Mordor" means "murder" in Old English.

Tolkien studied classics and English literature at Oxford and, after a stint working on the *Oxford English Dictionary,* went on to teach Old English and English literature there. He was interested only in the oldest English literature — *Beowulf* was one his favorites. He knew a pile of medieval languages, including Old English, Old and Middle German, and Gothic.

Dwarves

Dwarves were nasty little human-like creatures who lived underground. They had to stay out of the sun, because it would turn them to stone. They were the finest metalworkers anywhere; they could create magical objects, such as Freya's gorgeous necklace and Thor's powerful hammer, and this caused the deities to associate with them on relatively amicable terms. Dwarves could cohabit with deities, too; four of them slept with the goddess Freya, their price for the necklace of the Brisings.

Other fanciful beasties

The Norse cosmology was also populated with various other magical creatures. There were elves, light and dark; the dark elves seem to have been similar to dwarves and the good light elves. They get mentioned in myths from time to time but don't do much. There were trolls; Thor occasionally did battle with them. There were dragons — see Chapter 23 for more about them.

A Big Tree House: The World They Lived In

For all their warlike reputation, most of the Norse people really spent most of their time in peaceful pursuits, farming, hunting, fishing, and making up stories to pass the long winter nights. Their myths reflect the hardship of living in the far north — gods must travel vast distances from one house to another over rugged terrain, plagued by snowstorms and hunger. See Figure 13-3 for a map of where these cold-weather folks lived.

Figure 13-3:
Northern
Europe and
the north
Atlantic.

The Scandinavians, like most people, came up with a view of the universe that seemed to fit they way they lived. In the Norse cosmology, everyone had their own home; humans knew exactly where they fit in between the gods and the dead and on the same level as the giants.

The Norse visualized the universe in three main parts, joined by a magic tree named Yggdrasill. On top of everything was Asgard, home of the gods and goddesses; the deities each had their own houses within the wall of a citadel. *Vanaheim* was up here, too; that's where the Vanir (the old fertility gods) lived until they merged with the Aesir. *Alfheim,* home of the light elves, was also up there.

In the middle was Midgard, home of humans. It was surrounded by an ocean with a giant snake encircling it: Jormungand, the Midgard Serpent. Jotunheim, home of the giants, was either on this level or across the ocean. The dwarves lived in *Nidavellir,* and the dark elves lived in *Svartalfheim.* Asgard and Midgard were connected by a flaming rainbow bridge called Bifrost.

On the lower level was Niflheim, home of the dead, a place of bitter cold and unending night. Hel, goddess of the dead, had her house here; it was also called Hel. Figure 13-4 shows how it all fits together.

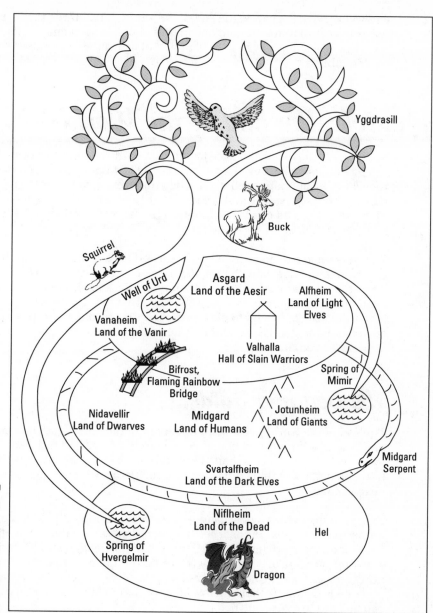

Figure 13-4:
Yggdrasill, the tree of life, and the nine worlds of the Norse cosmology.

All these places were comprised the "nine worlds" of the Norse cosmos. At the axis of them was Yggdrasill, a timeless ash tree. Yggdrasill had no beginning and will survive Ragnarok, the end of the world. It had three roots, one in Asgard, one in Jotunheim, and one in Niflheim. A dragon gnawed its lowest root. Various animals lived in or near it, and its fruit was supposed to ensure safe childbirth.

Ragnarok: The End of the World

Norse myths have a very clear description of the end of the world. The story is a bit confusing because Ragnarok, the big last battle and the destruction of the world, hasn't happened yet, though the events leading up to it have. That temporal oddity aside, the story is similar to other myths describing the end of the world and its creatures, followed by the resurrection of the human race by two survivors.

The Norse had a deep awareness of fate and life's transience and this is reflected in the tale. Long before Ragnarok happens, the god Odin knows how it will turn out; as part of his constant quest for knowledge he once asked the dead how he would die, and they informed him that the wolf Fenrir would eat him. Odin also knows that Loki the trickster is plotting to bring about the downfall of the good gods, and that he will succeed. This is the gods' fate; they can't avoid it.

The Death of Balder

The end of the world began with the death of the nicest god, Balder, everyone's favorite. To protect him, Balder's mother Frigg had traveled throughout the world and asked each and every substance to swear that it would not harm Balder; everything did except for mistletoe, which Frigg considered too insignificant.

This gave the deities a new game — they threw things at Balder and laughed uproariously when their missiles bounced right off without hurting him. Everyone was happy except Loki, the god of mischief; he loved trouble and suffering, and it drove him crazy to see Balder immune to attack. (Although in other stories Loki is a cooperative member of the gods of Asgard, at this point he is definitely their enemy. Like we said in his description earlier, Loki can be hard to figure out.)

Loki got some mistletoe and shaped it into a dart. He gave the dart to Balder's blind brother Hod, who was feeling left out of the game, and helped him throw it. It hit Balder and he dropped dead. The brave god Hermod rode to Hel, the goddess of the dead, to ask her to return Balder, but she refused.

Everyone wanted to get back at Loki. The gods caught him, dragged him into a cave and tied him to a rock. The goddess Skadi carried a live snake into the cave and hung it up above Loki so its venom would drip on to his face. Loki's faithful wife Sigyn stayed by his side, holding a bowl over his head to catch the venom before it hit his face. But sometimes she had to take the bowl away to empty it, and the venom hit its mark then. Loki would writhe in pain during those moments, and his writhing caused earthquakes. So he lay, and so he would remain until Ragnarok (see the following section).

The death of Odin's son Balder is the beginning of the end because it forces the gods to see that Loki is their enemy and that their power is limited — the lines of battle are drawn and it's easy to see who is on which side. The gods imprison Loki, but they now know that he and his three evil children (Fenrir, Hel, and the Midgard Serpent) will fight against them.

Ragnarok — the big finish

This is the way the world will end. First, Midgard will have wars for three winters. The family will break down: fathers will kill sons, brothers will kill brothers, mothers will seduce their sons, and brothers will seduce their sisters. Next will come three fierce winters with no summers between them.

Two wolves will eat the sun and the moon and the stars will vanish from the sky. The trees and mountains will fall down and the wolf *Fenrir* will run free. The sea will rise as the *Midgard Serpent* writhes around, working his way to dry land. The giants will set sail in a boat made from dead men's nails. Loki will take to the water, too, in a boat full of the dead from Hel (the land of the dead, headed by Loki's daughter by the same name).

Fenrir and the Midgard Serpent (Loki's sons) will advance side by side; Fenrir's lower jaw will scrape the ground as his upper teeth brush the sky, and the Midgard Serpent will spew venom everywhere, poisoning all the earth. All the giants and the dead and all other members of the evil team will assemble together.

Meanwhile, the gods will arm themselves and assemble all their warriors from Valhalla. They will march to meet the enemy, Odin and Thor at their head. Yggdrasill, the tree of life, will wave its limbs and shiver as two humans hide inside it.

Odin will immediately attack the wolf Fenrir; after a long fight, Fenrir will swallow Odin and that will be the end of the Allfather. The Midgard Serpent will go for Thor; they will kill each other. The fire giant Surt will kill Freyr. Tyr and a fierce hound will kill one another, as will longtime enemies Loki and

Heimdall. Odin's son Vidar will grab Fenrir's jaws and rip the wolf apart, avenging his father.

The fire giant Surt will fling fire in every direction, and everything in the nine worlds will burn up. Everyone and everything will perish and the earth will sink into the sea.

Everyone will die, that is, but the two humans who hid in Yggdrasill (and a few gods who rise again, including Balder): a man and a woman called Lif and Lifthrasir. The earth will rise out of the sea again, lush and green, and the birds and fish will return. The two humans will have children, who will have children, and life will begin again.

Chapter 14

Dragonslayers: The Big Northern European Sagas

Sitting in the cold and dark all winter long, the people of Scandinavia and Northern Europe had to do something to pass the time. So they wove complex tapestries, made elaborate pieces of metalwork, and they also made up poems. Every party had entertainment in the form of a *scop,* or poet, who would chant for hours about the tales of great heroes and beautiful women, of dragons and monsters and battles fought long ago, and of love affairs gone wrong.

The poets memorized these poems. Poems weren't written down; paper and ink were scarce, and most people couldn't read anyway. For hundreds of years, poets developed prodigious memory skills to retain incredibly long stories. They used little tricks to help; for example, the last word of one line would start with the same letter as the first word of the next line to jog to the memory. But unwritten works change and develop, so it's impossible to say what the "true" version of any ancient or medieval saga is. All we have is a text written by some random person that happened to survive long enough to get copied by more modern readers.

Famous poems, such as *Beowulf* and the *Saga of the Volsungs* were combinations of history and legend. In the *Saga of the Volsungs,* verifiable people such as Attila the Hun and various actual ethnic groups turn up; historical figures such as Gregory of Tours get mentioned in *Beowulf.* But the stories also feature definite mythical elements, like all the monsters in *Beowulf* and Odin's frequent appearances in the *Saga of the Volsungs.* (A poet in *Beowulf* actually tells the story of the Volsungs at a party.)

Scholars have debated the significance of Norse heroic tales for the last two hundred years, and a lot can be said about them. But the main reason people still read these poems today is the same reason medieval folks would have requested them from poets of an evening: They're really cool stories.

Prime Time Programming: The Saga of the Volsungs

The *Saga of the Volsungs,* or *Volsungsaga,* is the story of a family of heroes. The character who gives the saga its name, Volsung, makes only a brief appearance early in the tale, but he's important: All of his descendants call themselves Volsungs, and they are the strongest, bravest, and most ambitious of heroes. Medieval Scandinavians would all have known this tale, with its dragon and ring of power and confused lovers. They also would have known what life under constant warfare was like — Vikings didn't exactly lead a peaceful existence. All of this would have made the *Volsungsaga* a crowd-pleaser.

A *saga* is a story that deals with the myths and legends of early Germanic heroes or with historical kings; lots of sagas were written in Iceland between 1200 and 1400. Nowadays the term can refer to any similar story.

The *Saga of the Volsungs* was written down by an unknown author in Iceland in the thirteenth century. His story came from older Norse poetry and traditional lore. He combined events from ancient wars with the Huns, Burgundians, Goths, the mythic deeds of Sigurd the Dragonslayer, and added betrayal, unrequited love, and the vengeance of a barbarian queen. The story is set somewhere in Northern Europe during the fourth and fifth centuries CE. This was a time when different groups of people were wandering throughout Europe, as the northern frontiers of the Roman Empire collapsed and Germanic tribes and the Huns from Asia invaded most of the previously civilized parts of the continent.

In this saga, the Burgundians were the tribe of Gudrun's brothers Gunnar and Hogni, good guys. The historical Burgundians would have been in Germany near Worms at this time. The Huns were pastoral nomads from Central Asia; they united under Attila in the fifth century and marched into Europe. The Goths came from north of the Black Sea and wreaked havoc among civilized Europeans; the Huns mostly destroyed them. Does this matter? Not especially, because most of the original audience for this poem had little sense of geography or history. They just wanted to know about good guys and bad guys.

Events preceding the birth of Sigurd

Once upon a time, the king of Hunland and his queen couldn't have a baby. Frigg, goddess of childbirth, asked Odin (see Chapter 13) to help them; Odin brought a magical apple to the king and the queen got pregnant. The king died in battle, and the queen was pregnant for six years without giving birth. She finally asked her servants to cut the child out of her body; her six-year-old son kissed her before she died. His name was Volsung, and he was the ancestor of the Volsung race.

Volsung married, and he and his wife had twins, a girl named Signy and a boy named Sigmund. They had nine more sons after that. Volsung built a huge palace with a giant tree called Barnstock standing right in the middle of it, its branches reaching through the roof.

Be careful who you marry

After Volsung and his wife had kids (see the preceding section), Volsung gave Signy to Siggeir, king of Gautland (a region of Sweden), to marry. During the wedding banquet, an old man with only one eye strode into the hall, stuck a sword into the tree Barnstock, challenged everyone to pull it out, and walked out again. All the warriors tried to pull the sword from the tree trunk, but no one could. Finally Sigmund stepped forward and pulled it out easily. King Siggeir was angry because he had wanted the sword, and he vowed to get revenge.

The old man with one eye was Odin, king of the Norse gods. He tended to show up on earth from time to time to help heroes or to stir up trouble. Read more about him in Chapter 13.

The next day, Signy told her father that she didn't like her new husband, but he insisted that she go home with him. Husband and wife sailed away, and Siggeir invited all the Volsungs to come visit in three months. When they arrived, Siggeir attacked them, killed Volsung, and seized his ten sons. Signy begged him not to kill them, so he put them in stocks in the woods. Every night for nine days a wolf came and ate one of them, until only Sigmund was left. On the tenth night, Signy covered Sigmund's face with honey. The wolf came and started licking the honey off; Sigmund grabbed the wolf's tongue with his teeth, ripping it out and killing the beast.

Sigmund took up residence in the woods. Signy sent him her two sons to see if they could help him, but they proved cowardly, so she told Sigmund to kill them. One day she changed bodies with a sorceress, went out to see her brother, and slept with him for three nights. After nine months, she gave birth to Sigmund's son, Sinfjotli. When he grew up, she sent him to Sigmund (who thought he was Siggeir's son), and Sinfjotli proved brave and tough as could be. Sigmund thought that he would spend a while toughening the boy before they went to seek revenge. They found magical wolf skins that let them transform themselves into wolves and spent some time rampaging around the woods as wild beasts, which proved to be a good training program for a young warrior.

Sigmund and Signy's revenge

After spending some time with Sinfjotli (see preceding section), Sigmund finally decided that Sinfjotli was ready to help him avenge his father Volsung's death. The two of them went to the castle and attacked the king, where they were captured. The king had them buried underground, but Signy managed to throw in Sigmund's sword before they were sealed up. They used the sword to saw their way through the rocks holding them underground, climbed up into the hall where all the king's men were sleeping, and set the place on fire.

Signy now told Sigmund that Sinfjotli was his son. Now that she had vengeance, she decided to die with her husband Siggeir, and walked into the fire. Sigmund and Sinfjotli went home and had various adventures.

Sigmund married a woman named Borghild. Sinfjotli and Borghild's brother got into a fight over a woman, and Sinfjotli killed the other man. Borghild poisoned Sinfjotli in revenge, and Sigmund drove Borghild away from the court; she died soon thereafter.

The story of Borghild's poisoning Sinfjotli is very similar to the tale of Medea trying to poison the hero Theseus at his father's court. See Chapter 6 for that story.

Sigmund then married a second time. His new wife was Hjordis, the daughter of a powerful king named Eylimi, and the fairest and wisest of all women. Another man wanted to marry her, and her father knew that there would be trouble whoever he chose, so he let Hjordis choose. She picked Sigmund, even though he was very old by now.

Shortly after Sigmund and Hjordnis married, his rival for her affections went to war against him. Sigmund was mortally wounded (after a battlefield visit by Odin; see Chapter 13 for more on Odin's interest in fallen warriors) and his famous sword broke. After the battle, Hjordnis found him dying on the field. He told her that she would bear a son who would be the foremost of the Volsung line. He asked her to save the pieces of his sword, which would be made into a new sword named Gram; his son would use that sword. Then he died.

The great Dane Sigurd (the guy, not the dog)

After Sigmund died on the battlefield (see the preceding section), the king of the Danes came to the battlefield, saw Hjordnis, and heard her story. He took her home with him and married her. She had her baby boy and named him Sigurd. He was the biggest and strongest boy around, and everyone loved him.

A man named Regin was largely responsible for Sigurd's education, teaching him several languages, sports, chess, and runes. He and Odin helped Sigurd choose a horse, a descendant of Odin's horse Sleipnir; it was called Grani. Then Regin told Sigurd that he needed more wealth, and told him just where he could get it: from the hoard of the dragon Fafnir. (Fafnir happened to be Regin's brother, but Regin was ready to kill him for his wealth.)

Runes were Germanic and Norse letters that people used for carving inscriptions on wood or stone. They had both practical and magical uses. J.R.R. Tolkien made ample use of them in *The Lord of the Rings.*

Now for that big ol' dragon

After making the decision to get himself some more wealth (see the preceding section), Sigurd needed a good sword if he was going to kill a dragon. He went to his mother, who gave him the pieces of his father's sword. Regin put these back together into a sword named Gram that could cut anything. After a detour to kill the king who had killed his father, Sigurd set out to find Fafnir.

Regin showed Sigurd where the dragon lived and told him to dig a ditch to hide in. Then Regin (who was no fool) ran off to hide. While Sigurd was digging, an old man — Odin — walked by and told him he was doing it wrong — he should dig several ditches for the dragon's poisonous blood to run into and then hide himself in another one to stab it. Then the man disappeared. Sigurd dug the ditches like the old man had suggested. (This practice of appearing briefly to make a suggestion and just as quickly disappearing was typical of Odin; see Chapter 13.)

Fafnir came crawling out to get a drink, shaking the earth as he went, and Sigurd hid in his ditch. When the dragon stepped over him, Sigurd plunged his sword up to the hilt into the dragon's chest. Fafnir thrashed and raged, destroying everything around him, and then he died.

A little bird told me

Regin came back and congratulated Sigurd on his victory, but moped a bit because his brother was dead and it was his fault. He asked Sigurd for a favor: cut out the dragon's heart, roast it over the fire, and give it to him to eat. Sigurd agreed, but as he was cooking the heart, he touched it and put his finger in his mouth. As soon as the blood from Fafnir's heart touched his tongue, he could understand the speech of birds.

And what were the birds saying? That Regin was going to betray him and that Sigurd should kill Regin, take the dragon's treasure for himself, and then go see the beautiful Brynhild. Regin was feeling guilty about having his brother killed and thought he could blame Sigurd for it; then he could have the dragon's treasure all to himself. (The saga doesn't explain how the birds knew this.)

So Sigurd killed Regin with his sword. He ate some of the dragon's heart and saved the rest for later. Then he rode to the dragon's lair, where he found mounds of treasure. He loaded it onto his horse and rode off to see Brynhild.

Love's losers and the psychic hotline

After Sigurd took Fanfir's treasure (see the preceding section), he went to see Brynhild. She was a Valkyrie, a warrior maiden. Sigurd found her asleep in a tower, dressed in armor. He sliced it off her body, which woke her up, and introduced himself as one of the Volsungs. Brynhild told him that she had made a vow that she would only marry someone who knew no fear.

In addition to her warrior skills, Brynhild could also foretell the future. Sigurd told her he wanted to marry her, and she said that she would. They went their separate ways for a while: Sigurd to fight more battles, and Brynhild to make a beautiful tapestry depicting his heroics. Sigurd then went to her house, and they renewed their commitment to one another. But Brynhild warned Sigurd that he would marry a woman named Gudrun instead of her.

Trapped by the ale of forgetfulness

After Sigurd's psychic reading from Brynhild, it just so happened that Gudrun now arrived on the scene. See the preceding section for inside track about this. She was the daughter of a king and a friend of Brynhild's. She came to visit Brynhild to ask her advice about a dream. Brynhild told Gudrun about Sigurd, and then predicted her future: Sigurd was going to visit Gudrun, her mother Grimhild would give him a potion that would make him forget everything, he would marry Gudrun but die shortly after, then she would marry King Atli, whom she would kill at the end. Gudrun was daunted by this prediction and rode back home.

And it all came to pass just as Brynhild had said. Sigurd came calling at Gudrun's house, and Gudrun's mother Grimhild thought he would make a nice husband for her daughter. She mixed up a special ale of forgetfulness. Sigurd drank it and immediately forgot Brynhild. He married Gudrun and swore allegiance to her family.

A burning ring of fire

After Sigurd drank the ale of forgetfulness and married Gudrun, Gudrun's brother Gunnar needed a wife. Sigurd offered to help him find one. They decided he should marry Brynhild (remember, Sigurd and Brynhild had promised to marry each other, but then he forgot about her). Brynhild had ensconced herself in a tower surrounded by a ring of fire; she had set this up as a test, declaring that she would only marry a man who would ride through the flames to her.

Gunnar couldn't persuade his horse to gallop through the fire, so he and Sigurd exchanged bodies and Sigurd galloped through the flames on Grani, the magical horse he had found with Odin's help (see above). He introduced himself as Gunnar, spent three nights with Brynhild, and then went back home with his brother-in-law.

Brynhild went to her father, told him that a man had ridden through the ring of fire and said that she would marry him because obviously he knew no fear. Then she went to Gunnar's castle and married him.

One day when Brynhild and Gudrun were bathing in the river, they got into a fight and Gudrun revealed that it had been Sigurd, not Gunnar, who rode through the ring of fire. Brynhild got all bent out of shape about this and took to her bed. Everyone tried to cheer her up and get her to go on with her life, but she refused; she had been tricked into marrying an inferior man, and didn't want to live anymore.

Brynhild asked Gunnar to kill Gudrun's husband Sigurd. Gunnar was torn, but eventually sided with his wife and got his brother Guttorm to murder Sigurd. Guttorm stabbed him while he lay in bed with Gudrun; Sigurd managed to kill his assassin before he bled to death. Desperately unhappy, Brynhild stabbed herself. Before she died, she asked Gunnar to burn her and Sigurd on a pyre together, which he did.

Gudrun and Atli (otherwise known as Attila the Hun)

Following the death of her husband Sigurd (see the preceding section), Gudrun left home and moved into the Danish royal court for seven years. Her mother Grimhild finally contacted her and told her she needed to marry again and get compensation for the loss of her husband. She gave Gudrun a drink that made her forget her troubles. Then she announced that Gudrun would marry Atli. (Atli was Attila the Hun.) He is shown in Figure 14-1.

Figure 14-1:
Attila the
Hun or Atli.

© Hulton-Deutsch Collection/CORBIS

Who would want to marry Attila the Hun?

Gudrun said she didn't want to marry Atli because he would be cruel to her brothers, but her mother insisted. So the wedding took place, but it wasn't a fond union. Atli spent his time plotting to get Sigurd's gold, which was now in the hands of his wife's brothers, Gunnar and Hogni.

He invited them to come visit; Gudrun tried to warn them not to come, but they showed up anyway. Atli ambushed them. He cut out Hogni's heart and showed it to Gunnar. Atli then put Gunnar in a pit full of snakes. Gudrun sent Gunnar a harp; his hands were tied, but he played it with his toes until a snake bit him and he died.

Atli tried to reconcile with Gudrun, but she was pretty upset about her brothers' deaths. She got her revenge, though. She killed the sons she had had with Atli (with their consent; they told her that she could do what she liked with them) and served her husband their blood and hearts. After she told him what he had had for dinner, their relationship was even more strained. She finished things off by stabbing Atli in his bed one night; but she did give him a nice funeral. Then she set his hall on fire, and all his soldiers killed one another in their frenzy to escape.

Giving it up too soon: The end of Gudrun's line

Despite her rather dramatic split with her second husband Atli (see the preceding section for the grand finale), Gudrun managed to find herself yet another husband and have several sons with him. Her busy life seems to have slowed down a bit now, and she found time to arrange a marriage for the daughter she had with Sigurd, a beautiful woman named Svanhild. Svanhild's prospective husband's son insinuated to his father that Svanhild had already slept with him, and the king ordered her trampled to death by horses.

When Gudrun heard of her daughter's violent death, she urged her three sons to avenge her; she charmed their armor, so it couldn't be harmed by iron. Two of the brothers killed their other third brother on the way there, though they soon decided that it had been a mistake. Those two found the evil king and cut off his hands and feet. Then the king's men found them and attacked them, but they were impervious to iron. A one-eyed man (Odin, of course) walked in and suggested that the king's soldiers use stones against the brothers and that was the end of Gudrun's last children. It was also the end of the story — the *Saga of the Volsungs* definitely ends on a down note.

Something for Everyone: *Beowulf*

Beowulf is the earliest full-length poem in any Germanic language. Only one copy of the manuscript of *Beowulf* survives. People started taking notice of it in the late 1700s, when all of Europe was trying to come up with stories that explained the existence of their nations — an *Iliad* for every nation (see Chapter 7 for the story on the *Iliad*, and Chapter 11 for a discussion of national foundation myths). The Germans claimed the *Niebelungenlied* (the Song of the Niebelungs), the French took the *Chanson de Roland* (the Song of Roland), and the English claimed *Beowulf.* So did the Danes and the Germans. The Danes claimed it for its setting in Denmark, the Germans claimed it because it was in the pre-Christian North, and the English claimed it because it was written in English — Old English.

The name "Beowulf" may come from the Old English words for "bee" and "wolf," which combined yielded a word that meant "bear."

Old English is not readable by a modern English speaker unless he or she has studied the language. It's not the same language that Chaucer used in the *Canterbury Tales,* which is Middle English and fairly easily read by modern folks after a little getting used to. Old English is also called Anglo-Saxon, and it's much more like German than modern English. The English spoken today has a lot of French mixed in with it from the years that the Normans spent living in England after William the Conqueror's conquest in 1066.

The poet who wrote down the story seems to have been a Christian (it's very likely that he was a monk, because they could write and had ink and paper), looking back at a pagan age. Tidbits of what seem to be pagan beliefs are also sprinkled throughout, such as Beowulf's belief in fate and his desire for praise and glory during his life, not after death. The evil Grendel is connected with Cain, but also with the evil Norse giants.

Anyway, *Beowulf* is the story of a guy named Beowulf who is brave and good at killing monsters. Beowulf was a Geat. The *Geats* lived somewhere in Sweden.

Grendel and the Heorot drive-thru

A king in Denmark named Hrothgar was immensely successful in battle. He built a huge hall named Heorot, and all his young soldiers stayed there with him when they weren't battling.

One day a monster arrived — Grendel. Grendel lurked outside the halls of humans, hating the sound of their merrymaking inside. He lived in the marshes. He was a descendant of Cain and the giants, condemned by the Creator, along with all other trolls, elves, and the living dead who strove against God.

When night fell, Grendel went to take a look inside this hall where people were having so much fun. He saw all the warriors lying on the floor asleep after their feast. He grabbed 30 of them and took them home to eat. At dawn, the other warriors woke up and noticed that a bunch of their number were missing. They all mourned for their lost companions, Hrothgar most of all.

Grendel turned up the next night and took another group of warriors for dinner. After that no one wanted to sleep in Heorot, and it stood empty for twelve years. The Danes didn't know what to do — even praying to their pagan gods didn't help.

Beowulf meets party-crasher Grendel

So Grendel had been eating Hrothgar's men, which was a real downer to the Danes. Enter Beowulf the Geat. He had heard of Grendel's misdeeds and came sailing over from Sweden to help out; Beowulf was a great hero with ambitions to be even greater, and heroes always need to do dangerous, flashy, crowd-pleasing feats to advance their careers. Hrothgar's guard met Beowulf and his men at the port, and after Beowulf had introduced himself and stated his purpose, the guard led the Geats to Hrothgar.

Beowulf told the king that he and his men wanted to cleanse Heorot of its monster, and Hrothgar couldn't say no to that. Hrothgar showed Beowulf and his men to the hall. Beowulf announced that because Grendel didn't use weapons or armor, he wouldn't either. Beowulf told the king where to send his armor if he died and said that he accepted whatever his fate would be.

Beowulf used the word *wyrd* to mean "fate." The word survives in modern English (through William Shakespeare's *Macbeth*) as "weird."

That evening everyone had a party in Heorot, with golden ale and a poet singing the stories of heroes (including the *Volsungsaga*). Beowulf used the opportunity to brag about past heroics on his resumé, such as the time he spent five days swimming in the ocean killing sea monsters. Hrothgar's beautiful queen went around the hall greeting everyone, and Beowulf pledged to her that he would kill Grendel or die trying. Then everyone went to bed, all the Danes departing for their own homes while Beowulf and his team bedded down in Heorot.

Everyone fell asleep. In the darkness Grendel crept in, angry at all the humans. He saw the warriors sleeping and laughed to himself, planning to eat them all. He grabbed one and immediately gobbled him up. He reached for another and found his own arm being grabbed. Beowulf had his arm and wouldn't let go!

Grendel screamed and writhed, but he couldn't get away from Beowulf. Finally his arm tore away from his shoulder. He ran out the door and escaped into the marsh, where he soon died.

Mother of Grendel

The seemingly effortless downfall of Grendel (see preceding section) made everyone really happy, and Hrothgar gave Beowulf a bunch of presents. They had another big party with Grendel's arm as a decoration. But that night, after everyone had gone to sleep, another monster showed up: Grendel's mother. She wasn't as big or as strong as her son, but she was still pretty scary, and ultimately proved to be at least as tough as Grendel. She grabbed up Hrothgar's favorite warrior and ran back to the marsh with him. Everything went back to the way it had been before Beowulf killed Grendel.

So Beowulf got to do some more heroics. He put on his armor, picked up his weapons, and walked out to the seaside, where Grendel's mother apparently lived underwater. Beowulf jumped into the water, descended for a whole day, and found the monster deep below the waves. (Evidently he could hold his breath for a really long time.)

Beowulf swung at Grendel's mother with his sword but couldn't hurt her. So he grabbed her with his hands and flung her to the seafloor. She fought back and tried to stab him with a knife, but his armor protected him. The Beowulf grabbed an ancient giant sword, part of the collection of armor and weapons she kept in her underwater cave (they were souvenirs of warriors she had killed in the past), and struck her in the neck with it; that killed her.

Now Beowulf had a chance to look around her house, and who should he see lying on a couch but Grendel, cold and dead. He used the sword to chop off Grendel's head and swam back to the surface.

After more parties, poems, and presents, Beowulf and his team of warriors left Hrothgar's court in Denmark went back to their home, Geatland (in Sweden). Beowulf became king.

A dragonslayer's last stand

After finishing up his monster-killing exploits in Denmark (see preceding section) Beowulf reigned peacefully as king of the Geats for 50 years. Then one day a dragon pulled into town.

This dragon had a collection of treasure in a cave in the hills and had lived there peacefully until a thief had come and stolen a cup. The dragon left his cave to find the thief, and when he returned, he discovered that his treasure had been looted again. So he went to war against the Geats, burning their homes and fields with his fiery breath.

Beowulf was an old man now, but he rose to the occasion. He took up arms and went out to the dragon's lair. Though he had marched out with a group of men, most of his warriors were afraid to approach the monster. Beowulf stood alone in front of the dragon's cave. He shouted a challenge to the creature, who came out to meet him; each was horrified by the other.

The dragon breathed fire at Beowulf, and Beowulf stabbed it with his sword. His shield stopped some of the fire, but his sword didn't give the dragon the death-blow he had hoped for and only enraged it. Beowulf was in trouble.

Now a young soldier named Wiglaf announced to his companions that it wasn't proper to let his lord die alone and ran out to help him. Beowulf struck at the dragon again, but his sword broke and the dragon grabbed him by the neck. Wiglaf plunged his sword into the dragon's chest, and Beowulf revived enough to stick his dagger into its belly. Together, they killed it.

Wiglaf bathed Beowulf's wounds, but Beowulf knew that he was dying and said a little speech about how sorry he was not to have a son to leave his dragon-slaying gear to, but that he didn't regret how he had lived his life. He gave Wiglaf his gold necklace and armor, and then his soul floated away to meet its judgment.

Beowulf's other soldiers now showed their faces and found Wiglaf sitting by his dead lord's side, trying futilely to revive him with water. Wiglaf told them that their lives as heroes were over, because they had dishonored themselves by failing to support Beowulf. He also said that the Swedes wouldn't be long in seeking them out now that their leader was dead.

The soldiers all went together to take care of Beowulf's body, but first they came upon the dragon, 50 feet of fire-breathing flying snake lying dead amidst its treasures. Wiglaf had the men build a pyre and cover it with gold and armor, and they burned Beowulf's body, singing a sorrowful song. They buried his ashes in a *barrow* (a cave-like tomb) with more treasure, and that was the end of Beowulf the Geat.

Chapter 15

A Seat at the Round Table: King Arthur and His Court

No single, definitive version exists of the story of King Arthur, the legendary king of England, and his chivalrous Knights of the Round Table. The story has been so popular for so many centuries that almost every western European country for the last 1,000 years has had a shot at the legend.

So this chapter doesn't have everything there is to know about Arthur. We've tried to summarize some of the more famous stories (especially from Malory, whose work influenced most authors who came after him) and describe a few of the better known characters, but we didn't get them all. We don't claim to have gotten them "right," either; there are so many versions of the stories, no one can say which is "correct." Malory said one thing, Tennyson said another, and Monty Python still another, and all of them are allowed to do this — it's a legend, and you can tell it as you like.

Searching for King Arthur

Who was King Arthur? No one knows. There has been far too much poetry and prose written about him in the last 1,000 years for anyone to tell for sure. There aren't any accurate records from the time when he supposedly lived.

The historical Arthur probably lived in the fifth, sixth, or seventh century CE, at a time when Roman rule in Britain was in decay and the Welsh and English kingdoms that replaced Roman government were still in the development stage. Various tribes fought one another and a group called the Saxons invaded much of Britain.

Arthur may have been a leader of the Britons, the native British people who tried to repulse the Saxon threat. He may have been a Welsh hero. Some people suggest he was a descendant of the occupying Romans. A popular explanation is that he was a British cavalry general named Arturius who fought the Saxons and defeated them in the battle of Badon Hill in 517.

Back in the twelfth century, people found a cross in Glastonbury Abbey with a Latin caption on it reading "Here lies buried the famous King Arthur, in the Island of Avalon." See it in Figure 15-1. The cross was last seen in the eighteenth century, but drawings of it survive today. Was this Arthur's actual tomb or a publicity stunt by the monks of Glastonbury Abbey? No one knows.

Figure 15-1:
Arthur's
Cross from
Glastonbury
Abbey.

No one can tell for sure who Arthur was or what he did, if he even existed. Does that matter? Not really. Instead of being a king out of history, King Arthur is a literary figure with a long and popular lifespan. Everyone loved tales of Arthur right from the very beginning (in medieval times, that is) and writers have yet to stop embellishing his story.

Everybody loves Arthur: Medieval sources

Geoffrey of Monmouth's *History of the Kings of Britain*, written around 1135, gave Arthur his place in medieval history — it was kind of an official biography. A literary history with a romantic flavor, much of it was adopted from Welsh history and legend; Monmouth seems to have written it to give the Welsh and

Britons a bit of national pride. Julius Caesar and Brutus make appearances in the tale, but Arthur and his sidekick Merlin get most of the coverage.

The French fell in love with Arthur and composed their own stories about him. They wrote courtly poems, setting the tales in a sophisticated world of courtly love, philosophy, and chivalry. The poet Chrétien de Troyes wrote the most famous of the French poems. He lived in the French court in the twelfth century and wrote his most famous works between 1170 and 1190. These were _Lancelot (The Knight of the Cart), Yvain (The Knight with the Lion),_ and _Perceval (The History of the Grail)._ The Germans had a shot at Arthur, too. Hartmann von Aue's version of _Iwein (Yvain)_ and Wolfram von Eschenbach's _Parzival,_ both written around 1200, take their plots from the French versions.

Courtly love was an elaborate form of romance practiced by medieval nobles; courtly relationships were secret extramarital affairs in which the man wooed the lady with gifts, songs, and other tributes, and she would occasionally glance at him. Chivalry was the code knights were supposed to follow; it included things such as loyalty to the Church and one's country, kindness to the weak, honesty, and generosity.

The most famous version of the Arthurian legend is the one in Sir Thomas Malory's _Le Mort D'Arthur,_ written in1485 while Malory languished in prison (he'd committed a number of crimes, including highway robbery, cattle theft, and attempted murder). Malory appears to have used most of the sources available to him, including Monmouth's history and the French romances.

Arthur himself doesn't play much of a role in the majority of medieval "Arthurian" literature. Writers preferred to focus on his court and the exploits of his knights. Arthur appears at the beginning and end of a lot of the stories as a rather remote and majestic figure who can't be bothered with mundane adventures.

His star power continues!

Lots of stuff was written about Arthur in medieval times (see the preceding section). The Arthurian legend has been consistently popular for the last ten centuries or so, embodying different ideals at different times. While the earliest stories described civilization emerging from chaos, the medieval people saw Camelot as a kind of chivalric utopia. Victorian poets used the story to express Victorian ideals, and modern authors tend to portray it as a battleground in which noble ideals can rise above misery.

Arthur had a big resurgence in popularity in nineteenth century England. The English poet Tennyson wrote a long poetic version of the King Arthur story called _Idylls of the King._ Tennyson based his story on Malory's _Morte d'Arthur,_ but put his own Victorian spin on the tale. He emphasized Arthur's goodness, his insistence on harmony, chastity, peace, and selflessness — all favorite Victorian virtues.

Interest in King Arthur has yet to die. The twentieth century produced a huge amount of Arthurian stuff: books (fiction and nonfiction), plays, movies, and historical tours of England. There's no reason to expect it to stop anytime soon.

Who's Who in Camelot

The Arthurian legends have an enormous cast of characters, far too many to list here. There were kings, sorceresses and wizards, beautiful ladies, the occasional hermit, and lots and lots of knights.

One thing that makes the story more confusing is some characters' inconvenient habit of going by different names in different sources. Lancelot sometimes appears as "Launcelot;" Mordred occasionally goes by "Modred"; the Lady of the Lake seems to have had a bunch of different names; and at least two different princesses who fall in love with Lancelot are named "Elaine." Don't let it throw you; just read the stories and don't worry about getting them to match.

Macho men of yore

You can't have heroics without men, and the Arthurian stories had a bunch of them — good, bad, and in-between. Here are a few of the major players:

✔ **Arthur:** Arthur was a great king of England. In the stories, Arthur unified all Britain and brought an age of prosperity to the kingdom. His Round Table at his court at Camelot provided a place for all rival knights to sit on equal footing, none higher or lower than the other. The knights of his court loved to go out on quests for honor and adventure, such as the search for the Holy Grail. Arthur himself was a great and heroic warrior, but he was also a little of everything else: generous, indecisive, forgiving, unfair, wise, and stupid.

✔ **Merlin:** Merlin was a magician. He helped Uther Pendragon seduce Igraine and make Arthur. He gave baby Arthur to a trustworthy knight, Sir Ector, to raise far from the dangers of court. (See "A Medieval Daytime Drama: Arthur's Beginning" a little later in the chapter for more.) In some versions, Merlin tutored the young Arthur and arranged for the sword-in-the-stone contest that proved Arthur's kingship. He also got the Lady of the Lake, Nyneve, to give the sword Excalibur to Arthur. Toward the end of Arthur's life, Merlin fell in love with the sorceress Nyneve (the aforementioned Lady of the Lake; more on her later in the chapter), who persuaded him to teach her all his magic and then imprisoned him in an enchanted cave or glass tower. So much for the loyalty of former students!

Some knights were closer to Arthur for various reasons than the others. Here are the most important and influential knights in Arthurian stories:

- **Lancelot of the Lake:** (So-called because his foster mother raised him under the water of a lake.) He was a late addition to the King Arthur legend, appearing for the first time in the works of Chrétien de Troyes (though there is some reason to believe that earlier stories of him existed). He was Arthur's best and favorite knight and was loyal to the king in all ways but one: he and Queen Guinevere carried on an illicit relationship for years. (His name was also spelled "Launcelot.")

- **Galahad:** He was Lancelot's illegitimate son with Elaine. He was sinless and invincible, the only knight worthy to sit in the Siege Perilous and the only one to find the Holy Grail. (The *Siege Perilous* was a seat at the Round Table reserved for an appointed knight — before Galahad arrived at Camelot, no one knew who this knight would be, but no one ever sat there because if the wrong person sat in the Siege Perilous, he would die.)

- **Gawain:** This was Arthur's nephew, son of his half-sister Margawse. Before Lancelot entered the myths, Gawain was one of the most valiant and honorable of the knights. Later he became less exalted and morally upright, and in some accounts actually led Lancelot in an attack against Arthur. Gawain was under an enchantment that made him get stronger as the morning went on until he peaked at noon, and then his strength would decline in the afternoon.

- **Mordred:** He was Arthur's illegitimate son with Arthur's aunt Margawse (she seduced him; he didn't realize who she was). He was a major troublemaker in Arthur's court; he exposed Lancelot and Guinevere's adultery (everyone had known about it for years, and had tactfully avoided saying anything), which forced Arthur to take action, and then tried to marry Guinevere when Arthur was in France. In the last battle, he fatally wounded Arthur, who then killed him. (His name was sometimes spelled "Modred.")

- **Uther Pendragon:** He was Arthur's father and king of all England. He had Merlin transform him into the shape of the Duke of Cornwall so he could sleep with the duke's wife, Igraine. He then gave Merlin the child of that union: Arthur.

Independent women

Sure the men had a lot of knightly stuff to do (see the preceding section), but you can't have chivalry without ladies to love and fight for. Arthurian stories have their fair share of women, all of whom have minds of their own. Don't let those pretty faces fool you! Here they are:

- ✓ **Guinevere:** She was Arthur's wife. She was desperately in love with Lancelot. Many of the stories describe her romance with him — meeting him in castle towers where she was imprisoned, berating him for his dalliances with other women, longing for his return from adventures. Her relations with Lancelot range from pristine courtly love in the poems of Chrétien de Troyes to no-holds-barred adultery in Malory's book. She had no children.

- ✓ **Morgan le Fay:** She was the daughter of Igraine and the Duke of Cornwall, which made her Arthur's older half-sister. She was a sorceress; Merlin taught her magic. In some stories she helped Arthur, and in others she plotted against him.

- ✓ **Elaine:** This young lady was a beautiful princess who seduced Lancelot and became the mother of Galahad. Guinevere hated her. At least one other character named Elaine also fell in love with Lancelot: the doomed Maid of Astolat.

- ✓ **Igraine:** She was Arthur's mother. She was the faithful wife of the Duke of Cornwall. Merlin disguised Uther as her husband and Igraine welcomed him into her bed, where they conceived Arthur; the Duke of Cornwall was killed that night. Igraine then married Uther and gave birth to Arthur.

- ✓ **The Lady of the Lake:** She was Lancelot's foster mother. She seems to have been the same person as the character called Vivien, Nimue, or Nyneve in various sources. She presented the magical sword Excalibur to Arthur and took it back from him as he was dying. Merlin fell in love with the Lady and taught her all his magic. In the end, she knew so much she imprisoned Merlin in a glass tower (or cave).

A Medieval Daytime Drama — Arthur's Beginning

Arthur had to come from somewhere; the story of his birth and youth is exciting and well known. It all started with lust.

Uther and Igraine

Uther Pendragon was king of all England. The Duke of Cornwall had fought against him for many years. Uther invited the Duke to come for a visit to talk things over and maybe reconcile. The Duke brought along his wife, Igraine. The negotiations went pretty well, but Uther fell in love with Igraine and tried to seduce her. She told her husband about it, and the pair left at once.

When the king discovered that they had slipped away, he flew into a rage. The Duke hid his wife in a castle named Tintagel. He and his army battened down at another castle, which Uther attacked. The battle raged and many people died.

But Uther was sick with lust for Igraine. One of his knights, Sir Ulfius, went to the wizard Merlin to ask for help. Merlin came up with a plan: He would make Uther look like the Duke of Cornwall, so he could visit Igraine in the night. She would have a son from this union, and Merlin demanded that they give him this baby as soon as he was born.

That very night Merlin disguised Uther as the Duke of Cornwall, and Uther went to Tintagel castle. Igraine thought he was her husband and welcomed him to her bed. He left early in the morning. And as it happened, the Duke died that same night, three hours before Uther visited Igraine. When Igraine heard this news, she was troubled. Who had come to her in the night?

With the Duke dead, all the other nobles reconciled with Uther. He married Igraine to seal the pact, and in due time, she gave birth to a son. Merlin took him away, christened him "Arthur," and brought him to a knight named Sir Ector to raise. Two (or 15) years later Uther died, having first declared little Arthur to be his heir.

That weird sword stuck in the stone

After Uther died and Arthur went to live with Sir Ector (see the preceding section), Arthur grew up thinking he was Sir Ector's own son. He thought Sir Ector's son Kay was his older brother.

When Arthur was a teenager, something weird happened. A sword stuck in an anvil appeared in the greatest church in London; on it were the words "Whoso pulleth out the sword of this stone and anvil is rightwise king born of all England." Plenty of men tried to pull the sword out, but no one could. So they decided to hold a tournament to decide who should win it.

A *tournament* was a contest of knightly skill. The knights would be divided into two teams and fight with swords, axes, or whatever weapons they liked. There would also be *jousting,* in which two knights would gallop at each other with long spears and try to knock each other off their horses.

Sir Ector and his son Sir Kay were going to participate in this tournament, and Arthur came along as Kay's assistant. When they got to the jousting site, Kay realized he had forgotten his sword at home, and he sent Arthur back to get it. But no one was home, and Arthur couldn't get in to get the sword, so he thought he would go to the church and get the sword he had seen sticking out of a stone — he had no clue what it was.

Arthur galloped to the church, ran up to the stone, pulled the sword out easily, and dashed back to his brother. Kay immediately recognized it. He brought it to his dad and said, "Shouldn't I be king, since I have this sword?" Sir Ector was no fool; he asked Kay outright how he had gotten the sword, and Kay said Arthur had given it to him. So Ector asked Arthur how he had gotten it, and Arthur said he had just pulled it right out of the stone.

Ector had known his adopted son was unusual, but he hadn't realized just how unusual; now he knelt down and hailed Arthur as king. All the other knights came to the church, and everyone took another try at pulling the sword out of the stone; Arthur was the only one who could do it. Ector now made Arthur promise that his foster brother Kay would always be his *seneschal,* or steward, which Arthur was glad to do.

The beginning of Arthur's reign

That weird sword sure opened a big door for Arthur (see preceding section). He and Ector went to the archbishop, told him the story, and after some squabbling and disagreement among knights who didn't want a boy king, Arthur was crowned.

How to make a kingdom

Young Arthur went to work stabilizing the kingdom from the chaos that had reigned since Uther's death. He soon incorporated Scotland and Wales. He used the Round Table to give a place to all important nobles — at a round table, all of them were equal and none could claim to sit above another.

The seed of a bitter prophecy

While Arthur was just getting the court going (see the preceding section), his mother's sister Margawse came to visit with her sons, including Gawain. Arthur and Margawse fell in love (or lust, perhaps? Remember, Arthur was quite a young man at this point) and spent a month together, and Mordred was conceived. Merlin later told Arthur that the bastard Mordred would cause the downfall of Arthur's court. Hoping to avert this prophecy, Arthur issued a decree that all noble babies born around May Day should be brought to court. He put them all on a boat and set it adrift. It eventually sank, but one baby survived and a man found him and raised him — that was Mordred.

Another sword: Excalibur, the magical sword

Shortly after the Mordred business (see the preceding section), Merlin and Arthur went riding one day and came upon a lake. In the center of it was an arm grasping a jeweled sword and scabbard. Merlin told Arthur that this was the sword Excalibur and that the Lady of the Lake wanted to give it to him. Arthur rowed out to get it. On the ride back home, Arthur claimed that he liked the sword better than its scabbard (the sword's covering or sheath), but Merlin told him he was a fool — as long as he had the scabbard, he would lose no blood, no matter how badly he was wounded.

A king needs a queen

After Arthur had gotten his kingdom in order, his thoughts turned to love. He told Merlin that he wanted to marry Guinevere, daughter of his ally King Leodegan. Merlin warned Arthur that Guinevere was destined to love Lancelot, but went and asked her father if Arthur could marry her anyway. Leodegan was delighted with the match, and Guinevere married Arthur. But as Merlin had predicted, she never did love anyone but Lancelot. See the following section for the story of their escapades.

Sex, Lies, and a Good Jousting

After Arthur got his court started, he and his knights had to come up with appropriate knightly activities. Though the Knights of the Round Table spent their time looking for adventure, the plotlines of the legend actually hinge more on sex than heroics.

Lancelot and Guinevere

Guinevere loved only Lancelot, and Lancelot loved only Guinevere. What her relationship with Arthur was is hard to say. Arthur did know before he married Guinevere that she would fall in love with Lancelot; Merlin warned him. The couple tried to keep their relationship secret, or at least discreet, but everyone at court knew about them. Generally, though, everyone courteously turned a blind eye to their affair; the king had evidently chosen not to criticize them, and most of the court let it go. After Arthur's death, Lancelot and Guinevere both repented their years of adultery and joined religious orders.

Ladies' man Lancelot — to die for!

All the ladies fell for Lancelot, and though he spurned them all, Guinevere was forever getting extremely jealous. His most famous affair was with Elaine, the mother of Galahad — see "Lancelot and Elaine" for that story — but he also won the affections of another Elaine, the fair maid of Astolat.

King Arthur announced that he would hold a huge tournament in Camelot. Guinevere stayed behind in London, claiming she was ill. Lancelot happened to be staying, too, and everyone assumed the two of them wanted to be together. But the queen decided that was just too suspicious, so she sent Lancelot off to the tournament.

He rode away, and to further dispel suspicion, decided to fight against King Arthur and to carry another lady's token. He fought for Elaine's father, and carried her token into battle. He was badly wounded and stayed with Elaine for a while, getting nursed back to health.

The doomed Elaine

When he was healed, Elaine told him she was in love with him and asked him to marry her. When he refused, she offered to be his mistress. When he said no to that, too, she claimed to have no more joy in life. She wasted away and died, and her father sent her body down the river to Camelot on a barge. With it was a note stating that she was a virgin and asking Lancelot to bury her. Guinevere started to get angry, but Lancelot told her to back off. *The Lady of Shalott* was Tennyson's poem about the story.

Lancelot and Elaine

One day a hermit came to court and announced that the man who could sit in the Siege Perilous (see "Galahad" earlier in the chapter) would be born that year and that he would also find the Holy Grail.

A king's little scheme: Seduced in the night

Right after the hermit's visit, Lancelot went off adventuring, as he was wont to do. He came to a town where the people begged him to save a lady who was perpetually scalded by hot water, the result of a curse by Morgan le Fay. (The victim was also beautiful and completely naked.) Lancelot saved her and met the king of the land, King Pelles.

Pelles wanted Lancelot to get his daughter Elaine pregnant. He himself was a descendant of Joseph of Arimathea (the man who had created the Grail), and he knew that his daughter's son would be Sir Galahad, the purest knight ever and the one who could win the Holy Grail. He knew Lancelot loved only Guinevere, so he enlisted the help of a sorceress, Lady Brusen, to help.

Lady Brusen sent a message to Lancelot that Guinevere was waiting for him in a nearby castle. Lancelot immediately went to see her and spent a great night with her, but was astonished the next morning to discover Elaine in bed with him instead. He pulled out his sword to kill her, but she jumped out of bed naked and begged his forgiveness, telling him that she would have his son. She was young and beautiful, and it wasn't long before Lancelot was kissing her again.

Around a year later, after Lancelot had come back home, Guinevere and the rest of the court heard the news about the birth of Elaine's baby Galahad; everyone knew he was Lancelot's son, and Guinevere was furious. But

Lancelot explained that he had been enchanted and had thought he was making love to her, his own true love Guinevere, and she forgave him.

A bowl of milk for table two: Catfight!

After Lancelot explained himself and made peace with Guinevere (see the preceding section), Elaine came to visit. All the men at court admired her beauty (except for Lancelot, who was mortified to see her) and Guinevere pretended to welcome her. Elaine was heartbroken because Lancelot wouldn't talk to her, so her sorceress friend Lady Brusen promised to arrange for Lancelot to come to her bed. Lancelot had promised Guinevere he would go to her that night. But Lady Brusen got to him first! After Lancelot went to bed in his own room, Lady Brusen came and told him that Guinevere was waiting for him; then she led him to Elaine. As before, he was fooled (castles were very dark at night).

Guinevere had her own maid go get Lancelot, but the girl came back and reported that he was gone. She was furious and lay sleepless, sure that he was with Elaine. After some time, Lancelot fell asleep and started calling for Guinevere. She recognized his voice and coughed to wake him. (He was only in the next room; it's surprising she hadn't heard him earlier.) He realized where he was and ran into the hall in his nightshirt, where the queen laid into him. Overcome with the shock of it all, he fainted.

When he awoke, he was insane. He jumped out of the window in his nightshirt and spent two years running around the woods out of his mind. Guinevere and Elaine had words, and the queen kicked Elaine out of the castle.

Guinevere spent tons of money sending knights out to find Lancelot, but no one could. He wandered around insane for a while and eventually ended up back with Elaine, though it seems they weren't lovers. Finally some of the Knights of the Round Table found him and brought him back to Arthur. Arthur forgave him for his absence and commented that he figured the madness was due to Lancelot's passion for Elaine. Lancelot didn't say anything, but everyone knew who had driven him insane.

Everybody's Working for the Weekend: Knightly Heroics

The Knights of the Round Table had a ton of adventures — it was one of their reasons for existence, after all. The Arthurian world was populated with strange knights and sorceresses who always kept things hopping. And there was the quest for the Holy Grail, a quest with an ostensibly Christian purpose but with lots of magical adventures along the way.

Sir Gawain and the jolly Green Knight

The story of Gawain and the Green Knight is one of the older Arthurian tales. It was written in the late 1300s by an unknown author. The style is similar to that of Scandinavian epics and Anglo-Saxon verse, in contrast to the more sophisticated courtly poetry that came later.

King Arthur and all his knights were at Camelot for the Christmas holidays. They had a tradition that no one could eat on New Year's Day until some adventure had happened, so all the guys were sitting around waiting. They didn't have to wait long; a giant green knight walked into the court and proposed a bargain: He would let any knight cut off his head, but that knight had to promise to return the favor and let the Green Knight cut his (the knight's) head off in a year.

Gawain accepted the challenge and cut the knight's head right off. Then, to everyone's amazement, the Green Knight picked his head up, reminded Gawain to meet him at the Green Chapel in a year, and strode out.

Making good on an old challenge

The next year at Halloween, Gawain set out; he had no idea where the Green Chapel was, so he left early to give himself lots of time. At Christmas, he found himself in a dreary forest. He knelt and prayed, and a castle appeared before his eyes. The lord there gave him a bed for the night, told him that the Green Chapel was just down the road, and said he would take Gawain there for New Year's Day, which was in just three days.

In the meantime, he proposed an odd challenge: For the next three days, he would go hunting and Gawain would stay in the castle with the lord's wife. At the end of the day, they would exchange their spoils.

Kiss and tell-all confessions

Every day the lord went off hunting, and at the same time his wife came to visit Gawain in his bed. He put her off, but she managed to get some kisses in. On the first evening, the lord gave Gawain several deer and Gawain gave him a kiss. On the second night, the lord gave Gawain a boar, and Gawain gave him two kisses. On the third night, the lord gave him a fox skin and Gawain gave him three kisses. But Gawain broke his pact, because that day the lady had given him a magic green belt that would protect him from harm, and Gawain, thinking ahead to his previously scheduled beheading extravaganza, kept this magic green belt a secret.

On New Years Day, one of the lord's servants took Gawain to the Green Chapel, where the Green Knight was sharpening his axe. Gawain bent to receive the blow. The Green Knight swung twice without hitting him and then grazed his neck with the axe on his third blow.

The Green Knight now revealed that he was the lord of the castle and that he had instructed his wife to try to seduce Gawain. The first two swings of the axe were payback for Gawain's kissing his wife, and the third was for cheating by keeping the magic belt to himself. Gawain was embarrassed and tried to give the belt back, but the Green Knight made him wear it to remind him of his disgrace. And then he told him that the whole bizarre scenario was a scheme by Morgan le Fay to test the Knights of the Round Table and frighten Guinevere.

King Arthur puts a good spin on it

Gawain returned to Camelot and told everyone his story. And Arthur announced that from then on, all knights would wear a green *baldric* (a belt worn over a shoulder and across the chest) to commemorate Gawain's adventure.

Sir Galahad and the quest for the Holy Grail

Arthur and his knights had just sat down to the Pentecost feast when a young woman rode into the hall and asked for Sir Lancelot. Lancelot rode away with her to an abbey, where his son Galahad, all grown up, was waiting for him. Galahad wanted his dad to make him a knight. Lancelot did this, and then he rode back to Camelot.

Time to try out the Siege Perilous

The next day, Galahad arrived and sat in the Siege Perilous (see "Galahad" earlier in this chapter), the seat at the Round Table that was reserved for his sinless self. Everyone marveled that Galahad must be the knight who would find the Holy Grail. They all caught the urge to go searching for it, especially after everyone saw a vision of the Grail hovering over the table at dinner.

The Holy Grail, also known as the *Sangreal,* was supposed to be a silver cup in which Joseph of Arimathea collected blood and sweat from Christ's wounds as he hung on the cross. Joseph of Arimathea then brought the cup and the lance that pierced Christ's side to Britain, where he founded the first British Christian church. Elaine, Galahad's mother, was one of Joseph of Arimathea's descendents. (See the section "A king's little scheme: Seduced in the night" earlier in this chapter.)

The ladies were all set to accompany the knights on this quest, but a hermit told them they couldn't go — this was a holy mission and women were not welcome. So the knights got their armor and weapons together, and everyone set off in different directions — no one had any idea where the Grail was, so one direction was as good as another.

Galahad heals all and finds the Holy Grail

All the knights had various exciting adventures, but Galahad was the star of this show. Because he was without sin, he had no trouble defeating the knights who attacked him occasionally. He rescued the Maidens' Castle, where seven knights had been raping young ladies. He entered a tournament on the spur of the moment and wounded Gawain. He found a king who was hundreds of years old and made him young again before he died. He found a well whose waters were boiling with lust, but at his touch they cooled down (Galahad was chaste as well as sinless, or maybe being sinless supposes chastity). All in all, he was a very busy do-gooder.

Galahad arrived at last at the castle of Carbonek, the home of the Grail and the end of his quest. There he fixed the spear that had pierced Christ's side. Joseph of Arimathea performed mass with the Holy Grail, assisted by several angels and Christ himself. Galahad thanked God for granting his wish to see the Holy Grail and requested that he now be allowed to leave the world. He got this wish, too. A group of angels took his soul up to heaven. A hand reached down and pulled up the Holy Grail and the spear, and they have not been seen since then.

The Last Days of King Arthur

One day in May, Mordred, the brother of Gawain and bastard son of Arthur, denounced Lancelot and Guinevere to the king. To prove his point, he waited until Lancelot went into the queen's chamber and burst in on the lovers moments after Lancelot walked through the door; he didn't catch the pair in any adulterous activities, but he claimed his proof nevertheless.

The breakup of the Round Table

Lancelot and Guinevere said their goodbyes, and Lancelot fought his way out of the castle. Somewhat against Arthur's will, the queen was sentenced to be burned at the stake. Her captors led her out to the fire in her underwear, customary attire for execution by burning. As everyone expected, Lancelot rode to her rescue and carried her off (and gave her a dress to wear), but not before killing a huge number of knights, including Gawain's unarmed brothers.

Lancelot and Guinevere set up shop at a castle called Joyous Gard, along with many supporters. Arthur and Lancelot fought for a while, but eventually Lancelot brought Guinevere back to Arthur, who would probably have forgiven him but for Gawain, who was angry about the deaths of his brothers. The king banished Lancelot from England, and Lancelot went to France where he had many relatives.

Arthur took his army over to France to fight Lancelot, leaving Mordred in charge back in England. Mordred thought this was his chance to claim the throne. He forged messages announcing that Arthur was dead, and then asked Guinevere to marry him. She fled and barricaded herself inside a castle. Back in France, Gawain and Lancelot had been fighting, and it looked like Lancelot was winning, but because he wouldn't strike Gawain while he was down, the contest was still on.

King Arthur identifies his real enemy

Mordred kept pestering Guinevere to marry him. Off in France, Arthur heard about what Mordred had been doing in his absence (see the preceding section), and finally realized that Mordred was his enemy. He decided to head back to England for revenge against his traitorous son.

Arthur and his army arrived in Dover, England, and Mordred met them with his army. They fought a battle, which Arthur's army won handily. Gawain died after that battle; the wounds he had received from Lancelot had opened again. As Gawain died, he forgave Lancelot and regretted having instigated war against him.

Arthur continued to pursue Mordred and his forces, fighting several battles. Finally he offered Mordred a treaty. They were supposed to sign it in front of their armies, but, suspecting treachery, each ordered their soldiers to attack if they saw a naked sword. As luck would have it, a snake bit one of the soldiers, and he drew his sword to kill it. The battle went badly for Arthur's men. Finally Arthur and Mordred met each other on the field. Arthur thrust his spear through Mordred's body, and Mordred chopped Arthur's head open before crashing down dead.

King and sword depart forever

As Arthur lay dying, he made a request to Sir Bedivere, the only knight left near him. He asked him to throw Excalibur into the nearby lake. After two false starts, Bedivere threw the sword in, and reported that he saw a hand reach up from the water, wave the sword three times, and disappear beneath the surface.

Now Bedivere carried Arthur to the water's edge, and they found a barge carrying a queen, Arthur's sister Morgan le Fay, and her ladies. They loaded Arthur onto the barge and sailed away and out of sight. The next day Bedivere found a fresh tomb with a hermit kneeling by it; the hermit said that the previous night a group of ladies had brought a body and buried it. And that was the tomb of King Arthur.

But not everyone believed Arthur was dead. Some people thought that he would return one day and bring fresh glory to England.

Part V

Some Sunblock, a Sacrifice, a Monster, and Thou: Non-European Mythology

The 5th Wave   By Rich Tennant

"Ooo-this inscription speaks of a time when Shu, the god of air, and Tefenet, the goddess of moisture, were on a date down a dark lonely road. News comes of an escaped evil god who has a hook for a hand..."

In this part . . .

Back when Europeans were running around naked and painting themselves blue, great civilizations were arising in other parts of the world. The Egyptians and folks of the Middle East (Sumerians, Babylonians, and so on) were building cities, fighting battles, and composing myths. This part does a quick-and-dirty job of covering the major myths of a bunch of places — Egypt, the Middle East, India, China, Japan, and North and South America.

Chapter 16

Floods, Mud, and Gods: Mesopotamian and Hebrew Mythology

*M*esopotamia means "the land between the rivers." The rivers in question are the Tigris and the Euphrates. Mesopotamia, which is now Iraq, was the cradle of civilization and the source of many of the oldest myths known. By the way, "Mesopotamia" refers to the whole area; in that area a variety of civilizations rose and fell — a really good description of that would take a whole book — but the biggies were the Sumerian, the Akkadians, and the Babylonians. Also in the general vicinity (but farther west, toward the Mediterranean Sea) were the ancient Hebrew people, who were not a mighty empire by local standards but became important for other reasons.

The story of Gilgamesh is just about the oldest written epic in existence. From around 3000 BCE, it tells of a Sumerian hero dealing with gods and monsters and creating a new civilization. It has some striking similarities to stories in the Bible. The Enûma Elish is the Babylonian creation myth, a wild and violent story similar to the wild and violent story of creation by the Greek poet Hesiod. The mythological creation stories in the Hebrew Bible (the Old Testament) are radically different from anything seen in Greek or Mesopotamian mythology. The Flood story in Genesis, while similar to the one in Gilgamesh in its details, is different in its depiction of human beings and their relationship with divinity.

Gilgamesh: The Sumerian Creation Story

The story of Gilgamesh is over 4,000 years old. It was common to all the peoples of Mesopotamia, and it shows up in Sumerian versions and Babylonian versions. Unfortunately, we don't have a single really good ancient text that tells the whole story of Gilgamesh. Any version of the story has to be put together out of parts. Some are older, some are newer, and some are in different languages from different places. That's possible, more or less, so the story of Gilgamesh, King of Uruk, still lives.

Gilgamesh the King: Big man in Uruk

Gilgamesh was the legendary king of the city of Uruk. He was the son of the previous king Lugalbanda and the goddess Ninsun. According to the story, he was actually two-thirds god and one-third human, which is miraculous in itself. According to the Hittite version of the story, he was 11 meters (36 feet!) tall, but the other versions don't say anything about extraordinary height.

At the beginning of the story, Gilgamesh was bored. He was king, better looking and stronger than everyone else, but he didn't have enough to do. So he got into trouble and acted like a jerk. He abused his subjects, had sex with all their daughters and sons, and became increasingly unbearable until the people of Uruk begged the god Anu to do something.

A new drinking buddy who's a total animal

Anu arranged for Aruru, a goddess of creation, to make a friend for Gilgamesh. This friend was Enkidu. At first, Enkidu was mostly an animal. He lived in the wilderness and talked to the other animals. But one day he ran across a prostitute from the city and had sex with her. After that, the animals wouldn't have anything to do with him.

So he went back to the prostitute, who taught him how to be civilized — he learned to stop drinking milk and start drinking wine, how to wear clothes, and how to comb his hair. Then he entered the city to find Gilgamesh, because he had heard that the king was being a jerk.

When Gilgamesh and Enkidu saw each other, they immediately fought. They punched and wrestled, and eventually Gilgamesh got the better of Enkidu. But the fight was so close that Gilgamesh knew that he had met his match. As guys will do, they stopped fighting and became best friends.

A major hunting trip

Enkidu suggested that they might enjoy having an adventure, so the two
set off to kill Humbaba, a monster that lived in the great cedar forest to the
west. They took their axes. As they walked, Enkidu had second thoughts, but
Gilgamesh ridiculed him into continuing. But as they approached the monster,
Gilgamesh himself got scared, and Enkidu threw his earlier words back in his
face. In the end they held hands for moral support, approached Humbaba
together, and killed him.

Just say no to Ishtar

When the two buddies got back to Uruk, Gilgamesh got all dressed up to let
the people admire their heroic king. He looked *good,* and Ishtar, the goddess
of love and war, saw him and developed a huge crush on him. But when she
propositioned Gilgamesh, he laughed in her face: "Yeah, right!" he said, "I
remember all the other guys you had sex with and look what happened to
them!" Gilgamesh reminds Ishtar of how she turned one ex-lover into a wolf,
and another into a mole. "Forget it!" he says.

Ishtar, disappointed and embarrassed, set the Bull of Heaven loose to tear
up the crops and terrorize the people of Uruk. Actually, the god Enlil tried to
stop her, but she threatened to open the doors of the underworld and let the
dead have dinner with the living (which she had actually done once before),
so Enlil gave in. Gilgamesh and Enkidu successfully killed the Bull.

Bittersweet realizations: The price of male bonding

But then Enkidu died. Gilgamesh was distraught. Enkidu's death reminded
him that he, too, must die some day, despite being such a he-man. So he
set out alone on another quest — to find the secret of immortality.

Searching for immortality

Gilgamesh traveled a long, long way, far outside the known world. On his journey, he fought various lions and dragons, negotiated with the Man-Scorpion to
pass through the dark mountain, and finally came to a . . . restaurant.

The proprietor was Siduri, the Woman-Who-Makes-Wine. She first tried to talk
Gilgamesh out of his journey, but eventually gave him a tip — why not go talk
to the one guy who actually became immortal, Utnapishtim? So Gilgamesh
went off to find Utnapishtim, which required crossing the Water of Death.

After a scary journey, Gilgamesh met Utnapishtim, who looked just like a
normal guy. Gilgamesh and the journey he had just made didn't impress

Utnapishtim. Instead, he called Gilgamesh a fool and urged him to call off his search. But Gilgamesh insisted on hearing Utnapishtim's story.

Utnapishtim tells a flood story

Utnapishtim told Gilgamesh of a time long before, when the people on earth made too much noise and annoyed the gods, and the gods decided to kill everyone. But the god Ea tipped off Utnapishtim, so he built a boat and survived the flood. The flood was so fierce that it terrified even the gods, and Ea took that opportunity to suggest that (a) the gods think twice about doing anything like that again, and (b) that they make it up to Utnapishtim and his wife by making them immortal.

Coming home

After the story, Utnapishtim's wife suggested that Gilgamesh try a simple experiment — staying awake for six days. Gilgamesh said, "No problem," and promptly fell asleep six days. The point of this isn't particularly clear. Perhaps it means that immortality is like never, ever sleeping, and Gilgamesh wouldn't like it if he got it. Or perhaps the point is that Gilgamesh isn't remotely capable of acquiring immortality and is just wasting his time looking.

Anyway, when he woke up, Mr. and Mrs. Utnapishtim took pity on him and told him where he could find a plant called All-The-Old-Men-Are-Young-Again, which would enable him to live forever. Gilgamesh found the plant, but as he took (another) nap next to a river, a snake came along and ate it.

But the story has a happy ending after all. As Gilgamesh approached his city, Uruk, he looked at its impressive walls that he had built and realized that he *would* have a kind of immortality — he built a city and a civilization, which would survive him, and the story of his adventures will keep his name alive forever.

And, so far, it has!

Enûma Elish: The Babylonian Creation Story

The *Enûma Elish* is also called the "Babylonian Genesis," but it's older than the Babylonians. The story is recorded on clay tablets that archaeologists found at the ruins of the city of Nineveh, the old capital of the Assyrian Empire. Other tablets, with other bits of the story, turned up in the ruins of the city of Uruk. These tablets are not that old by Mesopotamia's standards of "old." They date to between 1000 and 500 BCE, so they were "written" after civilization had existed in the area for about three thousand years already. But the story is much, much older than that. It certainly goes back to the First Babylonian Dynasty, when King Hammurabi wrote his famous code of laws — he was king from 1792 to 1750 BCE.

But a lot of the names in the Enûma Elish are Sumerian, and the Sumerian Empire, perhaps the earliest political empire in the world, lasted from 3800 BCE until around 2000 BCE, when Sargon combined Sumer with Akkad. Akkad, to the north of Sumer, would be the source of the Babylonian empire a couple of hundred years later. So we're dealing with a really old story here.

The name "Enûma Elish," by the way, simply comes from the first two words of the story, which is in the form of poetry: "When above enûma elish the heavens had not yet been named. . . ." The "family tree" of Enûma Elish can be found in Figure 16-1.

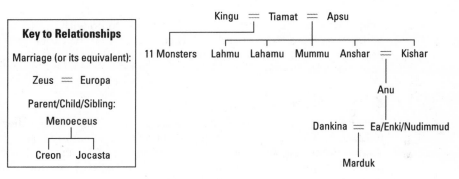

Figure 16-1: Grandma Tiâmat and her divine kin: a Family Tree of the Enûma Elish.

This version of the creation of the gods is not entirely consistent with other stories about the relationships among the gods, but that's the way it is with mythology.

Just one big happy family

The story starts off nicely enough. Before there was heaven or earth, or anything else, there were Tiâmat and Apsû, and their son Mummu. Tiâmat was female, the god of sweet water (as opposed to salt water). Apsû was male, the god of salt water. Their son, Mummu, was the mist that rises from the water.

Then Tiâmat and Apsû had four more kids, two sets of twins. First they had Lahmu and Lahâmu, and then they had Anshar and Kishar, who were smarter and stronger than the first set of twins. Anshar and Kishar had a child together named Anu. Anu became a sky god.

Anu then had a kid named Ea, who also went by the names Nudimmud and Enki. Ea was far and away the best of all the gods, even though he was the youngest. He was god of underground water, magic, and making good plans.

House party

Now, most of the younger gods — Lahmu, Lahâmu, Anshar, Kishar, Anu, and Ea — took to partying and staying up late, which prevented Apsû and Tiâmat from getting a good night's sleep. Evidently the only god who wasn't in on the ruckus was Mummu, the first-born son of Apsû and Tiâmat. Apsû and Mummu complained to the younger gods, but they didn't listen. So they decided that more drastic steps were necessary. Father and son described their plan to Tiâmat — they were going to kill all the other gods and get some sleep.

Tiâmat was outraged and would have nothing to do with it. But Apsû and Mummu decided to go ahead with their plan. When the other gods learned of it — it evidently wasn't a secret — they panicked and wandered around aimlessly with no clue.

Ea in the house

Only Ea knew what to do. He made a magic circle around the other gods to protect them, then uttered a spell and put the whammy on his great-grandfather Apsû. Apsû fell asleep, and Ea took off his crown and his shining power and put them on himself. Then he killed Apsû, imprisoned Mummu, and built a house on Apsû's body, which he named (in a fit of originality) Apsû. He didn't do anything to Tiâmat because she wasn't in on the plot.

With his nice new house built, he got a wife, Damkina, and they had a son: Marduk (see Figure 16-2). Ea made his son Marduk "doubly equal" to the gods — if "doubly equal" doesn't seem to make sense, remember that Ea has magical powers, and don't worry about it too much.

Mamma's turn

Tiâmat was broody, though, and started getting angry about the death of her husband. She had a new husband, too, a god named Kingu, and he egged her on. She decided to get some revenge and started having snake-monster babies to serve in her army. When she had given birth to eleven of these, she was ready to make her move.

© Bettman/CORBIS

Figure 16-2: Marduk: the young upstart who saved the gods.

A corporate reorg and some new leadership

After Tiâmat and Kingu began plotting revenge (see the preceding section for more info), Ea found out about Tiâmat's plans, and panicked at first, but then pulled himself together and went to his granddad Anshar for advice. Anshar suggested that he use his magic to defeat Tiâmat — it had worked with her first husband, after all. Ea tried, but his magic didn't work at all.

Then Ea's father, Anu, tried to reason with her, but that didn't work either. Because magic and negotiations had both failed, it seemed that physical force was all that was left.

Marduk to the rescue!

Who could take care of business? How about Marduk? That seemed like the best plan. Anshar, Anu, and Ea called the young Marduk and told him of the problem. Ea and Anu trained him, giving him super-magic-god-powers until they thought he was ready. When he was trained, Marduk agreed to take on the war with Tiâmat but demanded complete authority as the Number One God if he was successful.

Starting a fighting war with their matriarch and acknowledging young Marduk as the king of the gods required the approval of all the *Annunaki* (the word the gods used to describe themselves). So Anshar sent Kaka, his secretary, to call Lahmu and Lahâmu and Kishar and Damkina to join them. They were all terrified when they heard of the problem, but a good meal with lots of wine made everyone feel better.

Finally, Marduk came in to show his stuff. They put a robe on the floor, and Marduk spoke a spell and blew it to bits. He then spoke another spell and fixed it. All the gods were impressed and bowed to Marduk, praising him as their king.

The final showdown: Bridges to earth, sky, and Babylon

Marduk went off to face Tiâmat and her new hubby Kingu. Kingu was terrified and put up no resistance, but Tiâmat was made of sterner stuff and put up a good fight. Marduk finally beat her by blowing a terrible wind into her mouth, causing her to puff up, and then shooting an arrow down her throat and into her heart.

Marduk took the "tablet of Fate" from Kingu and wore it around his neck. He divided Tiâmat's body into two pieces and made one piece into the sky and the other into the earth. He set up constellations in the skies and got the calendar running properly. He then killed his captive, Kingu, and made human beings out of his blood.

He ordered half of the Annunaki to be sky gods and the other half to be earth gods. They were so grateful to him for saving them from Tiâmat that they built the city of Babylon in his honor.

Mesopotamian Gods: Okay, We Fear You . . . You Happy?

The characters in Mesopotamian mythology worshipped their gods, but they didn't particularly like them. When the old man Utnapishtim offered a sacrifice to the gods after the Great Flood, he said that they "swarmed like flies over the sacrifice, attracted by the sweet smell." When the goddess Ishtar suggested that the hero Gilgamesh have sex with her, he said, "Are you crazy? Get lost!" See the earlier section "Just say no to Ishtar."

This attitude — fear mixed with contempt — may have come from the harsh environment of the world between the Tigris and Euphrates rivers. The summers were brutally hot and the winters were fiercely cold. While the Nile River in Egypt flooded in a predictable and beneficial way, bringing new rich soil to the people, the Tigris and Euphrates flooded at odd times, and it was catastrophic. Check out the map of the region in Figure 16-3. Huge thunderstorms lashed the plains of Iraq. So perhaps it isn't too surprising to find the characters in the mythology of this harsh world offering sacrifices to appease the gods but not singing many hymns of praise to them. There certainly aren't any human heroes being buddies with the gods, such as Odysseus and his friend Athena.

Figure 16-3:
The Ancient "Near East" was home to big important civilizations and some small important ones, too. What was it near? The Europeans, who gave it that name.

Who were these gods? Any list will have to be incomplete, because there were many civilizations over many thousands of years in Mesopotamia: Sumerians, Hittites, Assyrians, Babylonians, and Persians last of all. But the famous myths, the ones such as the Enûma Elish and the story of Gilgamesh, were common to Sumerians, Assyrians, and Babylonians, and they feature some of the following gods. You should note that most of these gods have different names in Sumerian and Akkadian; if one of the names occurs in another myth that we describe in this chapter, we put that one first. They are:

✔ **Anu** (or sometimes just An): The father of the gods, but not the king of the gods. He was the god of the top part of heaven. He was the most powerful god, but also the most remote — he didn't have much business with folks on earth. He mated with Ki.

✔ **Ki** (who also went by the names Ninhursag, Ninmah, and Nintu), who was the Earth. Her relationship with Anu produced Enlil.

✔ **Enlil,** who was the Air. Enlil was less powerful than Anu, but more active. He made things happen on earth. When Enlil was born, everything was dark and boring.

- **Nanna** (or Sin), who was the moon. She gave birth to Shamash.

- **Shamash** (or Utu), who was the Sun (the Arabic word for "sun" is still *Shams*). She, in turn, gave birth to Ishtar.

- **Ishtar** (or Inanna), the goddess of love and war.

- **Ea** (or Enki) was the wise god, the one who kept peace among the other gods. He had a lot of work keeping Ishtar in line, since she was usually nothing but trouble in the myths that survive from Mesopotamia.

- **Marduk,** *the* god of Babylon. In many of the earlier myths, Marduk doesn't appear at all. It seems that he was particular to Babylon, and came to rule the other gods when Babylon came to rule the other peoples of Mesopotamia. The "Babylonian Genesis," or *Enūma Elish,* is the story of how Marduk came to be King, and that poem was probably written to legitimize Babylonian rule over other people — "Our god beat up your gods!"

- **Kur** was the god of the underworld. He shared the underworld with Ereshkigal.

- **Ereshkigal** was Ishtar's sister.

Some stories say that Ereshkigal was allowed to be queen of the underworld as a present, but others say that Kur raped her and carried her down there by force. One particularly nasty story shows how gods could raise sibling rivalry to new heights. Ereshkigal was married to Gugalanna, the Bull of Heaven. When he died, the goddess Ishtar decided to go to his funeral — he was her sister's husband after all. The funeral was to be in the underworld, of course, but evidently Ereshkigal didn't like the idea of her sister entering her domain. So Ereshkigal told the guards of the underworld at each of the seven gates to demand that Ishtar take off one piece of her clothing before she could pass. By the time Ishtar got to the funeral she was naked. This was disrespectful, of course, so Ereshkigal killed her and hung her on the wall. Eventually, Ea rescued her and brought her back to life — it wouldn't do for a goddess to die for good. But Ishtar had to find someone to replace her among the dead. She picked Tammuz, the king of Uruk. He wasn't thrilled with the idea of being dead, so it was agreed that he would have to be dead only six months out of the year, and his sister Geshtinanna would be dead the other six (no one mentions what Geshtinanna thought about this "deal").

Hebrew Mythology: A is for Apple, B is for Babel

Probably the myths most familiar to people today are the myths of the ancient Hebrews, particularly the ones found in the book of Genesis in the

Hebrew Bible (which is itself the part of the Christian Bible known as the Old Testament).

We should be really clear, here, by what we mean when we call the stories in Genesis "myths." We do *not* mean that they are lies, or irrelevant, or not to be taken seriously. We do not even mean that they are necessarily not historically factual. (Some stories are historically factual *and* mythological at the same time — think of the story of Paul Revere's ride through the suburbs of Boston.)

What makes myths different from other stories is that myths are true in a fundamentally meaningful way. We, Amy and Chris, think that to call something a "myth" is to *increase* its importance, rather than to diminish it. Any old story can be factual, but only a few are true. We, personally, don't think that it's particularly important whether the events described by a myth really happened or not, as long as the story offers something meaningful and true.

We will not spend too much time on the myths of the Hebrews, only just enough to show them in the context of all the other mythologies that were around them.

In the beginning

The Hebrew account of creation is very different from the Babylonian story (see the earlier section "Enûma Elish: The Babylonian Creation Story") or the Greek version that Hesiod tells (see Chapter 3). According to the Hebrews, there was no squabbling among the gods, no gods eating their own children or plotting against their parents. There was only one god, who doesn't have a name other than God, who created everything simply by speaking (well, almost everything — you can see the interesting exception in a minute).

In the beginning, there was only water and wind. God started by making light and separating it from darkness. He then built a solid dome to hold the water back and made dry land under the solid dome (the story of Noah and flood reveals that this dome has windows in it, and when the windows open up, the water pours through). Then he made the plants and animals, and finished by creating human beings. All of this took six days. See Figure 16-4.

The creation of humans

Genesis actually has two creation myths side by side:

✔ In the first one, the god spends six days making everything, and he does all the creating merely by speaking. In the first version, two humans are created simultaneously, both a man and a woman.

✔ In the second creation myth, he makes earth and heaven on one day, and on that same day, before creating plants and animals, he makes a human being. But in this version, he doesn't make the human merely by saying "Let there be a human being." He gets down and molds the human out of dirt. In the second version, man comes first, and then God creates a woman out of the man's rib. This second version is very much like the Greek account, in which Prometheus molded humans out of mud.

Figure 16-4:
God creating Adam, as painted by Michelangelo. Is Adam reaching toward God or toward Eve, who is already waiting in the wings?

© Bettman/CORBIS

One apple and you're out of the garden

Just as Hesiod blamed all humanity's troubles on a woman, Pandora (see Chapter 3), so, too, did the ancient Hebrews. Eve, the first woman, was tempted by the serpent — who was the smartest ("the most subtle") of all the animals. Pandora (whose whole story is in Chapter 3) opened the box, letting a bunch of evils and one good thing (hope) into the world. Eve, by eating the fruit (the apple) from the tree of the knowledge of good and evil, caused people to (a) stop being immortal, and (b) have to work for a living. But she also gave people moral judgment and made people more like gods — which is why the immortality had to go. Immortality plus moral judgment equal god, so humans can't have both at once.

Yet another flood

It seems that every culture that existed anywhere near the Mediterranean Sea (and some in other places) had a story in which a great flood killed everyone but one couple. The story of Noah is the most famous, but the Mesopotamians told of Utnapishtim and his boat (see "A flood story" earlier in the chapter), and the Greeks and Romans knew of Deucalion and Pyrrha (see Chapter 12), who survived a world-ending flood.

Noah's ark and company

Because these stories are, on the surface, so similar, their differences are all the more interesting. In the Hebrew story, God sees all the wickedness in the world, and regrets having made human beings. He singles out Noah as the only one worth saving. When the story gets to the building of the boat, all of the instructions and details come from the mouth of God. The text says only that "Noah did what God told him." So the Hebrew version really focuses on God, and Noah isn't much of a character, just an instrument of God's wishes.

The Tower of Babel and different languages

Of course, one common function of myths is to explain the origins of things, and the best example of this in the Hebrew Bible is the story of the Tower of Babel.

Once, the story goes, everyone spoke the same language, and the humans decided to build a brick tower that would reach to heaven. God noticed, and got worried that they might succeed at this task, and who knew what other ambitious project may be in the future.

So he issued a command, and all the people started speaking different languages. Unable to communicate, they abandoned their construction project and went their separate ways.

Common Threads in the Three Creation Myths

The Mesopotamian flood story is very different from the Hebrew flood story. Utnapishtim gets tipped off to the upcoming flood by Ea, but nothing is made of Utnapishtim's being particularly good — he was just lucky. (See the earlier section called "Utnapishtim tells a flood story.") No god gets credit for anything in that story. Utnapishtim designed the boat and tells Gilgamesh all about it.

He even mentions that the flood scared the wits out of the gods, but he wasn't scared. So the Mesopotamian flood story focuses on the human hero, who thumbs his nose at the nasty, sneaking, cowardly gods.

The Roman poet Ovid begins his poem *Metamorphoses* with the story of a flood, in which Deucalion and Pyrrha are the only survivors. (See Chapter 12.) In Ovid's account, Zeus has been treated outrageously by a human king, and decides to kill everyone. No reason is given as to why Deucalion and Pyrrha survive; they just come floating into the story on a boat. Ovid's account focuses on how strange it is to have the world covered with water — dolphins swimming through fields of grain, schools of fish building nests in trees — and how sad and lonely the two survivors felt.

This Tower of Babel story has a lot in common with the story of Bellerophon, who tried to ride the winged horse Pegasus up to Mt. Olympus, or the story of Phaethon, who demanded to drive the chariot of the sun. Both of those guys got killed for their ambition. (See Chapter 6 for more on these guys.)

One common theme in mythology is that human beings are definitely not allowed to try to become gods — the gods occasionally grant someone immortality, as they did with Heracles and Utnapishtim, but you shouldn't try to take it! (See Chapter 6 for more on Heracles.)

Chapter 17

Three Cheers for Egypt: Ra, Ra, Ra!

• •

• •

*E*gyptian civilization has been around for a very, very long time. The Egyptian dynasties got their start about 5,000 years ago, long before the rise of Greek civilization. And they held sway over the Nile region for almost that entire time, creating a sophisticated civilization, an elaborate system of writing, a complex group of gods, and noteworthy burial practices.

Egypt was actually two Egypts, Upper Egypt and Lower Egypt. Lower Egypt was in the northern part of the country and encompassed Memphis and the Nile Delta. Upper Egypt was much larger, extending all the way to Elephantine Island near Sudan. The important city of Luxor and the Valley of the Kings (home of the big pyramids) were there.

Lower Egypt was north of Upper Egypt; that can be confusing to Americans, who traditionally put north above south on their maps, but that's just a convention. Upper Egypt was at a higher altitude than Lower Egypt; the Nile flowed down from Upper Egypt into Lower Egypt and the Mediterranean Sea.

Write Me a Really Big River

The Nile was Egypt's defining feature. The entire Egyptian civilization existed within a few miles of the great river; just outside that fertile area was dry desert, but the Nile's banks were lush with plants and animals. Every year the Nile would overflow, flooding the land around it, and when the waters receded, the plants sprang up like magic. It was a relatively easy place to live (for those times, anyway) and thus was fertile ground for culture. Check out the map of Egypt in Figure 17-1.

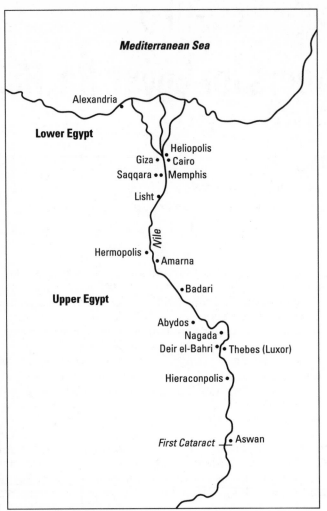

Figure 17-1:
Ancient
Egypt.

This endless cycle of destruction followed by fertility became the foundation of Egyptian religion. Creation was an ongoing cycle of renewal repeated every day, and the Egyptian people's job was to help the gods ward off destructive demons who might prevent the cycle from progressing as it should.

One thing to remember about Ancient Egypt — scholars of the subject, called *Egyptologists,* can't say for sure what went on most of the time. Even though experts have unearthed a huge body of archaeological and textual evidence, no one can say for sure exactly what it all means. So scholars argue and disagree and debate. If you want definite "facts," you won't find them here — but then again, that's mythology!

The Egyptians didn't have the same sort of mythology as the Greeks did; deities were real entities, but they didn't engage in shenanigans like the immortals on Mount Olympus. A few stories about them have survived into our time, but some of the best (such as the story of Isis and Horus) come from Greek writers. The Egyptians themselves didn't start writing down their myths until about 2000 BCE, after Egyptian civilization had already been around for a while.

Egyptians, like most peoples in this book, didn't insist that any one version of a story or description of a god was the "true" one. They would adapt myths to fit different circumstances, and a god such as Seth could go from being the protector of Upper Egypt to the enemy of the gods, deserving of destruction. And there wasn't exactly a "national" religion. Though several deities did have national status, many more were strictly local concerns. So when we talk about Egyptian mythology, we are really just assembling pieces of information from many different places spread over several thousands of years.

In keeping with that, the Egyptians didn't have a single creation story. Instead, people in different parts of the country told different stories of how the world came into existence and of the creation of gods and people. For example, in the story we tell below, the world develops from a mound in the primeval waters; in other versions, though, a lotus flower emerges from the waters and opens to reveal a baby god. Depending on the account you read, humans emerged from the tears of the first deity or were sculpted out of clay or metal by one of the gods. It's all very confusing if you try to reconcile the different versions with one another. So we recommend that you don't try; just read the stories for themselves and don't attempt to make them fit together.

Order from chaos: One version of how the world began

In the beginning, there was the primordial water of creation. A mound rose out of it. Atum, the creator god, emerged from the water all alone. Apparently having nothing better to do, he masturbated. He caught his semen in his mouth, and spat out two children: Shu, god of air, and Tefenet, goddess of moisture. These two went off to explore, and Atum couldn't find them, so he sent his daughter, a fiery goddess also called Atum's divine Eye to see if she could. She brought them back, and Atum wept to have his children back safe. His tears turned into the first humans.

Shu and Tefenet had two children: Nut, the sky goddess and Geb, the earth god. Nut and Geb fell in love and embraced one another so tightly there was no room between them. Nut got pregnant, but there was no room for her children to be born. Their father, Shu, the air god, separated them and held Nut high up over the earth (which you can see in Figure 17-2), so there was room for living creatures and air for them to breathe. Water surrounded the earth and sky. Every night Nut swallowed the sun, and every morning she gave birth to it again.

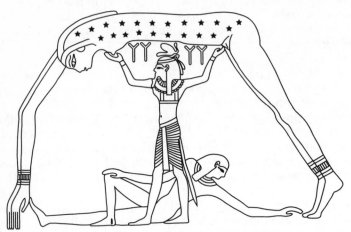

Figure 17-2:
The air god, Shu, is separating the sky goddess, Nut, from the earth god, Geb.

Nut had two pairs of twins, Osiris and Isis, and Seth and Nephthys. Osiris and Isis fell in love in the womb, but Nephthys (a girl) hated her brother Seth. Nevertheless, Nephthys became Seth's wife and Isis became Osiris's wife. As first-born male, Osiris was destined to rule Egypt, and he did for a short time.

Other myths having to do with creation

In addition to having a few creation stories, the Egyptians also had four creator gods, each with his own cult. The story of the origin of the world and the creation of humans on it came out differently for each of them.

Another take on Atum

The Atum worshipped at Heliopolis was a snake that emerged from the primeval chaos (like Amon — see the next section), though he was usually depicted as human. He had both male and female attributes. He was sometimes called Ra-Atum, and represented the evening sun who returned to Nut's womb — see the story in the "Order from chaos: One version of how the world began" section of this chapter. In that story, humans formed from his tears.

Amon-Ra fusion

Amon-Ra became a national god in the second millennium BCE, when the fertility god Amon, worshipped in Thebes, fused with the sun god Ra. In his myth, he was the first being in existence. In one story, he took the form of a goose and laid the cosmic egg from which life came. In another, he emerged from the primordial chaos in the form of a snake, just like Atum (see the preceding section).

Khnum, sculptor of humans

Khnum had a cult on Elephantine Island. He controlled the yearly rising of the Nile and its life-giving power. His sacred animal was the ram, and he was usually depicted as a man with a ram's head. Khnum was a potter; he made humans and animals out of clay and breathed life into their bodies.

Heavy-metal god Ptah

Ptah was worshipped at Memphis, where he was considered the god who existed at the beginning of time and created everything. He created all gods by thinking of them and speaking their names aloud. He fashioned gods and kings out of gold and other metals, which also gave him the position of the god of crafts.

Gods and Goddesses of the Sands

The Egyptians had a huge number of deities. Some had more stories attached to them than others, but they were all fairly important.

Major Players

However, there were some that were simply more significant than the rest. They just seem to pop up at a greater frequency than the others. Here are a few of the biggies.

Ra, the sun god

Generally, the sun god was the main god of Egypt. He was born from Nut every day at dawn, grew up by noon, and was old by evening, when he went to the underworld for the night, before being born again the next morning. He took the sun over the sky in a boat. Osiris and sky goddess Nut joined him on his boat at night.

The sun god took many forms; one of the most popular was a dung beetle, a creature that pushes round balls of dung around, imitating the sun's progress across the sky. See Ra in Figure 17-3.

The Egyptians believed that the world would eventually end and that Ra himself could age. In one story, as Ra was getting older, people began plotting against him, and he decided to punish them. He sent the goddess Sekhmet to kill them, but he stopped her before they were all destroyed. But he felt so tired that he decided to retire. He appointed the god Osiris to be ruler over humanity (see the "Osiris, first among equals" section later in this chapter for more on this god).

The sun god generally went by the name "Ra" (or "Re"), but this name was usually fused with another deity's name. For instance, the midday sun was called Ra-Harakhty, and the evening sun was Ra-Atum. Really, his name was secret. When Ra was getting old, Isis tricked him into revealing his secret name to her, but she promised to tell no one but Horus, so no one ever found out what it was.

Isis, a mover and a shaker

Isis was the wife and sister of Osiris and the mother of Horus. Egyptians worshipped her as the great mother goddess. She was one of Egypt's earliest goddesses; her name is mentioned in the Pyramid Texts, some of the earliest records of Egyptian religion (2465 to 2150 BCE).

Isis was a political mover. As Egypt passed from the rule of its native kings to the Ptolemies, Isis became the official goddess of the new state cult. She also traveled through the Greco-Roman world, becoming identified with Demeter, Selena, and Hera.

In one myth (which is extremely similar to a story about the Greek goddess Demeter; see Chapter 5), Isis got a job nursing a baby boy for a noblewoman. She took a liking to the child, and every night would put him in the fire to make him immortal. One night, the mother saw her doing this and screamed. The baby died and Isis left.

Osiris, first among equals

Osiris was the brother and husband of Isis. He and Isis were both children of Nut and Geb. He was the ruler of the underworld, and, incidentally, the first mummy. His jealous brother Seth murdered him to take over his throne, and Isis mummified him, after which he went to his new job with the dead.

Osiris was the god of agriculture and taught people how to farm. The Egyptians compared his death and dismemberment with the annual harvest and cutting down of crops. His reanimation was the sign that crops would rise again the next year.

When Ra retired, he passed his throne to Osiris. (See above, "Ra, the sun god.") Osiris had a brief reign as king of the earth, in charge of deities and everything else. He reigned with his sister/wife Isis at his side, and presided over a golden age.

Seth

Seth was the brother of Isis and Osiris; after murdering Osiris and a lengthy disagreement with Isis and her son Horus, he finally accepted a job as the god of storms. See the next section for the full story. Seth lived in the desert. Egyptians depicted him as part wild donkey, part pig (or anteater).

Horus and his band of pharaohs

The son of Isis and Osiris, Horus was king of the gods and god of the sky, a position he had to fight his uncle Seth to acquire — see below for that tale. He was depicted as a falcon. *Pharaohs,* the Egyptian kings, were considered earthly manifestations of Horus.

Trouble in Paradise: Horus and Seth

The gods Horus and Seth both thought they should be king of the gods, Horus because he was the son of the former king Osiris and Seth because he was Osiris's brother and jealous that Osiris got to be king instead of him. So Seth killed Osiris, cut him into pieces, and seized the throne.

Assembly required, battery not included

Isis, distraught, gathered up the pieces of Osiris's body; she couldn't find his penis, so she made one out of wood. (The Greek writer Plutarch said that a fish had eaten it, and used this to explain why Egyptian priests didn't eat fish.) Then, with the help of the jackal god Anubis, she reassembled him and held everything together with mummy bandages. He came back to life long enough to get her pregnant.

Isis was afraid that Seth would kill her baby if he found him, so she went off to hide in the marshes of the Nile delta. There she bore her son Horus and raised him to avenge his father's murder and reclaim the throne. Seth told all the dangerous elements in the marshes — the plants, animals, insects and diseases — to harm Horus if they could. But Isis went around and learned all their names, which gave her power over them, and so she kept Horus safe.

She taught Horus the names of all the dangerous beasts, and he grew up immune from harm by them.

Isis acts as counsel for her son Horus

When Horus was grown, he and his mother went before a tribunal of gods to demand his throne. Seth argued that he was the only god strong enough to defend the sun-boat, but Isis persuaded the deities that he was wrong. Seth refused to continue the trial with Isis there, so the gods reconvened on an island. The ferryman wasn't supposed to take Isis there, but she disguised herself, bribed the ferryman, and managed to get over to the island. Then she turned into a beautiful woman, went to Seth, and complained that she was a widow and a stranger had stolen all her cattle, robbing her son of his inheritance. Seth agreed that this was a crime; Isis jumped on this and said he had incriminated himself.

The trial turns into a contest

Seth still refused to relinquish the throne and challenged Horus to a contest: They would each turn into a hippopotamus and stay under water for three months. Horus agreed, but Isis was worried that he might lose. So she threw a harpoon at Seth (though she hit Horus first). Horus got really angry at his mom. He cut off her head and ran off into the desert with it. Isis turned herself into a statue and returned to the gods; the god Thoth fixed her up with a cow's head as a replacement for the one Horus had taken.

The sun god punished Horus for hurting his mother by letting Seth tear out his eyes. The goddess Hathor restored them with a judicious application of gazelle milk.

The pen is mightier than the sword (harpoon?)

Horus appealed to the gods again. They wrote a letter to Osiris asking what to do. Osiris responded that he would send demons to plague the gods if they didn't give Horus the throne. Horus became king, Isis rejoiced, and Seth got a new home and a new job: He went to live with the sun god in his new position as god of storms.

Other deities, national and local

Although some deities were worshipped throughout Egypt, others had a more local influence. Different localities had favorite deities whom they worshipped specially, resulting in a huge number of gods and goddesses all over the Egyptian land. Here are a few more, though certainly not all, Egyptian deities:

- ✓ **Thoth:** He was the moon god. He was depicted as a baboon, an *ibis* (a large wading bird), or a man. He was associated with secret magical powers, many of which were written down in the mythical Book of Thoth. (Thoth is kind of equivalent to Hermes in Greek mythology.)

✔ **Anubis:** He had the head of a jackal. He received the souls of dead people and led them through the many trials the soul had to pass before reaching Osiris and paradise.

✔ **Hathor:** She was the goddess of lovers, fertility, and birth, and also the wife of the sun god. She had the shape of a cow. (Isis also had cow-like aspects; the cow was a common symbol for the life-giving female.) She nursed kings from her udder. Women wore *amulets* (charms) from her sanctuary to prevent prolonged labor.

✔ **Sekhmet:** The "Powerful One," was a lioness goddess. She killed rebellious humans for the sun god. Sometimes criminals were sacrificed to her.

✔ **Bastet:** The cat goddess, was the patron of love, sex, and fertility. She started out as a lioness like Sekhmet, but got milder as time went on and turned into a gentler pussycat.

✔ **Bes:** He was a fat dwarf with the mane and tail of a lion. His tongue stuck out of his mouth as a warning to enemies. He was the special helper for women in labor and safeguarded young children. People put his image on furniture and wore him as amulets around their necks to ward off demons.

✔ **Selket:** The scorpion goddess, was a guardian of the living and the dead.

Religion in Egyptian Life

Religion was very important to the ancient Egyptians. They had to observe all the proper rituals or the chaotic demons would wreak havoc over the land. This observation extended from the kings to the lowest walks of life.

Pharaohs: Nifty church-and-state combo

In Egypt, religion was a state matter. Egyptian kings, called *pharaohs,* were believed to be descendants of the deities Isis and Osiris, which made them divine. The pharaoh was considered a manifestation of the sky god Horus.

Kings and their agents the priests served the deities in their temples, which were built to embody creation on a grand scale. Egyptian temples are still very impressive, huge, and covered with carvings and paintings. The gods resided in these temples and priests took care of them, bathing and dressing their statues and laying out feasts for them to eat. Temples weren't like modern churches — most people never set foot in them — but more like machines to keep the cycle of the world in motion.

Pyramids: Houses of eternity

Like all other Egyptians, pharaohs wanted to be reborn after their deaths. And like everyone else, they had to prepare for the trip to the land of the dead. But kings could spend huge amounts of community money and mobilize millions of workers to help them out, and that's where pyramids come from.

Pyramids were tombs for kings. And that's all pyramids were. People have suggested that they were used as astronomical observatories, sundials, or for communicating with extraterrestrials, but the archaeological evidence and contemporary writings say that pyramids were tombs.

Over ninety pyramids can be found in Egypt, ranging from the Delta to the First Cataract of the Nile. Egyptians saw them as a symbolic representation of the mound of creation that appeared out of the primordial chaos at the beginning of the world. A king entombed in a pyramid went through the death-rebirth cycle and was reunited with the gods every day. Priests and other supporters performed rituals and made offerings to make sure that the pharaoh had a good afterlife. The tombs themselves were full of treasure and offerings of (formerly) living creatures, such as wives, servants, and pets.

Daily dose of religion

The Egyptians didn't know about the germ theory of disease, nor could they explain why bad things happened in life (any more than any modern person can). They figured that difficulties — medical problems or marital strife or hard luck in business — came from supernatural forces, angry deities, or demons on the loose.

So what to do? Worship the gods and goddesses, of course. While the kings and big priests took care of the big deities, ordinary people had their own ordinary gods. Villages had little village temples with regular guys serving as priests in addition to their day jobs. Each house had its little shrine to the family's favorite gods. Some popular ones were Ptah, the god of craftsmen, and Thoth, the god of writing. People would also worship the founders of their village.

Local areas had their own specialty deities. An area with a big poisonous snake problem could worship snake goddesses such as Meretseger. For good measure, people would put clay snakes down by their doors; not only would this keep snakes away, but it would also prevent nightmares.

Some charming prescriptions

If an Egyptian got sick, he or she would call in a priest or a doctor — often the same person. The priest/doctor would observe the patient, diagnose the problem, and consult his medical references to come up with a treatment.

Therapies included prayers, spells, medical procedures, or herbs. They had spells and prescriptions to treat pain, diseases of the eye, and other ailments.

Individual Egyptians would also treat themselves. For example, archaeologists have found a piece of papyrus with a spell against the headache-demon written on it. Evidently its owner would fold it up and put it on his headrest before going to sleep, hoping in this way to ward off headaches.

Protecting life and battling death: Childbirth

One of the most common medical concerns was childbirth, always somewhat dangerous for both mother and child. The demons that plagued Egyptians in general were especially likely to congregate around the house if someone was giving birth.

To avoid them, the mother would retire to a special secluded place to give birth and would spend the first couple of weeks after delivery there. This place, now known as a *birth box,* was a rectangular room with an opening on the side; on the walls were painted the images of the god Bes and the goddess Tawaret, both of whom helped women in childbirth. The goddess Hathor was also invited to the birth.

While the mother labored, her attendants worked on frightening off the demons, setting out figurines, banging ivory clappers, and drawing circles around the mother and, later, the baby with magic knives made from hippopotamus tusks. They would say various spells that seemed appropriate, such as a spell to release a child from its mother's belly or a spell to protect a child on the day of its birth. Attendants used other spells to restore the mother's health.

Mobile community oracles

Although ordinary folks didn't go into temples, the gods would sometimes come out to see them. For major festivals, the priests would dress up the statues of the gods and take them out on a parade. People danced and sang and vendors along the route sold food; the priests and gods had special rest stops along the route.

This was everyone's chance to ask the god a question. As the procession approached, a person would jump into the road in front of the god's statue and ask for a consultation. If the priests declared that the god agreed, the parade would stop and everyone would listen to the petitioner's question, which had to be a yes or no type, such as, "Should I buy this cow" or "Is my husband cheating on me?" If the god (carried by the priests) stepped forward, the answer was yes; a step backward meant no.

Animal cults

Most of the Egyptian deities were associated with some animal or other. Different animals embodied particular qualities — the lion was strong, the falcon fast and far-seeing — and the Egyptians matched animals with the personalities of their gods and goddesses.

At a place called Saqqara lies a huge burial complex filled with mummified animals. All the animals were identified with particular cults — baboons, cats, cows, dogs, hawks, and ibises (an ibis is a kind of bird). The ancient Egyptians would make pilgrimages there to make offerings to their gods. They would buy the deity's animal of choice and pay to have it mummified and placed in one of the underground galleries. They could also pay the priest to have a dream consultation with the god Thoth, though sometimes they would have to wait several days for the god's response.

Another popular animal cult was that of the Apis bull, which originated in the earliest dynasties. The Apis bull was considered a manifestation of the god Ptah, the creator of the city of Memphis (see above for more about Ptah). There was only one Apis at a time. He had to be black with a white diamond-shaped mark on his forehead. He lived a life of luxury served by special priests and spent his days performing oracles and prophecies (by doing basic bull things, which the priests would interpret) and making public appearances.

When the Apis bull died, everyone in Egypt mourned. The corpse would be embalmed and mummified and then buried in a gigantic sarcophagus with little trinkets to serve the bull in the afterlife.

Snakes and scorpions were associated with chaos, the dangers that constantly threatened civilized life. Egyptians had tons of spells to combat snakebites and scorpion stings.

Death and the Afterlife

The Egyptians took death seriously. They built elaborate tombs to protect their spirits after death, preserved their bodies so that they would remain intact, and communicated with ancestors. They all hoped to be reborn after death to spend time with the gods Ra and Osiris.

The dead had direct access to the gods and could intervene on behalf of their relatives, so people would set up household shrines to their ancestors and make offerings to them. They would write letters to their ancestors asking for help on all manner of problems — marital affairs, legal difficulties, and requests for children. Sometimes they just wrote to say "hi."

Or people would become convinced that their dead relatives were making trouble for them. For instance, a man in 1200 BCE became convinced that his bad luck was the doing of his dead wife. He wrote her a letter reminding her what a good husband he had been, insisting that it wasn't his fault that she died while he was away on business.

At night when people slept, they visited the world of the dead in their dreams. Of course, it's hard to know what to make of dreams, so some people established themselves as expert dream interpreters. The interpretations were a lot like modern horoscopes — vague enough so that people could see whatever they wanted in them.

Mummies and rebirth

All Egyptians wanted to be reborn after they died, and mummification was an important part of this. Without a physical body, a dead person's spirit would go hungry and be unable to find peace in the afterlife. Before a body was embalmed, people considered it an empty shell; but after mummification and a funeral, the dead person would be "reanimated" and could partake of offerings from his or her family.

Some of the earliest mummies formed when bodies buried shallowly in the desert sand dried out before they rotted. But this wasn't a reliable method, so the Egyptians worked out some more elaborate techniques. There were several forms of mummification, some more complicated and expensive than others. Basically, the embalmer would lay out the body, remove the brain through the nose with an iron hook, and pull the internal organs out through an incision in the body's side. The organs went into special containers that were protected by the gods. The embalmer packed the body with *natron* (a kind of salt) to dry it out. After forty days or so, the embalmer removed the natron, washed the body, coated it with oils and resins, and wrapped it in several hundred yards of linen.

The Book of the Dead

The trip to Osiris, king of the dead, was perilous. Monsters and traps lurked all along the way. A famous Egyptian document, *The Book of the Dead,* told people what they had to do to run the gauntlet and reach Ra's sun boat and the *Field of Reeds,* the Egyptian version of heaven.

The way to Osiris had several gates. The Egyptians imagined that they would encounter rivers, islands, deserts, and lakes of fire. Wealthy people had spells inscribed onto their coffins to help them through all this.

After a person got to Osiris, he had to declare himself innocent or guilty of various crimes. Anubis led the person to a set of scales and weighed his or her heart on it. The counterweight was a feather from the goddess of truth. If the heart weighed more than the feather, the person was obviously guilty, and a female monster called the Devourer of the Dead would summarily eat the deceased. This scene is shown in Figure 17-4. Anyone who passed the test got to move among the gods or even ride in the sun boat.

Figure 17-4:
Anubis
weighing
a soul.

Chapter 18

Land of a Thousand Gods: India

• •

• •

*I*ndia is a huge country with a very large and diverse population. Over the centuries, it has been home to an enormous number of deities and religious sects. India is also known for its religious tolerance; all of these religions have coexisted fairly peacefully throughout the ages.

A lot of Indian beliefs come from its geography and climate. The entire land has three basic seasons: a cool season from October to February, a hot season from late February to May, and a wet season from late May to September. The hot season is dreadfully hot and life slows way down. The wet monsoon season is a time of joy and abundance with great significance for Hindus. The land turns green and it's the season of rebirth. In the fall, the rain stops and the harvest is gathered. Indian people celebrate their major festivals. Myths and rituals both reflect this cyclical existence, which is fertile but unpredictable.

Though there have been people in India for millennia, their recorded mythology starts around 1500 BCE with the warlike Aryan invaders and their Vedic myths. A few centuries later, Vedic beliefs were gradually replaced by Hinduism, an immensely complicated body of deities and stories that's still widely practiced today. India also produced other religions, including Buddhism and Jainism.

The Vedic Invaders

Around 1500 BCE, India was invaded by a horde of light-skinned barbarians from the northwest. They called themselves *Aryans*. They were warlike and despised people with darker skins. They quickly conquered the dark-skinned natives of the Indus valley, who moved down south.

The Vedic religion had a highly developed mythology and a bunch of gods. Above the gods were abstract forces such as *Rta,* the force of order that coordinated the cosmic and the human. People prayed to the gods to ask for favors — material goods and long life — and also to maintain the natural order and keep the universe functioning as it should.

Creation of the world, animals, and people

Vedic mythology didn't exactly have a creation story. Instead, it had several myths explaining how order arose out of primordial chaos. Some of these stories used animal or human (or whatever) sacrifice as a metaphor for creation. For example, in one Vedic hymn the primal being Purusha was sacrificed and his dismembered body parts became all the aspects of the universe: the Vedic gods, the atmosphere, heaven, earth, animals, and humans. The parts that were left over constituted immortality in heaven.

Then there were stories of the *Golden Germ* or *Embryo,* which was an egg representing the world floating on the waters of chaos. The first deity rose out of this egg and formed the rest of the world. In one version of this story, the god Prajapati produced several children by himself, including his daughter Dawn. Eventually, he was overcome with lust for her and tried to rape her. She turned into a deer and ran away, and Prajapati turned into a stag. In this shape, he ejaculated on the ground, creating the first humans. In other versions, Prajapati and his daughter mated with one another in various animal forms, and she gave birth to all the different creatures on earth.

In some myths, Heaven and Earth are the divine parents of everything. In others, the divine carpenter Tvashtr, a minor Vedic god, created Heaven and Earth and everything else.

Warlike gods for a warlike people

The Vedic deities were called the *Devas.* Most of them were male, and they were very humanlike. Though their numbers varied, there were often 33 of them, evenly divided between heaven, atmosphere, and earth. Each had different responsibilities. They often used their powers to help humans, especially warriors.

Indra, the warrior chief

Indra was the best-known Vedic deity. He was the god of the atmosphere, huge, handsome, and strong — a great warrior. Indra was the child of Heaven and Earth, and separated them from one another in his position in the atmosphere. He often acted as the head of the Vedic deities, though he wasn't actually their king.

Indra spent all his time fighting battles, and the Aryans thought he helped them fight theirs; he was the special sponsor of the Aryan warrior class. He liked to drink *soma,* an intoxicating drink that made him swell to giant size and able to perform mighty deeds. In addition to defeating the hostile Asuras (see the "Devas versus Asuras and churning the ocean" section later in the chapter), he killed the evil snake Vritra with his thunderbolt. This deed separated land from water and made the sun rise every morning.

In later Hindu mythology, Indra turned into the god of rain. He lost a lot of his grand stature; the Hindu deities didn't think much of his warrior abilities, and he sometimes found himself humiliated and punished for his misdeeds. (In one story, Indra seduced a wise man's wife, and his testicles fell off as punishment.)

Varuna, the old king

Varuna was Indra's chief rival among the Vedic deities. He seems to have once been the head of the gods, but Indra gradually ousted him. He guarded the cosmic order and represented the static and orderly aspects of kingship, as opposed to the warrior-like and chaotic aspects that Indra espoused.

Devas versus Asuras and churning the ocean

One famous myth describes a contest between the Devas, the deities who help humans, and the *Asuras,* their opponents, sort of anti-gods. The two groups held a contest to see who would get the *amrita,* the elixir of immortality. They used a giant snake named *Vasuki* as a rope to stir up the ocean, the Asuras holding the head and the Devas the tail.

Turning the snake like a jump-rope, they churned the ocean into butter and the earth started to fall apart. Their churning created the sun, the moon, the goddess of fortune, and the divine doctor Dhanvantari, who had the elixir (which was the prize but evidently didn't exist until the contest started). The Devas were declared the winners; the Asura Rahu stole a drop, but the god Vishnu decapitated him as he swallowed it. That drop symbolized the moon, and its waxing and waning came from the drop of *amrita* disappearing and reappearing in Rahu's throat.

Memorized mythology: The Vedas

The Aryans didn't write down their mythology. Instead, their priests memorized and taught one another the sacred songs and prayers, called *Vedas.* These are some of the most important Vedas:

- ✔ *Rigveda:* This was the first of the Vedic hymn collections and is the best-known. It was written around the middle of the second millennium BCE in archaic Sanskrit. The god Indra features prominently in these hymns.

- ✔ *Sutras:* These are texts describing the practices of particular sects.

> ✔ *Bramanas:* These contain formulas to be recited during ceremonies, along with explanations and commentaries.
>
> ✔ *Upanishads,* or **"Equivalences":** These were written toward the end of the Vedic period, around the fourth century BCE. They use parables to explain that the *atman,* or individual soul, is identical with *Brahman,* or the universal soul.

Vedic religious practice also included many rites that weren't written down, secret rites that worshippers performed deep in the forest. These rites formed the beginning of some of the more mysterious teachings of later Hinduism (see the following section called "Hinduism: Room for Many Gods"), and were the origin of its emphasis on renunciation of the physical world.

The Aryans loved to make sacrifices of the burnt offering sort. Worshippers would conduct rituals, say prayers, and finally burn their offering in a fire. The offering could be plant or animal; most often it was the soma plant, which Vedic worshippers used to make an intoxicating drink. The point of the sacrifice was to enter into communication with the divine world.

Hinduism: Room for Many Gods

Hinduism gradually replaced and transformed the Vedic religion (see the preceding section "Memorized mythology: The Vedas"). The Hindu philosophy of life arose from peoples' perceptions of nature. The land could be abundant but then suddenly barren; creation and destruction, extreme climate, earthquakes, and constant invasions by barbarians made any state of existence precarious and impermanent. So people reasoned that everything they saw and felt in the world was only an illusion. They thought that some more powerful and eternal force must be based somewhere within the spirit.

Sources of Hindu myths

The first texts to explain Hinduism were the *Great Epics,* notably the *Mahabarata* and the *Ramayana,* which contain a huge amount of religious and mythic information. The *Mahabarata* is kind of like the Greek *Iliad,* a collection of war stories mixed with mythological scenes and moral lessons.

Most Hindu myths are in a collection called the *Puranas,* or "Antiquities," which was composed around the fourth century CE. The *Puranas* explain Hindu religious practices, mythology, and cosmology, mixed with information on more secular subjects.

Hindu myths were written in a language called *Sanskrit,* which was the language people used when they wanted their writing to be readable all across India. India is a large place and people spoke many different languages and dialects, but Sanskrit functioned as an international language (or *lingua franca*), much the way Latin did in Europe.

The creation of the world and Brahma, the creator

Brahma was the creator god and the god who would grant favors. He spent most of his time meditating, and while he meditated, he created the elements of the universe. His lifespan was identical to the duration of the universe (see the following section "The longest year?"). Brahma didn't do much besides meditate, and generally Hindus worshipped Vishnu and Shiva instead of him.

Brahma was usually depicted with five heads facing in all directions. He took on this characteristic when his beautiful daughter walked around him in a circle. Although at the time he had only one head, he now sprouted some new ones, the better to stare at her loveliness. He and his daughter had a son called Manu, the first man.

One reason Brahma was less popular than other gods is that people preferred a more personal and less philosophical form of worship. And, perhaps, most Indian people didn't see any reason to worship the sponsor of the ruling caste and guardians of tradition. Another reason was that he tended to grant favors too readily, like the time he granted invulnerability to a demon named Hiranyakashipu, who proceeded to terrorize the universe until Vishnu's man-lion avatar disemboweled him.

The longest year?

Brahma's life cycle had an important significance to Hindus. Hindus saw time in terms of vast cycles that repeated throughout eternity. These cycles included smaller ones such as the yearly renewal of the crops and the massive cycle of Brahma's life. His life was supposed to last 100 Brahmanic years, and each of those equaled 311.04 trillion (311,040,000,000,000) human years. (We'll let you figure that one out in dog years.)

Movin' on up to the Brahma side

Brahma was linked with the caste of *Brahmans,* the highest caste in Hindu society (see the later section "Knowing your place: The caste system"). He was also linked with the concept of *Brahman,* an impersonal abstraction of the union with the absolute, one of the more rarified forms of religious belief.

The big gods: Some okay guys

Hinduism had a ton of gods and goddesses, and we won't attempt to name them all. Its three major gods formed a sort of trinity: Brahma, Vishnu, and Shiva (although Vishnu was more than just himself; he also took the form of other creatures and gods, including the god-prince Krishna). See the preceding section for the scoop on Brahma.

Vishnu, the protector

Vishnu was the guardian of humanity and the protector of the *dharma,* the concept of cosmic order. At the beginning of the universe, he made three giant strides that marked the boundaries of the world for deities and humans. A good friend of the warrior god Indra (see the earlier section "Indra, the warrior chief"), Vishnu was also a friend to humans, always willing to grant favors to his worshippers.

Vishnu often came to earth to help out, especially when humans were threatened by evil. But he never came just as himself, preferring to take different forms called *avatars.* Most Hindus agree that there were ten avatars, although they didn't agree on exactly *who* they were. The ten avatars of Vishnu were:

- **Matsya,** the fish, protected the first man from the great flood that destroyed the world.

- **Kurma,** the tortoise, held Mount Mandara on his back when the gods were churning the ocean.

- **Varaha,** the boar, raised the earth out of the ocean with his tusk.

- **Narasimha,** the man-lion, killed the demon Hiranyakashipu.

- **Vamana,** the dwarf, saved the world from the demon Bali. Vishnu visited the demon as a dwarf and asked for as much land as he could cover in three strides. When the demon said yes, Vishnu turned into a giant and took back the entire universe.

- **Parashurama,** the Brahman, killed the hundred-headed Arjuna, destroyed the warrior class, and killed his own mother.

- **Rama** was the hero of the *Ramayana* and was (and still is) one of the most popular avatars; he had his own cult. His bravery in fighting demons and his compassion toward everyone, even to his foes, made him an example that Hindu parents held up for their sons to emulate.

- **Krishna** was another major figure in Hindu myth. See the next section for more about him.

- The **Buddha** helped punish the sinful; he's a bit different from the Buddhist idea of the Buddha.

✔ **Kalin,** the future avatar, will appear as a warrior on a white horse (or as a white horse) and will establish a new era.

Krishna

Krishna, Vishnu's eighth avatar, was a great favorite in India. Before Krishna was born, the king of his country heard a prophecy that Krishna would kill him. The king imprisoned Krishna's pregnant mother to prevent that from happening, but Krishna's parents smuggled him away after his birth. He was an adorable infant, always stealing butter for a snack and killing snakes and female demons. When he grew up, he killed two more demons and the king who imprisoned his mother.

Everyone loved Krishna. His skin was the beautiful blue of rain-bearing clouds, and he sparkled with jewels. He symbolized the link between nature, the land, and the faith of the people. He was the god of cattle and spent much of his time cavorting with the cow-girls in his native land. One night, he duplicated himself many times so that he could make love to a whole crowd of them.

Hindus have revered the cow for centuries. Aryans measured their wealth in terms of cows. Even today, cows are sacred in many parts of India.

Krishna's most famous speech was the *Bhagavad-gita,* or "Celestial Song," at the end of the *Mahabarata.* In the poem, the warrior Arjuna was about to start fighting a battle, but hesitated, wondering if it was okay to kill his relatives. Krishna, his charioteer, assured him that it was, promising him that everyone had to act according to his duty — no second thoughts were allowed. Life and death were an illusion, so duty was everything; if it was time to kill, then get killing!

Some historians think the *Bhagavad-Gita* was written after the *Mahabarata* and inserted into the larger work. Its message is a pretty clear justification for the caste system — do your duty and don't ask why.

Shiva, the sexy destroyer

Shiva was known as the destroyer of the universe and can be seen in Figure 18-1. He was aloof, far removed from humanity, and often depicted sitting alone on a tiger skin on top of Mount Kailas in the Himalayas, deep in meditation. He also was called Lord of the Dance, being seen as a four-armed man dancing on the back of a dwarf. The drum that beat his dance time was said to beat the rhythm of the universe. He wore a necklace of skulls, a garland of snakes, and had a third eye in the middle of his forehead.

Figure 18-1:
Shiva the destroyer.

Shiva represented the erotic side of life, and was often depicted as a *linga,* a phallic statute. (His tall hairstyle was pretty phallic, too.) Shiva once disguised himself and went into the forest where some wise men were meditating. The men thought Shiva wanted to seduce their wives, so they cursed him and his penis fell off. In retaliation, Shiva made the world grow dark and cold, and his attackers all became impotent. They didn't recover their virility until they built a *linga* as compensation to the offended god.

The goddesses: A mixed bag of tricks

Hinduism was rife with goddesses, too. Some were powerful warrior women, while others embodied more conventional female virtues.

Devi, the every-goddess

The goddess Devi was really a composite of various goddesses. She was linked with Shiva's main wife Sati/Pavarti. Devi also comprised some more fearsome goddesses:

- **Durga** was the warrior goddess, whose main job was to fight demons. She spurned all suitors. When she got angry, the terrifying goddess Kali sprang from her forehead. (See "Kali, the dark one" later in this chapter for more about her.) She and Kali were associated with Shiva, as his darker consorts.

- **Sitala:** She was the goddess of smallpox and other skin diseases.

- **Manasa:** She was the Bengali goddess of snakes.

- **Hariti** and **Shashti:** They were goddesses of childbirth.

> ✔ **Mata:** The mother goddess. She was associated with the earth and great rivers such as the Ganges. She nourished her worshippers, but also could bring death and disease.

Devi, in all her myriad forms, was one of Hinduism's major deities.

Shri/Lakshmi, goddess of prosperity

Shri was Vishnu's wife (or consort). She was born back in Vedic times when the gods churned the ocean with the snake Vasuki. She gradually became the ideal of the perfect Hindu wife — loyal and submissive.

Shri played an important role as an agricultural fertility goddess. When she sat next to Indra (see the earlier section "Indra, the warrior chief"), he poured down rain to make the crops grow. Her presence in Vishnu's life (see the earlier section "Vishnu, the protector") guaranteed the fertility of the earth.

Sati/Pavarti

Sati, the daughter of the cattle god Daksha, was Shiva's (see the earlier section "Shiva, the sexy destroyer") original wife. One day, all the gods were going to a sacrifice arranged by her father — all except for Shiva, who hadn't been invited. She told Shiva that she was ashamed because he wasn't included in the sacrificing party. She thought he was the best god of them all and ought to go. So Shiva attacked the sacrificing party. A drop of sweat fell from his forehead and a short, hairy man emerged from it: Disease.

Sati was so ashamed of Shiva's being excluded from the sacrifice that she burned herself to death. She was reincarnated as Pavarti (also known as Uma) and underwent great hardship to win Shiva back, refusing to be deterred by his uncouth behavior. Eventually she reclaimed him as her husband.

Once Pavarti had Shiva in her clutches, she went to work civilizing him and introducing him to family life. Many of the myths about Shiva and Pavarti feature little domestic details, such as their son Skanda playing with Shiva's skull necklace. The couple squabbled like any husband and wife. Shiva teased Pavarti about her dark skin, which she tried to lighten (in one story, she discarded her skin, which turned into Kali — see the following section called "Kali, the dark one"). This may have been a reflection of earlier Aryan prejudices against dark-skinned people — see the earlier section "The Vedic Invaders."

Pavarti and Shiva's son Skanda was conceived the first time they made love. The other gods interrupted them before they were finished, and Shiva's semen spilled out onto the ground. The gods passed it from one to the other, but it was too hot to handle. Finally it ended up in the Ganges, where it grew into Skanda. Little Skanda fought the demon Taraka and rescued the world and later became the general of the gods.

Pavarti accepted Skanda as her son, but she wanted a child of her own, too. So she collected the rubbings that came from her body as she bathed and formed them into her son Ganesh. She put him on guard outside her bedroom, but when he denied entrance to Shiva, Shiva knocked his head off. Pavarti demanded that Shiva give her son a new head, so he looked around and gave him the first head he saw — an elephant's! See Ganesh in Figure 18-2.

Figure 18-2:
Ganesh, remover of great obstacles.

© David Cumming; Eye Ubiquitous/CORBIS

Ganesh is still a popular Hindu god; he's the one who removes great obstacles. His brother Skanda is a favorite in southern India.

Kali, the dark one

Kali's job was to destroy demons. She was an ugly dark hag, with long fangs and a necklace of human skulls. She spent most of her time on battlefields or at cremation sites and sometimes became so intoxicated with blood that she'd try to destroy the entire world.

Shrines and statues everywhere

Some Hindu worship practices were (and still are) down-to-earth. Not only do many Hindu myths portray deities in human activities — baby Krishna stealing butter (see "Krishna" section earlier in this chapter), Ganesh protecting his mother, Shiva and Pavarti having domestic squabbles (see "Sati/Pavarti" earlier in this chapter) — but Hindus brought their gods right into their houses. They'd keep small statues of the deities and took care of them like beloved children, bathing, dressing, feeding them, and putting them to bed at night. They believed that the spirit of the god came to live in the statue and treating it kindly was one way of showing reverence.

Hindus also went to worship at shrines dedicated to particular deities. Hindu temples swarmed with colorful painted and sculpted images, flowers, food, and incense offered to the deities. Worship included chants, bells, drums, and dances, and sometimes the people carried their gods out in the streets in colorful, noisy processions. At certain times of the day, they engaged in a ritual called *darshan,* in which the shrine was opened and the people gazed directly into the eyes of the god. They believed that at that moment the god was looking back at them.

Hindus observed a number of festivals. They worshipped the goddess Durga (see the "Devi, the every-goddess" section earlier in this chapter) for nine days in October; the festival of lights called *Diwali* happened at the same time. *Holi* was a spring festival honoring Krishna (see "Krishna" earlier in this chapter). People also made pilgrimages to sacred sites, especially the Ganges River.

Life after life: What you sow is what you reap

Hindus believe that after a person dies, his or her soul immediately flies into another body that is being born. The new body doesn't have its own soul yet, and is ready to receive one from a newly dead person. Thus, a person who dies will immediately be born again. This process, the rebirth of a soul in another body, is called *reincarnation.* In Hindu belief, this cycle of birth, life, death, and rebirth goes on for eons.

Karma is the sum of a person's accumulated good and bad deeds and determines what happens in the next life. A Hindu can improve his or her karma by doing pure acts, thinking pure thoughts, and performing devotions — this can help them get reborn at a higher level. Likewise, someone who commits many sins can be reborn at a lower level or even as an animal. So the inequalities in life are nothing to worry about, and the privileged certainly don't need to feel guilty about their good fortune — all wealth, privilege, and suffering are the natural consequences of a person's good and bad acts in this life and in previous ones. The ultimate goal of life is to rack up so many karmic points that you don't get reborn at all but instead achieve enlightenment.

Hindus organize their lives around certain activities that are the goals of Hinduism. Righteousness in religious life is the most important. Material prosperity and gratification of the senses are also significant. Hindus who have renounced the world strive for liberation from the unending cycle of rebirth. Much of Hindu religious practice is aimed at achieving this higher internal reality. Prayer, meditation, and practices such as yoga are all methods to help believers focus on their inner world.

Competing Religions: Buddhism and Jainism

India never has had just one religion or one body of myths. It's always been incredibly tolerant, a fine place to worship and fertile ground for new religious thought. Buddhism and Jainism were two of the most important belief systems to come out of India. They both preached renunciation of worldly things, but in very different ways; the Buddha emphasized moderation in all things, but the Jains went all the way with the renunciation business — some of them even gave up clothes!

Buddhism and its start in India

Buddhism isn't practiced much in India these days; most Buddhists live in China and other parts of Asia. But it got its start in India, so we'll discuss its origins here.

Buddha and the journey to enlightenment

Legend has it that Siddhartha, the founder of Buddhism, was born to noble parents who decided that he should never see anything unpleasant so that his entire life would be happy. (He was born in Nepal around 563 BCE.) They raised him in a sheltered environment with all available luxuries, and he grew up and married.

The founder of Buddhism's full name was Siddhartha Gautama. Many English sources refer to him as Gautama; if you see the name Gautama in a discussion of Buddhism, relax, because he's the same person as the Siddhartha described here.

One day, the young prince went walking outside. For the first time in his life, he saw a sick person, an old person, and a dead person — all very shocking to his worldview. Then he saw a wandering holy man — intriguing. He became obsessed with suffering and ways to avoid it. At the age of 29, he left his wife and child and set off in search of truth.

Siddhartha embraced the ascetic life, starving and meditating and mortifying his flesh, and apparently was quite successful at it, even acquiring some disciples of his own. After a few years, though, he suddenly decided that this path, called *asceticism,* wasn't the path to truth, and he really didn't know what was.

So he abandoned his practice of discomfort, got something to eat, and sat down in the shade of a tree — the famous Bodhi Tree — resolving to sit there until he knew what life was all about. He meditated for 49 days, tormented by demons, but in the end, he achieved his ultimate goal — enlightenment! At this point he became the Buddha, the Enlightened One.

Do some moderation and don't suffer

He found his former disciples in the village of Sarnath, near the holy city of Benares, and there he preached his first sermon. His advice was surprising: He argued that moderation in all things was the key to avoiding suffering. People suffer when they can't have what they want, so the way to avoid that was to abandon all desire. The way to do that was to avoid extremes — though too much pleasure was unnecessary, too much self-denial was worthless because it only increased desire. He also claimed that reality was an illusion and that the universe was constantly changing. Because everything was transient, there could be no eternal soul, and therefore no reincarnation and no immortality.

Buddha listed eight rules, or *precepts,* for his believers to live by:

- Right views
- Right intention
- Right speech
- Right conduct
- Right livelihood
- Right effort
- Right recollection
- Right meditation

Buddhism didn't limit believers to any particular set of religious doctrines but instead aimed at transcending dogma and teaching a practical wisdom that could help humans attain an ideal state. Those who wished to become free from suffering had to free themselves from all attachments by following the eight precepts and meditating. Only then would they be able to attain perfect freedom or *Nirvana*.

Jainism: Give it up!

The Jains had their own version of Hindu mythology. Their history of the universe centered on 63 spiritual leaders called the *Shalakapurashas* and a number of saviors. They also had heroes whose stories resembled those of Krishna.

They saw the underworld as having seven layers and believed that cosmic time revolved on a wheel, alternating periods of prosperity and difficulty.

Another journey with a different ending

Around the same time that Buddha was enlightening his followers (see the preceding section "Buddha and the journey to enlightenment"), another young nobleman was creating his own sect that was nothing like Buddhism. Vardhamana, founder of the Jain sect, was born around 540 BCE. Like Siddhartha, he left his wife and child to seek truth.

Vardhamana joined a sect that practiced radical self-denial; he gave up all his possessions, keeping nothing but one robe to wear. After 12 years of wandering around seeking truth, he didn't even have that. And it was at that point, starving and naked, that he reached enlightenment.

The first vegan

Vardhamana adopted the name *Mahavira,* which means "Great Hero," and began to preach a doctrine of self-denial. His followers went naked and plucked out their beards. He refused to kill any animal, even insects, and even avoided onions because they might contain tiny, invisible creatures.

Mahavira spent the rest of his life proselytizing and increasing the membership of his sect, which caught on fairly well. Today in India, there are about two million Jains.

Chapter 19

China: Tao . . . Wow!

In This Chapter

▶ Creating the world the Chinese way

▶ Going with the flow Taoist style

▶ Following the rules of Confucianism

▶ Seeking enlightenment through Buddhism

China is a big place, and it has been civilized for a long time. Such a land is bound to have a bounty of deities, myths, and religious beliefs, including many ancient and mysterious stories about the origins of the earth and humankind.

China has three main religions — the "three teachings" of Taoism, Confucianism, and Buddhism. The Chinese blended these systems of belief: Most people had no problem blending the morals from Confucianism, the life philosophy of Taoism, and the idea of the afterlife from Buddhism. These belief systems work together and complement one another, creating a satisfying blend of religion and myth. In this chapter, we discuss ancient Chinese myths and the way the three more modern belief systems influenced Chinese mythology and ritual.

How the World Began and Where Folks Came From

More than 2,000 years ago, Chinese philosophers and scholars began writing down the traditional stories of how the world began and where people came from. But long before that, people had been passing the stories from generation to generation in the old-fashioned way — orally. Existing written versions of the oldest Chinese myths date from the third and fourth centuries BCE, but the stories themselves are considerably older.

These stories describe the formation of the earth, the creation of people, and the idea that the solar system has one sun rather than ten suns. And like most bodies of myth, China has a flood story, too.

Pan Gu, the first man

In the beginning, the universe was an egg. The egg split open; the top half, the lighter parts of the egg, became the sky, and the bottom half, with all the heavier, opaque egg parts, became the earth. The sky was called yang and the earth yin, of the yin/yang opposition; see "Effortless Effort: The Myths of Taoism" later in this chapter for more about that. Pan Gu, the first human, also emerged from the broken egg; people said he was the child of yin and yang.

Every day, Pan Gu grew ten feet. And each day that he grew, he pushed apart the earth and sky, so the sky grew ten feet higher and the earth became ten feet thicker. After 18,000 years, the earth and sky were in their proper places, and Pan Gu died.

His body split into many pieces, which all turned into parts of the world. His right eye became the moon, and his left eye, the sun. His blood became the rivers and seas; his hair, the forests; his sweat, the rain; his breath, the wind; and his voice, thunder. The rest of his body made rocks, rivers, plants, and mountains. Even the fleas on his body transformed — they turned into humans.

A melon goddess flings some mud: The first people

In yet another creation myth, Nü Gua was the creator goddess. She and the creator god Fu Xi were sometimes depicted as a married couple with human heads and snakes' tails. Their names come from Chinese words meaning "melon" or "gourd," a prominent symbol of fertility in Chinese culture.

Molded from mud

Nü Gua created humans out of mud. Once the earth was created, she moved down there but felt that something was missing from her life. One day, after glimpsing her reflection in a pool, she came up an idea. She grabbed some mud, sculpted a little statue of a creature that looked like her, and brought it to life. She created the first human.

The goddess liked her little creation, so she made some more humans. They all built homes and lived their lives, and Nü Gua didn't feel lonely anymore. She wanted to make some more people, but sculpting each one by hand was slow work. So, she came up with a more efficient method; she dipped a vine in the mud and flicked it so droplets flew off all over the place. Each tiny drop turned into another human.

Now the world was populated, and Nü Gua could rest. But after a while, some of her little people grew old and died. Instead of making them herself, she taught them how to reproduce themselves.

Fire and water make steam

Nü Gua continued to protect her creations. But one day, the fire god and the water god got into a fight; the fire god had been ruling the universe, but the water god decided that he wanted the job. The water god sent all the oceans and rivers to fight for him, but the water evaporated in the heat of the fire god's sun.

The water god became furious, and in his rage, he knocked over the Imperfect Mountain, the mountain that held up the sky in the northwestern corner of the world. This left holes in both earth and sky, and the world tipped over, its southeast corner toward the bottom. The incident caused great natural disasters, forest fires, and floods. All the water rushed downhill toward the southeast — people said that explained why rivers in China ran west to east.

Nü Gua came to the rescue of her little humans. She filled the hole in the sky with some stones. To make sure that it wouldn't break again, she killed a giant tortoise and used its body to prop up the sky where the Imperfect Mountain had been. Then she fixed all the riverbanks, ending the floods.

Saved by a gourd: A flood story

In another flood story, a farmer was at home with his two children, a boy and a girl, when it started to rain. The farmer decided to try and catch the thunder god to stop the rain, so he got a cage and a big fork and stood waiting by his front door.

With a great flash of lightning and a loud crash, the thunder god flew down, holding a giant battle-axe. The farmer caught him on his fork, shoved him in the cage, and locked him in. The rain stopped.

The bitter fruit of small favors

The next day, the farmer went to the market to buy ingredients to cook the thunder god. He had told his children not to give the god anything to drink, no matter how much he pleaded. While the farmer was gone, the god began to beg for water, so piteously that the children finally gave him some.

As soon as the water touched his lips, the thunder god broke the bars of his cage. To repay the children for their help, he pulled a tooth from his mouth and told them to plant it in the ground. Then he left. The boy and the girl planted the tooth, and it grew into a gourd plant bearing the biggest gourd anyone had ever seen.

The wrath of the water god!

The rain came back, and it rained harder than ever, so hard that the ground began to flood. The children's father came home from the market and told his kids to get inside the gourd. He himself built a boat and sailed it up to heaven to ask the king of the gods to stop the flood.

The king of the gods asked the water god to give it a rest. The water god stopped the flood so suddenly that the farmer's boat crashed down on the ground, killing the farmer. The boy and the girl in the gourd, though, bounced on the ground and landed safely.

A second start for people

When the children climbed out of the gourd, they discovered that they were the only people left on earth. The boy asked his sister to marry him. At first, she was hesitant because they were so closely related, but then she said that she would marry him if he chased her and caught her. He did, and they lived happily ever after.

The girl eventually gave birth to a strange baby shaped like a ball of flesh. The pair sliced it up into many chunks and carried the pieces up the ladder toward heaven. A gust of wind blew the pieces of flesh all over the earth; when they landed, they turned into humans, and the earth was populated again.

Effortless Effort: The Myths of Taoism

Tao means "the way" or "the path." Tao regulates the universe, enveloping and flowing through everything. (Think about Obi-wan Kenobi's explanation of the Force in *Star Wars*.) Taoism is not a unified religion in the sense that

Christianity is, but instead is a combination of teachings and a philosophy of life.

Taoism was supposedly founded by Lao Tzu (his name has a bunch of different spellings in English, including Lao-Tse, Laozi, and so on.) Lao Tzu lived in the sixth century BCE, around the same time as Confucius (see the "Confucianism: Myths of Devotion" section later in this chapter for the scoop on him.). Lao Tzu advocated a search for balance and claimed that changes can't be forced, only experienced and assimilated.

Little or nothing is known about Lao Tzu's life and teachings. According to legend, he rode around on a water buffalo, spreading his idea. His teachings are supposedly summarized in the book *Tao Te Ching*, but it's entirely possible that someone else wrote it.

At first, Taoism was more like a school of philosophy than a religion, but it turned into China's state religion around 440 CE. Taoism remained popular in China, peacefully coexisting with Confucianism and Buddhism (see the "Buddhism" section later in this chapter), up until the twentieth century when the Communists took over China and religion experienced a major upheaval.

Harmony of opposites: The beliefs

Taoism emphasized the harmony of opposites, such as male/female, light/dark, love/hate, and good/evil. It depicted this harmony with the concept of yin and yang. *Yang* (associated with maleness) is the pure light breath that makes up heaven. *Yin* (associated with femaleness) is the heavier, opaque breath that forms the earth. Neither force can exist without the other.

Taoists believed that the universe was constantly re-creating itself and evolving. *Chi* was the fundamental energy that flowed through everything, animating the world; it also meant "breath," the life force flowing through all living things. They envisioned the world as a sphere divided in halves, with each half corresponding to yin or yang.

Taoism itself had no real gods, certainly none that anyone could pray to (although Lao Tzu assumed godlike status, which must have disgruntled his ghost to no end). Instead, Taoists were supposed to seek answers to the questions of life through observation and meditation.

But even though Taoism didn't have any official deities, most followers persisted in believing that spirits pervaded nature, gods reigned in heaven, and demons lurked in hell. They treated the gods in the same way that they treated secular officials, and they bribed the demons for better treatment.

Taoism was keenly interested in health and the body. Taoists saw the organs and orifices of the body as corresponding to the five parts of the sky: earth, metal, wood, fire, and water. Chi, or breath, was important to physical well-being. Traditional Chinese medical wisdom said that illness resulted when the chi became blocked in someone's body and various techniques were used to keep it flowing properly. The martial art *tai chi* was a means for keeping energy moving through the body and massaging the internal organs.

Taoists emphasized advance planning and thinking before acting through the art of *wu wei* (which loosely translated means "effortless effort"). They wanted to act through minimal action. In life, they tried not to struggle against the stream but instead to stand still and let the stream flow by them.

Taoists worked to develop virtue, especially compassion, moderation, and humility, and they believed that humans were inherently compassionate. They tried to be kind to others, believing that their kindness was likely to be reciprocated.

Facets of humanity and the eight immortals

The Eight Immortals were legendary humans who achieved immortality by following Taoism. They represented all aspects of humanity, including youth and age, male and female (though most of them were male), and wealth and poverty. Some of the Immortals may have been based on actual historical figures. They inspired art and drama, and their stories served as proof that anyone could become immortal if they only did the right things.

Each Immortal had his or her own story and significance. They represented different groups of people (for example, the nobility or single women) and carried objects (or symbols) that helped identify them.

Military man: Han Chung-li, the hermit

Han Chung-li was a nobleman who became a hermit in his old age; he could turn base metals into silver, and he gave the proceeds to the poor. He carried a peach (symbol of immortality) or a fan made of feathers, and he represented the military.

Here's how he became immortal: One day, while he sat meditating in his cave, the walls cracked open and revealed a chamber lit with strange light. Inside the small room was a jade casket that contained the secrets of immortality. After he followed the instructions he found there, the cave filled with music and perfume, and a magical stork flew in and carried him away on its back, off to the magical island of P'eng-lai.

Chang-kuo Lao, the magically reborn

Chang-kuo Lao had a white donkey that he rode backwards. He could actually fold this donkey up and put it in his pocket. He carried a peacock feather or a peach. He represented the old and brought the gift of fertility to young couples.

Chang-kuo Lao was an old man. He went to have dinner with the emperor one day, but he fell down dead at the temple gate and began to rot. But then he miraculously revived and noticed that he had magical powers: He could turn birds to stone, drink poison, and become invisible. After some years, he died (again) in his mountain retreat. His followers buried him, but when his tomb was opened later, his body wasn't inside — he had become one of the immortals.

Lifelong student: Lu Tung-pin and fleeting material success

Lu Tung-pin was a government official preoccupied with advancing his career. One day, he met the first Immortal, Han Chung-li, while the great man sat sipping wine at an inn. Chung-li saw that Lu Tung-pin was not only an official but also a philosopher, so he invited him to drink. The two men talked about the Tao until nightfall, and Lu Tung-pin fell asleep at the table. He dreamed that the emperor had promoted him to a high position, but his dream turned into a nightmare; he gained enemies who convinced the emperor to fire him, and he was exiled without home or family, wandering from village to village. Then he awoke and saw Chung-Li smiling at him.

Lu Tung-pin now realized that worldly possessions and status had nothing to do with true Taoism. The next day, Lu Tung-pin sent away his servants, cancelled his appointments, and went off with the wise man. He studied with Chung-li for years and finally became an Immortal himself. He traveled the world selling oil and occasionally granting immortality to others. He had a magic sword that could make him invisible, and he sometimes held a fly-whisk to symbolize the fact that he could fly. He represented students.

The nobility: Ts'ao Kuo-chiu gets a second chance

Ts'ao Kuo-chiu was the brother of Empress Ts'ao. He achieved immortality after some major sinning. His brother had tried to rape a young woman who was visiting the castle, and Ts'ao Kuo-chiu advised him to kill her. The brother threw her down a well. She managed to escape and run away, but then she had the bad luck to approach Ts'ao Kuo-chiu with her grievances.

He had her beaten with iron poles until she nearly died. She revived and went to the Imperial Censor, who had the brothers arrested.

The younger brother was executed for murder. But before the executioner could get to Ts'ao Kuo-chiu, the emperor declared an amnesty, and he was released from prison. Realizing that his life had been empty and evil, he became a hermit. As an Immortal, he carried a writing tablet and represented the nobility.

Who needs sick days?: Li T'ieh-kuai and the iron crutch

Li T'ieh-kuai, called "Li with the Iron Crutch," learned Tao from Lao Tzu himself (the founder of Taoism; see "Effortless Effort: the Myths of Taoism" section earlier in chapter). Before Li T'ieh-kuai died, he told his assistant that he might come back from heaven, so he shouldn't burn the body until seven days had passed. The assistant watched for six days and then heard that his mother was dying. He figured that Li T'ieh-kuai wouldn't be coming back after so long, so he burned the body and went to his mother.

When Li T'ieh-kuai's soul returned later that day, he found his body nothing but a pile of ashes. The only available body was that of a beggar, crippled and filthy, who had starved to death. Li T'ieh-kuai wanted to exchange the body for a better one, but Lao Tzu suggested that he keep it and gave him some helpful gifts: a gold headband, an iron crutch, and a gourd that could restore life. Li T'ieh-kuai went to his assistant's house, found him weeping over his mother's body, and restored her to life with the gourd. As an Immortal, he represented the sick; pharmacists put his picture on their signs.

Culture club: Han Yu and a fortunate fall

Han Yu was a great philosopher and poet; he taught about the three elements in human nature — the good, the evil, and the balanced. When he complained to the emperor about the Buddhist influence in the court, he was banished to the wilderness in Canton (a region in China, also called Guangzhou), where he helped the people by killing a dragon. He tried to climb the tree of immortality but fell out; conveniently, he became immortal just before hitting the ground. He represented culture and carried a flower basket.

There will always be the poor: Lan Ts'ai-ho, the simple minstrel

Lan Ts'ai-ho may have been a woman, or she may have been a man "who didn't know how to be a man." In any case, we refer to her as female here. Her family sold medicinal herbs. One day, she found an old beggar covered with sores and took care of him. The beggar was really Li T'ieh-kuai in disguise (see preceding "Who needs sick days?: Li T'ieh-kuai and the iron crutch" section), and Lan Ts'ai-ho's reward was eternal youth. (In another story, she [or he] drank so much that she passed out and was carried away on a cloud.)

She wandered around in a torn blue robe with only one shoe, and she did lots of crazy things such as sleeping in the snow in winter and wearing thermal underwear in the summer. She was a minstrel, singing in different towns and urging people to seek the Tao. She carried a lute (or a basket of fruit) and represented the poor.

It's okay to be single: Good girl Ho Hsien-ku

Ho Hsien-ku was the only Immortal who was definitely female. In the myth, she had only six hairs on her head, but pictures of her usually show a full head of hair. She achieved immortality after dreaming of going to the mother-of-pearl mountains, where she ground up and ate a pearl that made her immortal. After this transformation, she spent her time wandering around the mountains, picking berries for her mother. The emperor summoned her to court so that he could see the immortal woman, but she disappeared. She carried a lotus and represented single women.

Confucianism: Myths of devotion

The founder of Confucianism was a man called K'ung Fu Tzu (but we call him by his English name, Confucius) who was born in 551 BCE in what is now Shantung province.

Confucius made himself an expert on etiquette and behavior, and he spent much of his life wandering China and advising different rulers on how to behave. He was obsessed with eradicating the "moral laxity" that he perceived all around him.

Confucius wrote a number of works on individual morality and the proper methods of ruling and using political power. He emphasized several values, including etiquette, love within the family, righteousness, honesty, benevolence, and loyalty to the state. Confucianism is not exactly a religion per se, but more of a system of ethics; practitioners don't worship a Confucian deity, but instead apply Confucian principles to daily life.

Offering the willow branch: Everyone loves a funeral

Funerals were almost more elaborate than weddings. The relatives would cry out to inform their neighbors that one of them was dead, and then they put on clothing made of coarse material. Mourners would bring incense and money and would place food and other gifts in the coffin with the body. A priest (Taoist, Buddhist, or even Christian) would perform the funeral ceremony and everyone would go to the cemetery with the coffin, carrying willow branches to symbolize the soul of the dead. The family would take these branches back home afterward and put them on their home altar. The funeral wasn't over yet, though; they would have more ceremonies for the deceased on the 7th, 9th, and 49th days after the death and again on its first and third anniversaries.

Respecting elders and valuing family

Confucian philosophy put great importance on how people treated the elders in their families, especially parents and grandparents. Many stories in Chinese literature illustrated the proper way to treat elders. The story of the origin of silk illustrated a daughter's devotion to her father, and the tale of a son searching for his father's remains showed an extreme case of what children should do for their parents.

Lady Silkworm loved her daddy

There was a girl who loved her father very much, and she was sorry that he was away on business so often. One day, while she was grooming her stallion, she said, "I'd marry anyone who brought father home." The horse immediately dashed away. He returned the next day with her father, who was relieved to find nothing wrong at home. The girl couldn't explain the horse's behavior and suggested that he must have known that she missed her father.

For the next few days, the horse got very excited every time the girl walked by, and finally, she remembered what she had said just before he galloped away. She told her father, who was furious that a horse would dare think of marrying his daughter. He had the stallion killed and laid its skin in the sun to dry.

While the girl and her friends were playing around the skin, it suddenly wrapped itself around her and flew away. Her father found the horse skin on top of a tree; inside the skin was a caterpillar. His daughter had transformed into Lady Silkworm. She waved her head and emitted a glossy white thread, which made the most wonderful cloth in the world.

A boy and his father's bones

The young man Chou had never known his father, who had been working far away throughout his childhood. When he was thirteen, his father died in a far-off province. The family performed many funeral rituals, but they were worried that the rituals wouldn't be effective without a body. When Chou's grandparents died, they made him swear to go retrieve his father's bones.

After several years, Chou decided that he had to find his father's body, so he left all his money with his mother and started working his way across the countryside. Everywhere he went, people were impressed with his devotion to his father but tried to persuade him to go home to his mother because his journey would be terribly long, and surely, he would never be able to find the body after so many years.

But Chou journeyed onward. He faced bandits and civil unrest and nearly died of hunger and the plague, but he kept going. Finally, he came to the spot where his father was buried; by this time, his dad had been dead some 20 years. The local officials tried to tell him that he had done well enough but that actually finding his father's bones would be impossible after so much time. Chou vowed that if he didn't find the bones within two weeks, he would throw himself into the river. And at that very moment, he saw his father's tombstone.

Chou spent the night digging up the body. He cut skin from his arm to close his father's mouth, he burnt money and incense, and he wrapped each bone for the trip back home. The return voyage was considerably easier; a general had heard his story and gave him money so he could travel by boat. When he arrived at home, his mother greeted him joyfully. They buried the bones with the proper funeral rites. News spread about Chou's devotion, and even the emperor sent words of praise.

Buddhism

Buddhism came to China from India in the first century CE. The Chinese adapted it to their own mythology, intertwining it with their native beliefs.

A myth about the beginnings of Chinese Buddhism describes how Emperor Ming dreamed that he saw a golden man flying in front of him as he looked out the palace window. He told his ministers about this dream, and they said there wasn't a golden man in India who could fly. The emperor sent messengers to India to find the man; they returned with Buddhist scriptures.

The Chinese translated the Buddhist scriptures from Sanskrit (an Indian written language; see Chapter 18) into their own language. The translations weren't exactly faithful to the originals; the Chinese modified Buddhist beliefs to fit their own view of human existence, especially Confucian logic. Gautama, the Indian founder of Buddhism, had preached that only those who renounced worldly things would achieve salvation and enter Nirvana (Buddhist paradise; see Chapter 18), but the Chinese didn't like the idea of such a speculative (not to say spiritual) religion or the notion of giving up family ties. Eventually, Chinese Buddhism became more concrete and put more emphasis on relationships with others, especially the family and the hierarchy of society.

A deity or two

The Chinese worshipped a manifestation of Buddha called Amitabha. He granted salvation to anyone who repented their sins and called his name — that is, salvation was attained through faith alone, which made it easier for the average person to achieve. Temples throughout China had statues of Amitabha sitting on a lotus blossom.

Amitabha was often accompanied by the goddess of mercy, the Bodhisattva Guanyin. She had originally been a male Indian Bodhisattva, but the Chinese saw her as depicting motherly virtues and made her female. Mothers would pray to her to help their children. She once saved some holy books that a Chinese Buddhist was taking from India to China. She could also break chains, counteract lightning, and remove the venom from snakes.

A little Buddhism, a little Confucianism: The myths

The Chinese Buddhists embellished on the myths about the Buddha, often adding details about filial piety to appeal to the Confucian mindset. In one famous tale, a disciple of Buddha named Mulian traveled through the layers of hell seeking his mother, who was suffering torment for failing to donate to the Buddhist monks during her life. He found her in one of the deepest levels nailed to a bed. The jailer refused to release her without the Buddha's permission. Mulian found the Buddha, who agreed to release his mother. She returned to earth as a black dog. (She later turned back to a human.)

Originally, Buddhism was popular primarily with immigrants that came to China from India, but by the third century, it had spread among the Chinese common people. During the Tang dynasty (618 to 907 CE), many Chinese renounced the world and joined Buddhist communities. The Zen Buddhist sect grew especially popular in China around the thirteenth century; Chinese Zen was started by a Buddhist monk named Bodhidma, depicted in Figure 19-1.

Figure 19-1:
Bodhidma,
the Buddhist
monk who
began Zen
Buddhism
in China.

Chapter 20

Japan: Myths from the Land of the Rising Sun

....

In This Chapter

▶ Combining Shinto and Buddhism for a balanced spiritual life

▶ Creating the world and settling sibling disputes

▶ Meeting monsters, mythical beasts, and beautiful maidens

....

*J*apan has always been a bit isolated from the rest of Asia, a group of islands surrounded by water as it is. It has always had a habit of opening its doors for a time to import ideas from abroad, mostly from China and Korea, and then shutting them again to concentrate on turning these ideas into uniquely Japanese ones.

Japanese mythology reflects Japan's uniqueness; it's full of the creation of islands, deities who have children faster than rabbits, and outlandish creatures. At the same time, though, other mythical ideas made their marks on Japanese beliefs. Buddhism, Confucianism, and Taoism all influence Japanese myths, adding ideas of peace with nature, social order, and the possibility of salvation to the native Shinto concepts. To the Japanese mindset, there was no problem mixing and matching religious beliefs and myths; they made room for them all.

The Creation of Stuff and Other Ancient Matters

Most Japanese mythology comes from a document called the *Kojiki,* the "Record of Ancient Matters." It was composed in 711 CE by a man named Ono Yasumaro at the request of the Empress Gemmei. He used several earlier texts to put together his work, which was written in a mixture of Chinese and old Japanese. Other sources of myths include the *Nihonshoki* (Chronicle of Japan), written in 720, the *Kogoshui* (Gleanings from Ancient Stories) of 807, and an anthology of poetry called the *Manyoshu,* compiled around 760.

The first gods and the first people

In the beginning, the earth drifted like a jellyfish. Five gods appeared on the high plains of heaven (their names are far too long for this book); these were the *Separate Heavenly Deities*. Seven more generations of gods and goddesses followed. Finally there appeared the first couple: a man called Izanagi and his sister/wife Izanami.

The gods told the pair to solidify the land. So they stood on the Floating Bridge of Heaven and stirred the waters with a jeweled spear. As they lifted the spear out of the water, drops fell from it and these drops formed an island called Onogoro.

The first marriage: How does that go again?

Izanami and Izanagi went down to this island and built a palace and a pillar. This seemed as good a time as any to start reproducing, so Izanagi asked his sister how her body was made. She said that she was missing something in one place. Izanagi replied that that was a great coincidence, because he had a little extra something in the same place. He suggested that they get together and unite these two spots.

First, though, they had to get married. They made up their own marriage ceremony: they walked around the pillar in opposite directions and exchanged compliments when they met on the other side. Then they had sex.

Sadly, their first child was the deformed Hiruko, or leech-child. They put the baby in a boat and set it on the ocean, presumably to die. They asked the gods what had gone wrong, and the deities decided that the problem must have been that Izanami, the woman, had spoken first during their marriage ritual, when in fact her husband should have.

Fire hazard: Birth of the fire god

So the pair returned to their palace and pillar and redid their marriage ritual, only this time Izanagi spoke first when they met. As the gods had predicted, this time Izanami gave birth successfully to many fine children: these were the many islands that make up the Japanese *archipelago* (a word that means "group of islands"), and the gods and goddesses of trees, mountains, and wind.

Her last child was the fire god, Kagutsuchi. Unfortunately, his birth burned Izanami so badly that she died, though she produced more gods and goddesses as she was dying — they emerged from her vomit, urine, and feces. Her husband Izanagi wept bitterly, and his tears turned into more deities. In a fit of anger, he cut off the fire god's head, and still more divinities arose from the dead god's remains.

Izanagi's trip to the underworld

Izanami descended to *Yomi,* the underworld. Izanagi decided that he simply had to go see her and to try to bring her back to life. His wife met him at the entrance to Yomi. When he asked her to come back with him, she said she didn't think she could because she had already eaten the food of the dead, but she would discuss it with the other gods. She warned him not to look at her, and indeed he couldn't see her at all in the darkness.

But Izanagi couldn't stand the thought of not seeing his wife, so he lit a torch to get a look at her. Much to his dismay and disgust, she was a rotting corpse, writhing with maggots. Izanagi turned and ran.

Furious, Izanami sent her hags to chase him, along with some thunder gods and an army. Izanagi got to the pass that led back to the land of the living, and turned to throw three peaches at his pursuers. He saw that Izanami, now a terrifying demon, had joined them. Just as she was about to reach him, he pushed a huge boulder over the pass, stopping her. The two had a brief argument — Izanami claimed that her husband had sinned against Yomi, and promised to kill people out in the world, to which he replied that for every 1,000 she killed, he would bear 1,500 more. And that was the end of their close relationship.

Men can have babies, too

Izanagi was understandably shaken by this experience, so he did what Japanese people always do when they feel stressed and polluted: He took a bath. He went to a stream on the island of Kyushu and took off his clothes. A number of new gods and goddesses emerged from his discarded clothing, and others arose as he bathed. The last three to be born were Amaterasu, the sun goddess (from his left eye), Tsuki-yomi, the moon god (from his right eye) and Susano, the ocean god, who came out of his nose.

Sibling rivalry between the sun and ocean

The sun goddess and moon god were happy to do the jobs they had been assigned. Susano, though, said he didn't want to rule the ocean but instead wanted to go be with his mother, Izanami. Izanagi banished him and then retired to heaven.

The sun goddess Amaterasu was one of the most important Japanese deities. The imperial family considered her their ancestor until after World War II, when they relinquished their divine status. The most important Shinto shrine in Japan is dedicated to her; it has stood in exactly same place in Mie Prefecture since the seventh century, and it gets rebuilt every 21 years.

But brothers and sisters should love one another!

Amaterasu got the idea that Susano wanted to take her possessions away from her, so she prepared for battle. Susano suggested to Amaterasu that they prove which one of them was mightier by seeing who could produce some male deities. Amaterasu took Susano's sword, broke it into three pieces, chewed them up, and spat out three goddesses. Susano took her necklaces and bracelets and turned them into five male gods. He declared himself the winner, but Amaterasu refused to concede, claiming that because the gods had come from her possessions, she was the winner. (In another version, the siblings did this exchange-of-possessions ritual to prove their honesty to one another and then each adopted the other's children.)

Susano replied by breaking up her rice fields, covering her irrigation ditches, and strewing his excrement in the hall where people celebrated the harvest. Then he took a heavenly pony and threw it through the roof of the hall where Amaterasu and her maids were weaving. One of the maids was so frightened that she hit her genitals on the shuttle of her loom and died (yes, that's weird, but that's the story). Amaterasu ran away and hid in the Heavenly Rock Cave.

The sun goddess goes on strike

This was a problem for the whole world — with Amaterasu on strike, the sun didn't rise and everything was plunged into total darkness. So the gods got together to discuss how to get her out of hiding. First they tried some loud singing birds, but that didn't work.

So they came up with an elaborate plan. They made a magical mirror and hung it from a tree. Then a young goddess called Ama-no-uzume got up on an upturned tub and did an erotic dance, displaying her breasts and genitals. The watching gods laughed uproariously at her antics, and Amaterasu peeked out of her cave to see what was going on. She asked why everyone was laughing, and Ama-no-uzume replied that it was because they had found a deity superior to the sun goddess.

While this conversation was going on, the other gods positioned the mirror so Amaterasu could see it. When she caught sight of her reflection, she left her cave and walked toward the mirror, captivated and wondering who this goddess was. The other gods grabbed her and stretched a rope across the entrance to the cave so she couldn't get back in.

Amaterasu apparently wasn't upset by this treatment. She went back to work running the sun, and life returned to normal. The other gods and goddesses punished Susano, who they blamed for precipitating the crisis. They fined him, cut off his beard and fingernails and toenails, and kicked him out of heaven.

Susano's second career

Susano wandered the earth, intending to go to Yomi, but he never got there. One day he came to the home of a family, where the father and mother were both crying. They told Susano that they had had eight daughters, but a dragon had carried off all but the youngest of them, a girl named Kushinada-hime. The dragon's name was Yamata-no-Orochi; it had eight heads and eight tails and was longer than eight mountains. Susano promised the couple that he would kill the dragon and save their last daughter.

Susano filled eight big jars with *sake* (Japanese rice wine) and put them in front of the house. Then he turned Kushinada-hime into a comb, put her in his hair, and hid in the woods. The dragon showed up and drank all the sake in the jars. It got drunk and nearly fell asleep.

The hero always gets the girl

Susano jumped out of the woods with his sword in his hand. He started to fight the first head, but the dragon's other heads only laughed at him. Susano was quick, and soon the dragon's other heads had joined the fight, too, but he managed to cut them all off one by one. Then he cut off all of its tails but one; that one had something in it that prevented him from cutting all the way through. He ripped it open and found a magical sword, which he later gave to his sister Amaterasu.

Susano and Kushinada-hime got married, and Susano composed the first *tanka* (a 31-syllable poem, similar to a haiku) to celebrate. The house where they lived is now the site of Suga Shrine in Izumo.

Susano has a culinary streak

Susano had other adventures, too. He once killed the food goddess because he found her method of cooking disgusting — she vomited or otherwise excreted the food she served. Many kinds of food came out of the wounds he inflicted on her. Susano also went to Korea to get seeds for different kinds of trees; he brought these back to Japan, planted them, and taught people how to use them for building. He was noted for his excessively long beard.

The hero O-Kuninushi

A long time after Susano and Kushinada-hime's heyday (see the preceding section) there came along another hero. One of Susano's descendants, a man named O-Kuninushi, was one of the great heroes of early Japan. He had many brothers who tormented him. However, they had a few adventures together despite this.

The ol' white rabbit disguise

One day, O-Kuninushi and his brothers went on a quest to find a beautiful princess called Yagami-hime, whom the brothers wanted to marry. They made O-Kuninushi carry the bags and suitcases.

The unencumbered brothers were walking faster than O-Kuninushi. They came upon a rabbit with no fur and asked what had happened to it. The rabbit said it had lived on an island and wanted to cross the sea. There was no bridge, but the rabbit came up with a clever ploy: It found a crocodile and promised to count the members of its family. The crocodiles lined up end to end across the water, and the rabbit hopped from back to back, pretending to count them. As he reached land, he muttered that the crocodiles were fools and that he had just used them as a bridge. The last crocodile heard this and ripped his fur off.

The brothers told the rabbit that it had been sinful, but if it bathed in seawater and sat in the sun, its fur would come back. That didn't work, and it proved pretty painful for the rabbit, too. Then O-Kuninushi turned up, heard the same story, and gave the rabbit a different prescription: He should bathe in fresh water, cover his body with cattails, and lie in the grass in the shade of a tree. This worked, and the rabbit got his white fur back. As it turned out, this rabbit was a god.

You can choose your friends but not your family

The brothers left the rabbit and eventually got to their destination. The princess Yagami-hime met them and said that she had heard the story about the white rabbit and wanted to marry O-Kuninushi. And so she did. The brothers got angry and vowed to hurt him. They got O-Kuninushi to go hunting with them, and they hurled a flaming rock toward him. O-Kuninushi was burned all over his body.

The white rabbit saw this and went running for O-Kuninushi's mother. She went to two shellfish goddesses, who put powdered shells on O-Kuninushi and saved his life. The brothers tried once more to kill O-Kuninushi, catching him in a snare, but his mother saved him again. She told O-Kuninushi that he needed to get away from his brothers.

O-Kuninushi visits Susano: Not exactly a luxury suite

O-Kuninushi went to visit Susano at his palace. Susano's daughter, Suseri-hime, greeted him at the door and the two fell in love instantly. Susano was less than thrilled with his visitor and made him sleep in a room full of snakes. Suseri-hime gave him a snake-repelling scarf and he passed the night safely. The next night Susano put O-Kuninushi in a room filled with centipedes and bees; another scarf did the trick.

Fed up with this unwelcome guest, Susano shot an arrow into a field and sent O-Kuninushi to retrieve it. Then he set the field on fire. O-Kuninushi was saved by a little mouse that took him to an underground cavern. After the fire went out, the mouse brought him the arrow, which O-Kuninushi presented to Susano.

Susano came up with one more trial — he told O-Kuninushi to stand behind him and pick the lice and centipedes out of his hair. Clever Suseri-hime gave him a bowl of nuts and clay, which he chewed and spit out as if he were chomping up centipedes in his teeth. Susano fell asleep under this treatment.

O-Kuninushi gets the girl and cuts out

Seizing his opportunity, O-Kuninushi tied Susano's hair to the rafters and ran away with Suseri-hime on his back, taking along Susano's sword and bow. Susano started up and pursued the couple but gave it up after a bit. Instead of chasing them, he called out to O-Kuninushi that he would be able to defeat his evil brothers if he used Susano's sword and bow.

When the couple arrived at O-Kuninushi's home, he installed Suseri-hime as his first wife. Poor Yakami, his first wife, left in a huff, abandoning his baby in the fork of a tree. And O-Kuninushi fought his brothers with Susano's weapons and finally rid himself of his tormenting siblings.

Supernatural Beings: Materializing in a Folk Tale Near You

Shinto mixed with traditional Japanese religion to produce a body of tales featuring various supernatural beings and occurrences. Many of these stories also illustrate a Buddhist and Taoist awareness of a world beyond the immediate physical one. There were also stories involving real historical figures who gained mythical status.

Bird ladies from heaven

In a number of stories, beautiful heavenly women wearing robes of feathers fly down to earth. The robes are called *hagoromo*, and they are the key to the goddesses' immortality.

In the traditional story, a group of goddesses descended from heaven for an outing in the world. They took off their robes and left them hanging on bushes while they went swimming in a stream. A man walked by and took one of the robes. When they saw him, all the women jumped out of the water, put on their robes, and flew back to heaven — all except the one whose robe was taken. She had to stay on earth and marry the man who had her clothes. She had a child with him, but managed to get back to her heavenly home.

Devils and bad plastic surgery

Oni were Japanese devils; they're easy to identify in pictures because they look just like devils should, with horns on their heads and cloven feet. Though they seemed scary, they weren't very smart.

Cutting a rug with the local devils

In one famous story, an old man with an ugly lump on his right cheek came upon a group of oni dancing around the forest at night. He joined right in with the festivities and proved a terrific dancer, much to the delight of the devils. They made him promise to return the next night and took the lump off his cheek as a bond. When the old man returned home, everyone wanted to know how he had lost his ugly lump.

Another old man had a similar lump on his left cheek, and decided to go dance with the oni the next night to see if they would take his off, too. But he wasn't nearly as good a dancer as the first old man. The oni were disgusted with him and gave him back the other man's lump; so now he had a big lump on both cheeks.

Momotaro, the Peach Boy

Momotaro, the Peach Boy, was a famous hero who fought devils. He came out of a peach — an old woman found a peach floating in a stream, took it home, and found a small boy inside it. When Momotaro grew up, he went off to invade the island of the devils. His mother packed him a bunch of dumplings for snacks along the way. As he walked, he met a dog, a monkey, and a pheasant who joined him in return for dumplings. The group attacked and defeated the devils together, and Momotaro returned home with a lot of treasure.

Earthbound ghosts: Boo!

In addition to devils, ghosts walked the earth in various forms. Some were angry and vengeful while others were more benign, but it was always unnerving to see one. A mask of a ghost is shown in Figure 20-1.

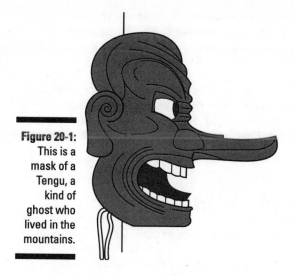

Figure 20-1:
This is a mask of a Tengu, a kind of ghost who lived in the mountains.

In the story *Mujina,* a man walking in Tokyo at night came upon a young woman weeping with her back to him. He put his hand on her shoulder and asked her what was wrong. She turned her face to him, and it was completely blank and smooth, just like an egg. He turned and ran into the darkness, toward the only light he saw. It was the lantern of a noodle-seller's cart. The salesman asked the man why he was running so fast, and the man said, "I saw a woman with a face like . . . like . . ." The salesman said, "Was it like this?" and turned his face into the light. The salesman's face was completely blank and smooth, just like an egg. At that moment, the light went out.

Mythical beasts and foxy foxes

Foxes and cats both had magical powers in Japanese myths — both could turn themselves into humans, and foxes specialized in being seductresses. An animal called a *tanuki,* similar to a badger but often called a "raccoon dog" in English, also appeared in a number of myths and folktales. Tanuki loved to get drunk and have loud parties. In statues and paintings, they often have jugs of sake and big genitals to go along with their leering expressions.

Japanese Rituals: A Little of Everything

Most traditional Japanese beliefs and practices come from Shinto, the only organized religion to arise in Japan. A number of foreign belief systems such as Buddhism, Confucianism, and Taoism came to Japan from the outside, but it all got "naturalized" into distinctly Japanese versions. The Japanese have never been big on exclusivity of religion, and they willingly make room for a myriad of deities, traditions, and rituals.

Most Japanese follow both Shinto and Buddhist traditions. The two religions go well together, because they share a sense of optimism and a pragmatic attitude toward human nature and the world. Shinto tradition regards the Buddha as a *kami,* or god, and Buddhism sees the various kami as manifestations of the Buddha.

The way of the gods: Shinto beliefs

Shinto is an ancient Japanese religion that started around 500 BCE or even earlier. The name "Shinto" comes from the Chinese words *shin tao,* which means "The way of the gods." It began as a mix of nature worship, fertility cults, and other religious activities. It had no real founder or written scriptures, and even now it has just a loosely organized priesthood. There isn't exactly a Shinto theology or a moral code, and Shinto ideas of the afterlife are vague.

The Shinto deities are called *kami,* a Japanese word meaning god or deity. Kami are everywhere, in food, rivers, rocks, places, and families. They are generally benign, protecting and nurturing people. People think of themselves as the children of the kami, and therefore they see human life as sacred. Practitioners of Shinto try to do the right thing, with a special emphasis on benefiting the group. (Harmony is extremely important to Japanese people.)

The four most important aspects of Shinto are tradition and the family, love of nature, physical cleanliness, and worship of the Kami. Shinto also emphasizes peace.

Ancestors are extremely important in Shinto. Many families keep an altar called the *Kami-dana* (Shelf of Gods) in their homes. There's even a yearly festival called *O-Bon* when all the dead ancestors come back to visit for a few days. People put offerings of food — potato chips and beer or sake — on their doorsteps for the dead to enjoy and make little horses out of eggplants and toothpicks for them to ride back home on.

Shrines to kami are everywhere in Japan: on mountaintops, at springs, in the middle of forests. Each shrine is dedicated to a specific kami who can answer the prayers of the faithful. A gate called a *torii* at the entrance of the shrine marks the boundary between the world of the gods and that of humans. Two statues of dogs stand guard. In the past, believers washed their bodies in a river near the shrine; these days, they only wash their hands and mouths at a fountain on the shrine grounds.

Charms from shrines are very popular in Japan. Shrines sell all kinds — charms for protection against traffic accidents, recovery from illness, successful childbirth, or good luck with exams. You can also buy little animal charms for your Chinese birth year, such as the year of the tiger or year of the monkey. Some charms come on key chains.

Ceremonies for the Kami include offerings, prayers, and ritual dances accompanied by musical instruments. Shrines hold annual festivals for planting, harvest, and special anniversaries. Some of the most important festivals are the New Year, the *Hinamatsuri* Girls' Festival (March 3), *Tango no Sekku* Boys' Festival (May 5), and *Hoshi Matsuri* Star Festival (July 7). National Founding Day falls on February 11, commemorating the date on which the first emperor ascended the throne in 660 BCE.

Japanese people visit shrines at important life passages. *Seijin-no-hi,* or coming of age day, is a day in January when everyone who will turn 20 that year becomes an adult. *Shichigosan* (Seven-five-three) on November 15 is a day when all girls aged three and seven and all boys aged five and three go to the shrine for a blessing.

Buddhism, Japanese-style

Buddhism arrived in Japan from Korea and China in the sixth and seventh centuries CE. Tradition has it that a Korean king sent a Buddhist mission to Japan around the year 552. (Modern scholars think it was probably earlier, maybe 538.) The emperor and some of his nobles embraced the new religion. Other members of the court claimed that the native deities would be offended if the Japanese people embraced a foreign religion. The two factions fought a battle over this issue (a real battle, with soldiers and weapons) and the supporters of Buddhism won.

Buddhism became the state religion in the 700s, and gradually more and more sects arrived in Japan. Each sect emphasized different aspects of worship and living; Japanese Buddhists espoused the beliefs of particular sects based on their individual social class and philosophical preferences. For example, the Tendai sect and the Shingon sect were popular with the aristocracy; they had highly developed philosophical systems and emphasized rituals. The Pure Land sect preached that faith and good works would allow believers to be reborn in the Western Paradise of the Pure Land. Members of the Nichiren sect were known for their religious zeal.

Zen Buddhism arrived in Japan in the twelfth century. Zen first arose in China and was heavily influenced by Taoism; it emphasized contemplation and meditation. Zen became popular among both the ruling classes and the common people. Practitioners of Zen split into various sects, taking aspects from other Buddhist sects (see the preceding paragraph) and incorporating them into their beliefs.

Japanese Buddhism emphasizes the importance of human institutions, practical morality, and a work ethic. It's incorporated into every level of Japan's hierarchical society, stressing family loyalty and reverence for ancestors. Believers worship the founders of various sects. Each sect or school of Buddhism tends to be exclusive, with strong emphasis on the master-student lineage.

Japanese Buddhists prefer to accept the world as it is instead of speculating on the meaning of life. They try to understand the absolute through reference to the physical world.

Buddhists in Japan have always been willing to incorporate ancient ritual practices and the native Shinto beliefs. Though Buddhist and Shinto priests are very different from one another, very few Japanese people see any contradiction in being Buddhist and Shinto at the same time.

Chapter 21

Latin America: It'll Tear Your Heart Out

· ·

In This Chapter

▶ Checking out the old Mesoamerican cultures

▶ Meeting the Maya — the calendar masters

▶ Cutting hearts out: Aztec sacrifices

▶ Interrupting an empire: The Incas and the Spanish

· ·

*P*eople lived in Central and South America long before the Europeans arrived. They had complex societies, large cities, and occupied themselves with their own affairs — pleasing their gods with offerings of blood, plotting the courses of the planets, maintaining a calendar, and conquering neighboring nations. This all came to an abrupt end in the early 1500s when the Spanish arrived and conquered the current empires of the era, the Aztec and the Inca. *Mesoamerica* is a fancy word for the region including Mexico, Guatemala, Belize, Honduras, and Nicaragua. It's more or less the same region as *Central America,* which encompasses Mexico through Panama.

Mexico and the surrounding area was the site of several successive civilizations. The major Mesoamerican cultures were

✔ **Olmec:** 1500 to 400 BCE.

✔ **Zapotec:** 500 BCE to 700 CE.

✔ **Teotihuacan:** 150 BCE to 750 CE.

✔ **Maya:** 250 to 900 CE.

✔ **Toltec:** 900 to 1180 CE.

✔ **Aztec:** 1325 to 1521 CE.

All of these cultures but the Maya were of the group called *Nahua;* Maya spoke Maya and the rest spoke Nahuatl. They all shared many cultural attributes, such as a very complicated calendar system. Many of the same gods appear in all their pantheons.

The Incas, another well-known group of Latin American Indians, didn't live in Mesoamerica. The Inca civilization was a separate culture in the Andes Mountains of South America. The Inca Empire lasted from 1438 to 1532.

Historians get their evidence about Latin American Indians from a variety of sources: documents that the people wrote themselves (in their own version of hieroglyphics), records written by Spanish colonists, ethnographic observations of modern Indians, and archaeological remains. The stories of the Aztecs and the Incas, in particular, illustrate how mythology can be important in daily life and indeed in the lives of empires. Both of these huge civilizations fell because of peoples' beliefs in the gods.

Footprints of a Lost People: The Old Cultures

Central America was home to a number of cultures during the 3,000 years before Europeans arrived. Modern people are more familiar with the Maya and the Aztecs because they lived more recently and some of them still are around today. However, their predecessors in that area also had significant civilizations. The Olmecs, the Toltecs, and other cultures had elaborate groups of deities and rituals that passed from culture to culture; thus, the relatively modern Aztecs still were worshipping gods that had been around thousands of years earlier. The city of Teotihuacan was home to a vast civilization and, since its decline, has been informative to subsequent cultures; both the Aztecs and modern archaeologists have marveled at it.

Olmecs

The Olmecs used to be called Central America's mother culture. That sort of term is unfashionable now, but the Olmecs definitely were a major force in cultural development. The Olmecs rose on the Mexican Gulf Coast around 1500 BCE and their empire lasted until 400 BCE.

The Olmecs imposed one government and one religion on the whole region. Famous Olmec archaeological sites include San Lorenzo, with giant big-lipped stone heads, and the ceremonial site La Venta. They may have begun keeping a calendar like later peoples did.

The Rain God was their most important deity. This god was a monster with human and jaguar features on his face. Carvings of him look sort of like a cross between a jaguar and a baby. Later civilizations also used this god, along with many other Olmec gods.

Teotihuacan

Teotihuacan was a city near present-day Mexico City, the first major city in the Western Hemisphere. In its heyday, it was almost the size of Rome and flourished for a longer time, from about 150 BCE to 750 CE. The Aztecs knew about it; they called it the Place of the Gods.

The city was laid out according to the movements of the stars and the position of nearby mountains. The Street of the Dead (named by the Aztecs) angled east from true north to point to a sacred mountain. The main east-west axis of the town lined up with the *Pleiades,* a cluster of stars important to the Mesoamerican calendar. The city had giant pyramids; under one of them is a cave that may have been used for secret rituals. Archaeologists have found skeletons of several soldiers wearing necklaces of human skulls, their hands tied behind their backs — human sacrifices, perhaps?

The locals worshipped the Storm God — paintings of this fanged, bug-eyed god with his trademark lightning bolt are all around the site. The people believed he could make summer clouds release rain to grow corn, beans, peppers, squash, and grain. He was also a war god; other paintings depict scenes of war and human sacrifice, including a procession of soldiers carrying knives with human hearts stuck on them. The Storm God's counterpart was a goddess, who sometimes was helpful and sometimes fierce.

Other than the evidence assembled by archaeologists, historians know little about the people who lived in Teotihuacan. No one knows where they came from, how their society worked, what language they spoke, or why they disappeared. But they do know the culture was influential — many images from Teotihuacan appear at the sites of later Mesoamerican cultures.

Toltecs

The Toltecs lived in central Mexico from 900 to 1180 CE. They supposedly sacked the city of Teotihuacan around 900. The Toltecs had a number of small states bound in an empire; they were known for their military prowess. Their king Topiltzin introduced the cult of Quetzalcoatl, the feathered serpent; Topiltzin also called himself Quetzalcoatl. The Toltecs had military orders named after animals, such as the Coyote, the Jaguar, and the Eagle, which showed up later in Mayan culture. The Toltecs were themselves invaded in the twelfth century; their conquerors included the Mexicas, who became the Aztecs. (See the "Aztecs" section later in this chapter.)

Quetzalcoatl, the feathered snake (or a real guy?)

Quetzalcoatl, the feathered serpent, is the most important figure in Mesoamerican mythology. He appears on the most ancient monuments over hundreds of years, and even today, Mexicans use him as a symbol of their culture. He may have been a real person, the Toltec priest-king Topiltzin-Quetzalcoatl (see the preceding section).

Quetzalcoatl was tall, strong, and fair-haired (blond or light brown). His face was covered with soot, and he wore a quetzal bird on his back. He sometimes appeared as the wind god Ehecatl.

Also appearing at the Sky Club as the planet Venus

According to the Toltecs, Quetzalcoatl had an argument with the god of night, Tezcatlipoca. Tezcatlipoca liked bloody sacrifices of humans, but Quetzalcoatl preferred more peaceful offerings, like jade or butterflies. Quetzalcoatl lost the fight, went to the Gulf of Mexico, and burned himself up on a pyre. He was reborn as the planet Venus, visible as the Morning and Evening Stars.

In another version of the story, the Toltec priest-king Topiltzin sailed away on the Gulf of Mexico, promising to return one day from the direction of the rising sun. The Aztecs assimilated Topiltzin as a god; they made him patron of priests and craftsmen and credited him with inventing the calendar. The Aztecs calculated the predicted date of his return as 1519. As it happened, that was the year that Cortés and his men arrived in the Yucatan. Cortés made good use of this mythological advantage that had dropped into his lap (see the "Montezuma and the fall of the empire" section later in the chapter).

Mesoamerican Indians loved a bird called the *quetzal*. They're beautiful iridescent green birds with incredibly long and very valuable tail feathers. South American Indians trapped them to get their feathers. Killing one, however, was punishable by death. The Guatemalan unit of currency is called the *quetzal*. Few quetzals are left in Central America, and they are highly endangered.

Maya

Though the Maya are still around today, it's the ancient ones of the Classic Maya period that most people remember. The Maya had one of the greatest civilizations in Central America during their heyday from 250 to 900 CE. Their empire stretched from hills in Guatemala, Mexico, and Honduras through Belize and across the Yucatán Peninsula. Mayan rulers, who believed they were descended from the sun, oversaw a society of farmers, craftsmen, and scholars. The Maya had several regional capitals; important ones included Tikal, Cobá, and Copán.

At the peak of the Mayan civilization, as many as two million Maya may have been living in Guatemala. The Mayan civilization declined rapidly after 900 CE; no one knows why. Though Maya continued to live in the area, by the time the Spanish arrived, they were no longer a great civilization, instead living in small farming villages and practicing the religion of their ancestors.

The Maya built giant stone temples and pyramids and were skilled at working gold and copper; some of their exquisite stone carvings provide much of the information that is known about their culture. They covered their buildings with sculptures and inscriptions based on their mythology and life.

For years, scholars assumed that the Maya were a peaceful people, growing their corn and getting by from day to day. Recently, however, they've revised this view. Mayan texts talk about victories in battles and list captured enemies, some of whom were sacrificed. Mayan cities had major fortifications of moats and towers — not exactly what peace-loving farmers would need.

Torture and human sacrifice were key parts of the Mayan religious rituals. They feared that the world would end if the gods didn't get human blood regularly. That also meant that the Mayan rulers periodically had to give the gods some of their own blood (which must have been lots of fun).

The interrupted creation of people

The Maya recorded their creation story and other mythology in a book called *Popol Vuh*.

In the Maya creation story, the gods spent a while creating humans. They weren't pleased with their first attempt, so they sent a flood to destroy them and turned the survivors into monkeys. Before the gods got a chance to try again, an imposter god called Vucub-Caquix entered the scene. He claimed to be the sun and the moon. The gods knew they couldn't finish humans until

Vucub-Caquix was gone, and the divine twins Hunapú (god of the hunt) and Ixbalanqué (Little Jaguar) took on the task of getting rid of him.

These twins came about in an unusual way. Their father had been lured to the underworld to play ball with the people there, the *Xibalba*. He had lost his game and therefore his life, and his head was hanging on a calabash tree to warn everyone not to mess with the Xibalba. This tree miraculously became covered with fruit. A young woman went to see it and had a conversation with the skull; the head spat in her hand and she became pregnant with Hunapú and Ixbalanqué.

The twins knew Vucub-Caquix would come to a fruit tree to eat, so they hid under it and shot him with an arrow. The monster tore off one of Hunapú's arms and ran away with it. The twins got an old man and woman to help them get the arm back. The old people found Vucub-Caquix and offered to help him. The monster said his eyes and teeth hurt, so the old couple pulled out his teeth and gouged out his eyes. After that, they took back Hunapú's arm and reattached it.

With the monster vanquished, the twins decided to avenge their father's death. They journeyed to the underworld, where the Xibalba subjected them to various trials. They won a ball game and they survived nights in the house of knives, the house of cold, the house of jaguars, and the house of fire. In the house of bats, however, they weren't so fortunate. Hunapú lost his head, and the Xibalba hung it in their ball court. It was okay, though, because a turtle volunteered to be a replacement head.

The brothers now played another ball game with the Xibalba, but they came up with a plan to win. They threw the ball to the end of the court and a rabbit ran after it; while the Xibalba were chasing it, Ixbalanqué stole back Hunapú's head. The game ended in a tie.

Now the Xibalba, fed up with their opponents, built a bonfire and suggested that they all fly over the flames. But the twins knew they were immortal, and they jumped right in. Five days later they rose from the dead and came back to visit their enemies disguised as fishermen. They put on a show, cutting themselves to pieces and putting themselves back together. Then they did the same trick to the leaders of the Xibalba, except they didn't put them back together again. The rest of the Xibalba surrendered, and the brothers punished them by (among other things) forbidding them to play ball.

Now the gods could get back to finishing humans. The cat (or jaguar), the coyote, the parrot, and the crow gathered up corn (maize), the special food for humans. And thereafter corn was essential for keeping people alive.

Dual "quadralities": The gods and their business

The Maya had a bewildering array of deities. The Mayan pantheon was complicated — most deities had four guises, one for each direction — and often they also had dual natures, being both young and old, male and female, and so on. Figuring out who was who is complicated because of the differences in Mayan paintings of deities and the descriptions of them by Europeans. Anyway, here are a few of the better-known ones:

- **Itzamná:** The creator and patron of knowledge.

- **Cizin:** The death god. He ruled the underworld.

- **Ah Kin:** He was the sun; he may have been an aspect of Itzamná. In the sky, he was just the sun, who could bring warmth or drought; in the underworld, he was a jaguar. The Sun god was the center of the Mayan universe. Rulers claimed to be descended from him, which justified their power over everyone else.

- **Ix Chel:** She was the moon goddess and Ah Kin's or Itzamná's consort. She was in charge of weaving, divination, childbirth, and medicine.

- **Venus:** A dangerous god, especially when he rose in the morning as the Morning Star.

Gods of corn and rain and patron gods for occupations and social groups were part of Mayan culture. All the deities together took care of human affairs.

Reptilian cosmology: The world where they lived

The Maya envisioned the universe as a united whole with all things intertwined within it — the heavens, the earth, the underworld, and everything in them. The deities in the Mayan pantheon and the many minor spirits (see the preceding section) each had their own place in the universe, though they all moved around constantly.

The Mayan world had four corners, with trees holding up the four corners of the heavens. Each quarter had a special color and particular gods associated with it. The heavens had 13 layers. The sky was a two-headed dragon whose body bore the symbols of the sun, the moon, the planet Venus, and the stars.

The earth was the back of a giant lizard floating in a pond. People entered the underworld through this lizard's mouth; the underworld had nine levels.

Time after time: The circular calendar

Time was central to Mayan thought. The Maya saw time as circular, not linear, and believed that as points in time reappeared, events associated with them could happen again — the past could predict the future.

The basic Mayan calendar, the *ritual almanac,* had 260 days; they used this calendar to schedule religious ceremonies and make predictions. It was divided into chunks of 20 days, each of which had an associated deity. The 260-day cycle doesn't seem to have had any particular significance and isn't attached to any natural phenomena. The Maya thought 20 and 13 were important numbers and 260 is what you get when you multiply them. This ritual almanac is the oldest known component of the Mesoamerican calendar. It was in use in 500 BCE and all the cultures in the region used a version of it.

The Maya also used another calendar that corresponded to the solar year. It had 18 months of 20 days each, and 5 extra days to make up 365. (The Maya had no provision for a leap year.) Each month had a patron deity who would affect people and events. We refer to this calendar as the *solar calendar.*

The ritual and solar calendars happened simultaneously. When Mayan scribes recorded dates, they either wrote down just the ritual calendar date or the two dates together; they never recorded just the solar date. The combination of the two calendar cycles repeated every 52 years.

Writing system

The Maya had an excellent system of writing that could convey just about anything they wanted to say. It combined phonetic symbols and pictographs, much like the ancient Egyptian system or modern Japanese. They wrote on paper made from the bark of fig trees. They created thousands of books but now only four are left. When the Spanish arrived, one of the first things they did was eradicate Mayan writing — they realized that writing was an intrinsic part of Mayan religion and social structure, and they knew they would have a better chance of Christianizing the Central American Indians without it.

The Mayan writing system wasn't deciphered until the twentieth century. Once scholars learned to read it, they discovered much more information about Mayan religion, the Mayan pantheon, and the priests who performed regular rituals. Mayan writing also revealed the details of their mathematical and astronomical knowledge; they compiled tables of the positions of Venus and the Moon and could predict solar eclipses.

Aztecs

The name Aztec came from the word *Aztlán,* meaning "White Land," which probably meant northern Mexico, their likely place origin. Their ancestors, the Mexica, probably started out as hunter-gatherers on the northern plateau and moved south around the same time as the Toltec civilization collapsed in the late twelfth century. The Toltecs experienced major social, political, and religious upheavals around this time, which left them vulnerable to attack by their various enemies. The Aztecs joined in the fray when they arrived in the area.

The Aztec Empire lasted almost exactly 200 years. By 1325, they had founded the capital of the Aztec Empire, Tenochtitlán. They allied themselves with some neighbors and conquered others, so that by 1519 there were about 6 million Aztecs — when Cortés arrived, Tenochtitlán was almost as big as London. Their civilization fell to the Spanish just two years later.

The name "Mexica" was applied to the city that grew up on the Aztec capital. Later it became the name for the entire country of Mexico.

How the world was created

The Aztecs and the Maya believed that the current sun is the fifth sun. The four previous suns, and the people who lived under them, died long ago. The people who lived under the first sun were eaten by *ocelots* (a kind of cat). The second sun was the sun of air; the humans who lived then turned into monkeys. The inhabitants under the sun of fire all died except for the birds, which flew away. Fish came into existence under the sun of water, but everyone else died in a flood. With the Fifth Sun, the elements of creation became integrated, but that was no assurance that this world would last any longer than the others; it, too, could die.

Gods for rain, corn, and sacrifices

The Aztecs, like the Maya, had a huge number of deities. A bunch of them had to do with agriculture and rain. Aztec deities included:

- **Tezcatlipoca, the "Lord of the Smoking Mirror":** He was the head of the pantheon of gods. He came to the Aztecs from the Toltecs (see the "Toltecs" section earlier in the chapter). The Toltecs thought that he corrupted Quetzalcoatl, making him get drunk. The Aztecs had a bunch of different identities for him. He was associated with war, death, and darkness, royalty and sorcerers. His alter ego was the jaguar.

- **Huitzlopochtli, sometimes called the Hummingbird of the South:** He was the Aztec god of sun and war; he didn't appear in any other Mesoamerican mythologies. He helped the Aztecs choose the site for Tenochtitlán.

- **Tlaloc:** He was an ancient rain god. People throughout Mesoamerica worshipped him. He got the majority of sacrifices.

- **Chalchiuhtlicue:** Tlaloc's wife, she was called the Lady of the Jade Skirt. She could stir up hurricanes and make people drown.

   The Tlaoques: They were Tlaloc's helpers; they made thunder by smashing their water jars.

- **Xipe Totec:** He was the god of springtime, seeds, and planting. He is known as the "flayed god," and in many statues he wears the skin of a sacrificial victim. His priests would skin their human sacrifices and wear the skins themselves. This made a direct connection between human sacrifice and fertility of the land, because these people were sacrificed to the god to make springtime come and the plants grow.

- **Ehecatl:** He was the wind god. His temples were cylindrical, to offer less resistance to the wind from any direction.

War for the land of the sun: Culture

The Aztecs were a warlike people. They sent armies throughout the countryside, conquering the locals and forcing them to contribute goods and captives for their sacrifices. The most successful Aztecs were generally the most successful warriors. They also had a very efficient farming and irrigation system and produced enough food to create a rich nation.

The calendar cycle festival

The Aztec religion incorporated aspects of most other area religions, including those of the Toltec (see the "Toltecs" section earlier in the chapter), Olmec (see the "Olmecs" section earlier in the chapter), and Mayan civilizations (see the "Maya" section earlier in the chapter). In particular, they used the same calendar system as the Maya, scheduling their rituals by its 52-year cycle.

Every 52 years, the people would hold a major festival to mark the end of one long cycle and the beginning of another one. They put out all the fires in the land, threw statues of gods into the water, and swept their houses clean. They would then set a captive's chest on fire; if the flames didn't burn high enough, this was a prediction that the world would end. The men locked up the women and children and put masks on them; they kept the children awake all night lest they turn into mice.

When the sun rose again, everyone rejoiced. They pricked their ears to get blood for the sacred fire, put on new clothes, redecorated their houses, and offered sacrifices to the gods. At noon they sacrificed some more captives.

Blood for the good of the gods: Human sacrifice

The Aztecs believed that their gods needed human blood and lives to stay happy. They thought they were the chosen people of Huitzilpochtli, the war god, and it was their mission to give him blood to keep the sun in motion. Huitzilpochtli was greedy; one year, his priests sacrificed more than 20,000 people to him.

The Aztecs sacrificed humans by cutting their hearts out with flint or *obsidian* knives (obsidian is an extremely sharp volcanic glass). They burned the hearts and threw the bodies onto an image of one of Huitzilpochtli's defeated victims. Aztec priests offered their own blood to the god, too — they would pull barbed cords through holes in their tongues, which must have been really gory and painful.

Montezuma and the fall of the empire

The Aztecs still were building their empire when the Spanish arrived in 1519, led by Hernán Cortés. Montezuma was emperor of the Aztecs. Although he was a successful king and led many wars of conquest to expand the empire and capture prisoners to satisfy his favorite god Huitzilopochtli's craving for blood, he supposedly had a fatalistic view of life. His astrologers had predicted an uncertain future for him, which was enhanced by his expectation that Quetzalcoatl would return in 1519 in the form of a white bearded man who would take over the empire.

Cortés quickly captured Montezuma, who died in his custody. Montezuma's successors didn't hold off the Spanish very long; in 1521, the Spanish captured the capital Tenochtitlán and that was the end of the Aztec empire.

Incas

The Inca Empire only lasted about 100 years, getting cut short by the Spanish conquest in 1532. But in that time, it managed to stretch 2,500 miles through the Andes Mountains down the Pacific coast of South America from Ecuador to central Chile. The Incas started as a small group in Cuzco, Peru, but extended their influence over 12 million people, who came from at least 100 different cultures and spoke many different languages.

Sun, moon, stars, and people

The Incas believed particular places were especially spiritual. The tops of mountain passes were especially important to them and people would make little offerings to local deities before continuing on their way. They had other, more formal, gods, too — the rulers claimed to be descendents from the Sun God, one of their main gods.

The creator god and the divine ancestors of the Incas

Viracocha was the creator god. He didn't concern himself much with the everyday lives of humans, preferring to let other deities worry about that. The Incas believed that he had traveled through the world teaching people how to live. When the Spanish arrived in 1532, some Incas thought they were Viracocha returned for another visit.

As is usual in creation stories, Viracocha didn't like his first attempt at creating humans and destroyed them with a flood, which one man and one woman survived. After he made a batch that he liked, he sent them into the world. He called up the sun, moon, and stars from the Island of the Sun in Lake Titicaca.

Our claim to fame

Viracocha then gave Manco Capac, the leader of the Incas, a headdress and a battle-ax to confirm his royal status. Manco Capac founded the city of Cuzco and the Incas later built their Temple of the Sun on the exact spot where he stood. He married his sister and they jumpstarted the Inca dynasty. The Inca rulers used this story to claim divine origins.

Skybound: The Inca deities

The Incas had a number of gods. Some important ones included:

- ✔ **Inti:** He was the sun god.
- ✔ **Mama Kilya:** The moon goddess, the wife of Inti, and mother of the Inca people. She regulated the passage of time.

> ✔ **Ilyap'a:** The god of rain. He took water from the Milky Way, which was a river across the sky. His sister kept rain in a jug that Ilyap'a would smash with a lightning bolt when he wanted to let some out.
>
> ✔ **Cuicha:** He was the god of the rainbow.

The sky and its changes were very important to the Incas, and their deities reflect this.

Children of the sun: Inca culture

The Incas left no written records; their historians memorized facts and passed their knowledge down orally. But the Spanish wrote many long documents about them and their culture at the time of the conquest, so some contemporaneous written information is available to scholars.

It's not easy running an empire

No empire can be built without some inconvenience and disappointment to the conquered. As the Incas conquered groups of people, they forced their subject peoples to move around and settle in different places — splitting up ethnic groups helped prevent rebellion (a trick the Soviets used when drawing boundaries for their central Asian republics). They built a sophisticated road network in and on the Andes Mountains throughout the empire, mainly for military purposes. The Spanish conquerors found these roads very handy for maneuvering through the Andes.

But the Incas weren't all harshness and bureaucratic unpleasantness. They offered gifts that impressed the heck out of less advanced civilizations — cloth was a favorite because the Incas were excellent weavers. They allowed local leaders to keep their positions and let people keep their old religions with some Inca rituals mixed in. The children of nobles went to Cuzco for training and jobs, which helped tie subject people to the capital.

Sun worship was the official state religion; the sun god's name was Inti. The Temple of the Sun in Cuzco had walls of gold; its garden was full of statues of animals cased in gold and silver. Several thousand women called the *Virgins of the Sun,* or the Chosen Women, lived in Cuzco, serving both Inti and the royal family. They were chosen for their beauty and skill at weaving and taken from their villages when they were about 8 years old. They made clothes, food, and beer for festivals, and slept with the emperor when he wished it.

Human sacrifice for the good of the empire

As part of their empire-building, the Incas selected children from everywhere in the empire and sacrificed them on mountaintops. This wasn't as bad as it sounds — people considered it an honor to have their kids chosen, so it was good for building ties with subject nations. They believed that these sacrificed children became deities themselves.

These children were dressed in the finest clothes and most expensive jewelry; they served as gifts for and messengers to the gods. They were killed by being buried alive, strangled, or hit on the head. They don't appear to have suffered much, which leads historians to believe that they were drugged with ritual alcoholic drinks and befuddled by the high altitude.

The Spanish conquer, an empire falls

The Spanish conquered the Incas in 1532, in search of the fabulous wealth they expected to find in the Andes (which did exist — the Incas had a huge amount of gold). Francisco Pizarro and his army of 168 men met the Inca king Atahuallpa and 80,000 South American Indians supposedly to negotiate; the Spanish had promised the Incas that no harm would befall them. Atahuallpa made the mistake of throwing a Bible on the ground, and the Spanish fell on the Incas, who were unarmed and not expecting a battle.

Although the Spanish were greatly outnumbered, they had steel weapons and horses, which was enough of an advantage to enable them to kill thousands of Indians and capture Atahuallpa. After holding him hostage and collecting a huge ransom for him, they killed him anyway and that was essentially the end of the Inca Empire.

Chapter 22

Coyotes, Thunderbirds, and Bears, Oh My: North American Indian Myths

. . . .

In This Chapter

▶ Solving marital problems with Little Turtle

▶ Living with the Bear People

▶ Stealing fire with Rabbit

▶ Tormenting giants with Coyote

. . . .

People arrived in North America sometime between 30,000 and 12,000 years ago. Most people think that the first Americans walked from Siberia to Alaska — across what is now the Bering Strait — over a "land bridge" (or perhaps an "ice bridge") that existed back then. Recently, though, some folks have questioned that idea — maybe some came in boats, paddling along the Pacific coastline. Some archaeologists even suggest that people may have crossed the Atlantic from Europe even earlier than first thought. In any case, they spread all over the continent (over South America, too), and adapted to the places where they settled. And, of course, they came up with myths.

Myths were sacred to North American Indians, because they explained the relationship between humans and the gods. Creation myths were especially important, as were myths that explained the origins of rituals. Many groups acknowledged a supreme spiritual being or Great Spirit. The spirits of ancestors helped the living and needed rituals. Other figures such as the Sun and Moon, Mother Earth and Father Sky, and creator/trickster animals such as Coyote frequently appeared in myths, as did other animal characters. It all added up to a complex set of beliefs.

North American Indians transmitted these myths orally — they memorized them and spoke them aloud instead of writing them down. The oral tradition of storytelling is very important to all groups of North American Indians.

Conquest by contagion

When the Europeans started arriving in the 1500s, they brought with them lethal weapons — germs for diseases such as smallpox and tuberculosis. The North American Indians hadn't ever been exposed to these germs and they died at an appalling rate, which made the European conquest relatively easy.

The Lush Green Forests of the East

Hundreds of years ago, the eastern part of North America was covered with forests. People lived in these forests from northern Canada all the way to the southern tip of Florida. These North American Indians had pretty complex cultures for people still using Stone Age tools.

The term "Stone Age" refers to technology; Stone Age people make their tools out of stone, not metal. That doesn't necessarily mean they're primitive; as we mentioned, the North American Indians had very complex cultures. Their stone tools were so effective that they could feed and clothe themselves and still have ample time for mythmaking and storytelling.

Northeastern woodlands: The Iroquois

The area from the St. Lawrence River to Delaware Bay and west to the Great Lakes was home to farming tribes, including the

- ✔ Iroquois
- ✔ Huron
- ✔ Delaware

These were some of the first North American Indians to encounter Europeans. Most records of Iroquois and other myths come to us from accounts written by European missionaries, so we know very little about their culture and mythology before the English and French arrived.

The Iroquois Confederation

We do know, though, that the Iroquois built up a federation of five Indian nations including the Cayuga, Seneca, Oneida, Mohawk, and Onandaga.

This confederation allowed them to farm and fight more efficiently. In its heyday, the Iroquois Confederation was the most powerful group of North

American Indians east of the Mississippi River; they took control of the Northeast and kept it from the mid-1600s on. On one occasion, they even raided the Black Hills in the Dakotas just to collect some prisoners to sacrifice at their festivals. They also tortured and occasionally even ate their prisoners as part of their rituals. They had a full body of myths and rituals and recorded them in their own way.

North American Indians in the Northeast recorded their tribal history in strings of beads called *wampum*. At tribal gatherings, the dignitaries in charge of the wampum would tell the stories associated with them. Wampum also served as a unit of exchange, both for trade and to maintain social and political equilibrium by making and confirming alliances.

The Iroquois said their dead went to a land far away; dead warriors went to the sky to become *Aurora Borealis,* or northern lights. According to some accounts, they believed in an All-Father similar to the Norse god Odin; this belief may have come from visits by Norse people to the Labrador coast in the eleventh and twelfth centuries. And they believed in an assortment of spirits that ran all natural phenomena, such as rivers, rain, seasons, and the growth of crops; many of their myths involve natural processes.

Domestic disputes between the sun and moon

In Iroquois myth, the sun and the moon were like husband and wife, and quarreled just as married couples will do. When the moon went down before her husband one day, he grew angry and beat her. She went and hid in the dark. Little Turtle went looking for her, and found her pining away for her husband; she had shrunk down to a mere sliver of her former rotund self. Little Turtle put her back on her course around the world. She gradually grew round again, but when the sun passed her without a backward glance, she again wasted away to nothing. And so the waxing and waning cycle of the moon continues every month.

Son of Thunder: Too hot to handle!

North American Indians said that Thunder lived in the sky; he was one of seven brothers and went by the name Heng. He showered blessings down on the people in the spring, but sometimes his children got out of control and brought destruction to the earth.

One of his brothers married a human woman. She had earlier inadvertently married a man of the Serpent People — he looked human for a while, but then turned into a giant snake. The woman ran away as fast as she could, the snake pursuing her through the forest, and she finally came to a lake where three handsome young men stood — Thunder and two of his brothers. Thunder threw his spear at the snake and killed it. The three young men brought the woman home with them. She married one of them and had a baby boy.

This boy had thunder power; by the time he was four, he could knock down trees with his toy arrows. His mother begged her husband and father-in-law for permission to take him back to her family to show them how strong he was. Thunder was worried about what would happen if the kid shot people with his arrows, but agreed to let them go.

The Thunder Boy enjoyed his visit, but the other little boys started teasing him because he wouldn't shoot his bow. Finally he couldn't stand it anymore and shot an arrow at them. Fortunately, it missed the other boys and only set some trees on fire, but that was enough for Thunder. He swooped down, grabbed the boy, and never let him go to earth again.

Southeastern woodlands: The Five Civilized Tribes

The Southern United States from the Atlantic to the Mississippi was home to a huge sophisticated population of North American Indians known as Mound Builders. As the Europeans settled, tribes became extinct from disease and their traditions were diluted. The Five Civilized Tribes of this area were the following:

- ✔ Cherokee
- ✔ Choctaw
- ✔ Creek
- ✔ Chickasaw
- ✔ Seminole

They adopted the ways of the invaders; this extended to their mythology, as they incorporated European and African folk tales into their traditional ones. Two of their myths are light-hearted accounts of how people got two of their most important possessions, which were fire and tobacco.

Rabbit steals fire

The Sky People (who weren't human) were about to celebrate the Green Corn Festival in their village square; by tradition, this was the only place fire was allowed. People didn't have fire, so they couldn't cook food or warm themselves. Rabbit thought this was wrong and decided to steal fire and give it to people. He came up with a trick: He made his hair stand on end so impressively that the Sky People made him leader of the dance. As he danced past the fire, he bent down low — so low that his hair caught on fire. He ran away with his prize.

The Sky People didn't want their fire to spread around, so they made it rain for four days. But Rabbit hid in a hollow tree and his fire stayed lit. The first humans saw the fire and came running to light firebrands. After that they had fire in their homes, and those with fire shared with those who didn't. Finally the rains stopped, everyone was allowed to have fire, and people remembered Rabbit fondly for his generous deed.

A cigarette after sex?

One day, a young man and a young woman walking down a path in the forest were overcome with desire for each other. They lay down on the side of the path and had sex, which was so satisfactory they decided to get married.

Later on, the man went out hunting and revisited the site of their first union. He found a pretty flower with scented leaves growing in the same place they had made love — the tobacco plant. He took it back to his people, and they all decided to dry it and smoke it; they named the new plant "Where we came together." The elders decided that because the man and woman were so happy and peaceful when the flower was created, they would smoke it at councils for promoting peace and friendship among tribes. And because of its origins, they believed thereafter that tobacco had both masculine and feminine energy.

Big Sky Country: The Great Plains

The people of the Plains in the central U.S. are the ones most people envision when they think about North American Indians. The Plains people were the ones who rode horses, hunted buffalo, wore feathers and headdresses on their heads, and lived in tipis. They belonged to tribes like

- Sioux
- Pawnee
- Blackfoot
- Cheyenne
- Comanche
- Kiowa

Funny thing, though — the Plains Indians didn't really live that way for very long. They didn't have horses until the Spanish brought them around 1600, and their way of life was pretty much destroyed during the westward expansion of the 1800s.

Land of the buffalo: The Lakota

People lived on the Great Plains for centuries, long before they had horses. They hunted buffalo on foot and planted corn. Buffalo were extremely important to the Plains Indians. Before Europeans arrived, there were vast numbers of the huge beasts roaming the prairies, herds sometimes covering the landscape as far as the eye could see. Hunting buffalo was a dangerous business, whether on horseback or on foot. It was imperative that the people observe the necessary rituals to ensure a safe and successful hunt.

Tribes had huge gatherings in the spring and fall, during which they made offerings to the spirits of the sky and earth and to tribal ancestors. They would perform rituals such as the Sun Dance, which was an occasion for seeking visions; sometimes participants would mutilate themselves by sticking skewers in their chests and hanging from them, offering their suffering to the sky spirits.

Not surprisingly, Plains mythology featured lots of buffalo. Plains people believed in a Great Spirit, such as the Wakan Tanka of the Lakota; the rituals for Wakan Tanka tied in with beliefs in buffalo spirits. They also believed in a rather vague supernatural power that surrounded everything and manifested itself in the sun, moon, stars, animals, and natural forces such as rain. Myths explained these powers, the origin of human rituals, and how it came to be that humans hunted buffalo and not the other way around.

White Buffalo Woman

The Lakota claimed that they learned all of their rituals when two Lakota hunters met a beautiful woman dressed in white buckskin. One of the men tried to hit on her, but she turned him into a pile of bones. The other hunter listened when she told him to go get his chief and build a large tipi for her.

Tipis (often spelled "teepees" or "tepees" in books about the "Wild West") were tents made of buffalo skin. The Plains Indians used these as portable housing while they hunted on the prairies in the summer. In the winter, they returned to their permanent houses made of earth; that was when they took care of growing their crops.

Speaking to Wakan Tanka

The woman walked into the tipi. She introduced herself as the White Buffalo Woman and showed the chief the pipe and small round stone she carried. The pipe, she said, was for speaking to Wakan Tanka, the supreme being. Its symbolism was important for the following reasons:

- The bowl of the pipe represented the earth
- The stem was made of wood and represented plants
- The feathers hanging from the pipe represented birds

> ✔ The stone was carved with a buffalo calf, representing all four-legged creatures
>
> ✔ The seven circles on the stone represented the seven rites that used pipes

She taught them the first rite that day and returned later to teach them the rest. The rites included ceremonies for releasing souls to the spirit world, purification in the sweat lodge, and searching for visions.

Many North American Indians believed that they could communicate with the spirit world by going off alone to fast and pray; young people did this as a *vision quest* to find their guardian spirits.

Shamans were people with especially close relationships with the spirits; *medicine men* were a step down from shamans. Shamans could enter a trance to talk to the spirits, and they could use their power to find game or heal the sick. (The North American Indians themselves didn't use the terms "shaman" or "medicine man;" these are words that Westerners use to describe North American Indian culture.)

The Arikara and the buffalo people

Once upon a time, buffalo looked like strong humans with horns. Instead of people hunting and eating them, they hunted and ate people.

The buffalo lived in a village near an ancient cottonwood tree with a big knot on it. When the buffalo priests prayed and knocked on this knot, humans came out of it. The buffalo hunted them like animals, clubbing them to death and cutting them up. The buffalo danced around a fire while their human meat dried, as the surviving humans huddled inside their cottonwood tree.

One young man had escaped the buffalo and hid from them in the wilderness. One day he met a lovely woman in white leather with horns on her head. She led him to a beautiful painted tipi and invited him to bed with her. She covered him with her white robe and gave him meat to eat. When he awoke the tipi was gone, but the woman, Buffalo-Girl, was still there.

She told him that the buffalo people were looking for a man to turn them into proper animal buffalo, and that he was the one to do the deed. She helped him sneak past the angry buffalo guards — some of them thought they could smell human meat, but the others said that was only because they were still splattered with human blood from their hunt — and brought him to the chief's tipi. He hid in a pile of animal skins.

Some pre-game rallying

The young man lay there and listened while the chief recited his hunting chants and practiced hitting the magic tree to get people to come out. The chief went out hunting the next morning, and Buffalo-Girl came back in. To give the young man courage and make him angry, she showed him the racks where the cuts of human meat were drying.

Then Buffalo-Girl took him to an ash tree and showed him how to make bows and arrows. He made as many as he could, enough for all the human warriors he hoped to summon. After that, she led the young man to the cottonwood tree and told the men inside that when the time came, each of them must take a bow and arrow and shoot a buffalo.

And they lived happily ever after

The next day, the buffalo chief and his warriors came up to the tree and struck it to make the humans come out. Each of the men grabbed a bow and shot the buffalo men. The buffalo were so frightened they ran away, carrying chunks of human flesh with them. As each one was hit with an arrow, he turned into a real buffalo, grazing on prairie grass instead of eating human flesh.

Buffalo-Girl married the young man. Their children founded the Arikara nation. Whenever the Arikara ate buffalo, they left the chunk under the buffalo's foreleg uneaten, believing that this was the lump of human meat the buffalo carried right before its transformation.

This myth had an important medicine bundle associated with it. *Medicine bundles* were portable shrines that commemorated the places where important spiritual events happened. They contained things like relics from ancestors or sacred objects from the gods. Medicine bundles had not only ritual uses, they were also an extremely valuable form of property.

The astronomical Pawnee

The Pawnee were very interested in astronomy. They venerated the North Star as a creator god and feared his opponent, the South Star. They thought the North and South Stars would come together at the end of the world. The Morning Star protected the Pawnee while the Evening Star was its enemy. They had a ritual associated with the Morning and Evening Stars: The young warriors would sneak to an enemy camp and capture a young woman. The tribe kept her prisoner for a while, treating her kindly so she would speak well of them to the gods. Then they would strip her naked, paint her red and black to symbolize the Morning and Evening Stars, and then shoot her with arrows. Her blood was supposed to revive an ancient blessing and ensure prosperity.

Saguaro Cactus Flower in the Southwest

The North American Indians of the southwestern part of the United States had highly developed mythologies. They included the pueblo dwellers such as the Hopi and the Zuni and the semi-nomadic Navajo and Apache. The people in pueblos ate food that they grew — the "three sisters" of corn, beans, and squash were their staples. The Apache and Navajo, on the other hand, didn't stay in one place for very long, so they didn't farm much; instead, they hunted and gathered wild animals and plants. The land was dry and fairly harsh; the people of this area used myths and ritual to keep nature working properly and the rain falling so they could have enough to eat.

Southwestern mesas: Pueblo people

The most highly organized tribes, including the Zuni and the Hopi, in the Southwest lived in large villages called *pueblos* built on top of mesas. Though these North American Indians now live in northern Arizona and New Mexico, before Columbus, their territory stretched from Texas to Nevada to northern Mexico. These tribes shared a common culture, with most of their efforts aimed at growing and storing enough food to survive in the harsh desert climate. Pueblo mythology focused on the relationships between humans and the natural world.

The Old Ones: The Anasazi

People started living in this area more than 2,000 years ago. Archaeologists don't know what they called themselves, so they use the name *Anasazi* (a Navajo word meaning "ancient enemies" — archaeologists don't always come up with the most politically correct names for people). The Anasazi are the ancestors of the modern Pueblo tribes, the Hopi and Zuni, who prefer to refer to them as the "Old Ones."

The Anasazi lived for centuries as hunter-gatherers. Around 900, they began living in villages near the Chaco Canyon in New Mexico. They traded with people from Mexico and California. Around 1200, they all moved into homes carved into cliffs in response to environmental stress and to be more easily defensible. Less than a century later, many of them moved away all at once. Historians think they were lured away by a new religion, the Pueblo *kachina* religion (see the following section).

Historians have traditionally thought the Anasazi were peaceful, but now it looks as though they might have waged war with the Pueblos around them. Archaeologists have found human skeletons with knife marks on them and the bones broken to get at the marrow inside. This suggests that these "peaceful" people might have indulged in cannibalism.

Underground religion

Pueblo families — members of groups such as the Hopi and the Zuni — lived in towns of apartments, built of mud or carved into rock; each family had to store reserves of food in case the crops failed. Below the apartments were underground chambers called *kivas,* where the tribe held its religious ceremonies. To Pueblo people, the group was more important than the individual; everyone was expected to aid anyone in need. Religion and rituals helped people live together, ensuring equality between and integration of social groups.

Zuni kachinas

Pueblo people believed that ancestral spirits, called *kachinas,* permeated the world. The Zuni believed that at one time gods and kachinas walked the earth along with humans; that is part of their creation myth.

Kachinas could help people with health, happiness, and successful crops. For religious processions, men would dress in colorful costumes impersonating kachinas, wearing elaborately decorated masks made of wood, hair, feathers, and leather. The kachina religion has been around for 700 years and is still practiced today.

Kokopelli, the flute player

Kokopelli, the flute-player, is a prehistoric deity dating from Anasazi times, over a thousand years ago. The Anasazi, or "Ancient Ones," were farmers on the Colorado plateau. The image of Kokopelli traveled throughout the southwest by trade and immigration. Now it's one of the Hopi kachinas and is common in North American Indian stories. See Figure 22-1 for what Kokopelli looked like.

Southwestern hunters: Navajo and Apache

The Navajo and Apache lived in what is now Arizona and New Mexico, a land of arid scrubland, high mountains, and oases in valleys. The North American Indians in this area lived by hunting and gathering, supplemented by a few crops they grew for themselves. After the Spanish arrived, they added sheep herding to this mix. They had a semi-nomadic lifestyle, living in temporary shelters in the summers and in earth and wood huts called *hogans* in the winter.

The Navajo had many long and complex myths. Their religion, much of which was borrowed from Pueblo tribes, was based on maintaining a harmonious balance between the human and spirit worlds. Imbalance could result in disaster, so the appropriate rituals were essential.

Figure 22-1:
Kokopelli
the flute-
player.

Coyote trickster myths

Some North American Indian myths might have had a moral purpose, but were also good entertainment. One popular character was the creator-trickster. Coyote was one of the most popular trickster characters, appearing in myths all over the Southwest and the Plains — he lives on to a certain degree today in the animated character Wile E. Coyote. Raven was a favorite in the Northwest. Rabbit was popular in the Southeast. The Lakota on the Plains liked Spider.

Tricksters across the North American continent exhibited many of the same traits — tricksters were clever but often bungled their enterprises through their own horseplay; they often ended up injured or dead only to rise again undaunted. Trickster myths could be extremely vulgar (too vulgar for this book!), which helped highlight the importance of moral rules. Trickster characters were often culture heroes as well, helping their people become civilized by giving them gifts such as fire or killing monsters that plagued them. Storytellers and listeners alike loved trickster tales, the storytellers because they were fine material for embellishment and the listeners because the characters and situations were so much fun. This made trickster tales an important part of the oral tradition.

Coyote and the giant

The Navajo say that a long time ago, giants were everywhere. They were a problem because they liked to eat human children. Coyote decided to do something about this. He invited a giant to take a sweat-bath with him. Inside the dark lodge, Coyote told the giant that he would now perform a miracle: he would break his own leg and heal it. He took a rock, pulled out a deer leg, and smashed it; he invited the giant to feel the broken part. Then he said "Leg, become whole!" and to the giant's astonishment, Coyote's leg was unbroken.

Coyote offered to perform the same stunt on the giant's leg, and the giant, having taken leave of his senses, agreed. The giant, of course, screamed in pain when Coyote smashed his leg with the rock, but Coyote told him all he had to do to fix it was to spit on it. Then he slipped out of the lodge, leaving the giant spitting on his leg and moaning in agony.

The Wealthy Pacific Northwest

The Pacific Northwest is rich in natural resources such as fish and wild berries — so rich, in fact, that the North American Indians who lived there had no need to waste their time on agriculture. They lived in large villages near the mouths of rivers, where they would take their canoes to catch salmon.

A generous people

The North American Indians of the Pacific Northwest were famous for their big parties called *potlatches*. At potlatch, the host family would serve their guests a great feast, entertain them with songs and dances (which also told the guests just how great the hosts were), and then give them presents. These presents were no mere party favors, but extremely valuable items; a host family might give away most of its net worth at a potlatch. That was okay, though, because all their guests would have to hold their own potlatches and invite their hosts from previous feasts; that way wealth got distributed to everyone. Many tribes held potlatches to commemorate special occasions, such as funerals or house dedications. Major tribes of the Pacific Northwest included the

- Tlingit
- Nez Perce
- Kwakiutl
- Coeur d'Alene
- Makah

Animal tales

The North American Indians of the Pacific Northwest felt especially close to animals. They adopted family animal totems (such as bears, salmon, killer whales) to acknowledge the role these beings played in the lives of their tribal ancestors. They used their totems like team emblems, decorating their houses and clothes with pictures of their totem animals.

Totem poles were tall wooden poles carved in the shape of various totems — bears, salmon, and so on. They commemorated special people or events and informed visitors about the history and affiliations of the tribe; they also let visitors know where they would be welcomed, because people who shared totems where considered kin.

North American Indians believed that animals had a close kinship with humans, because humans and animals used to be indistinguishable from one another. Their myths show the importance of respecting fellow creatures.

In Pacific Northwestern myths, the *Thunderbird* was a supernatural creature, an eagle with a head on its stomach. Lightning flew out of its beak and thunder roared when it flapped its wings.

Hunting is for food, not sport, my son

The Wolf Clan lived near a river where they could find many wild salmon and berries, which fed them well and made them wealthy. As time went on, the younger people grew careless and irresponsible; they would kill animals and leave them to rot, and they would slit the backs of salmon to put torches in them, so the fish would swim down the river lit up. The older people warned them that there would be trouble. And sure enough, at the end of the salmon season, the ghosts woke up and had their vengeance — the mountains broke open and fire gushed out, burning most of the forest and destroying most of the tribe.

Of bears and people

Princess Rhpisunt, daughter of the chief of the Wolf Clan, was gathering berries in the forest when she stepped in bear feces. She complained about this for hours, blaming all bears for being so nasty. She gradually wandered away from her friends, and ended up quite alone.

A young man found her and invited her back home with him; she agreed to follow him and ended up marrying him. The lodge where he lived was full of big people and bearskin coats; old slaves wandered around sleepily. A woman called Mouse Woman introduced herself and told Rhpisunt that she was living with the Bear People, who had been insulted at her criticism of them because she stepped in the bear mess; the bears apparently were touchy, because all the slaves were people who had once insulted them. Whenever one of the Bear People went out, he put on a bearskin coat and turned into a real bear. She warned Rhpisunt that she was in danger, but suggested something that could help.

Every time Rhpisunt went out to relieve herself, she had to bury her excrement and put a piece of copper from her bracelet on the ground. When the bears went to inspect her droppings, they were impressed at how nice they were — indeed nicer than theirs.

328 Part V: Some Sunblock, a Sacrifice, a Monster, and Thou: Non-European Mythology

Several months went by. Back home, Rhpisunt's family had been looking for her; they were afraid that a bear had eaten her. They began hunting bears enthusiastically. Rhpisunt was pregnant and her husband took her to a place in the mountains where she could have her babies safe from the hunters; she gave birth to twin cubs, strong and healthy.

Rhpisunt's brothers kept looking for her with the help of her dog. One day her husband told her that they would find him and kill him soon. Rhpisunt's brother soon arrived and killed the bear. Rhpisunt and her two cubs went back to her father's house; as soon as her sons entered the house, they took off their bear coats and became human. Their grandfather made them a tall pole that they could climb to see their other grandfather's house. And after Rhpisunt grew old and died, they turned back into bears and moved back in with the Bear People. From that time on, the Bear People and Rhpisunt's tribe remembered that they were relatives and helped each other hunt.

Part VI
The Part of Tens

The 5th Wave   By Rich Tennant

"...and so a great and powerful race of beings came across the land, and they were known as the Venture Capitalists..."

In this part . . .

This part contains information that didn't fit with the chapters on individual types of mythology but is interesting nevertheless. The next two chapters describe mythological places and fabulous mythological monsters.

Chapter 23

Ten Mythological Monsters

• •

In This Chapter

▶ Turning people to stone: Gorgons

▶ Rising up from the ashes: The Phoenix

▶ Sphinxes and The Sphinx in Egypt

• •

Myths are full of monsters. Heroes need monsters to fight — otherwise, how could they be heroic? Besides, gods use monsters to scare people. And in a mythological world where gods can take the shapes of animals and have kids with mortal humans, who knows what those offspring may turn out looking like.

Apart from being colorful characters and villains in mythological stories, many of these monsters have become symbols of abstract ideas — human ambition, death and rebirth, and (very often) the idea that the natural world can and does keep secrets from us humans.

Gorgons

According to Homer, there was only one *Gorgon,* a monster of the under-world. But the poet Hesiod mentions three of them: Stheno ("the Powerful One"), Euryale ("the One Who Sees Far"), and Medusa (the Queen of the Gorgons). They were the daughters of Phorcys, a sea-god, and his wife, Ceto. The people of Athens said that the Gorgons were daughters of Gaia, the Earth, which she produced to help her children fight against other gods.

Gorgons had wings and snakes for hair. They were so horrible-looking that anyone who looked directly at them would turn to stone — Medusa's name survives today as a symbol of supreme ugliness. The Greeks used artistic representations of Gorgons to ward off evil. The statue of Athena in the Parthenon in Athens held a shield bearing a Gorgon's face, which came from the tale of Perseus, who killed Medusa and gave her head to Athena. See Chapter 6 for that story.

Chimera

The *Chimera* was another female monster — female monsters have a hard time in Greek myths — that looked like a lion in front, like a goat in the middle, like a dragon in the tail, and could breathe fire. Bellerophon and Pegasus defeated her — see Chapter 6 for more about that.

In modern English, a "chimera" is a figment of the imagination. The word shows up as an adjective, too: "In the 1950s, a computer that could fit in a briefcase was considered to be a chimerical idea." Architects use the word "Chimera," or its French translation, *chimère,* to refer to any strange creature used as a decoration on a building.

The Phoenix

This mythical beast first appeared in Egypt, but you can also find it in Greek, Islamic, and later European mythology. A bird the size of an eagle with red and gold feathers, it sang beautifully. There could be only one Phoenix at a time, but each one lived for 500 years (or for a very long time, depending on the account you read). When it reached the end of its life, it would collect sweet-smelling twigs to build a nest, then would settle into the nest and burst into flames. After it had burnt completely away, a new, baby Phoenix would rise from the ashes and begin its long life.

For the Egyptians, the Phoenix represented death and rebirth, the immortal soul. Since then, the Phoenix has served as a symbol of eternal strength for any institution that claims the ability to overcome setbacks and keep on going — the Roman Empire was one.

Cerberus, the Hound of Hell

Homer mentioned a hound-of-hell that Heracles brought up from the underworld as one of his Twelve Labors. Later, Greek mythology got more specific. First, the hell hound got a name, *Cerberus.* Then it got a fuller description. Cerberus was like a dog, but with three vicious heads and, in place of his tail, a venomous serpent. He guarded the underworld — his heads would keep the living away, and his tail would keep the dead in their place. (The Roman travel-writer Pausanias, who was something of a dog-lover, objected to describing the underworld-guarding monster as a dog, because, after all, the dog is the "friend of man.")

Dragons

Dragons are huge and snaky, on that much everyone agrees. But because dragons appear in mythology from Europe, the Mediterranean, Africa, the Middle East, and Asia, a lot of variation exists. (Scholars have recently found pretty solid evidence that the ancient peoples of Greece and Africa were familiar with the fossil remains of dinosaurs. This evidence could explain why dragon myths are so common.)

Northern European dragons didn't have legs, but Asian dragons did. Greek dragons seem to have spent their time on the ground, like snakes, but Chinese and Japanese dragons are creatures of the air. Ironically, Asian dragons didn't usually have wings, while European dragons often did. Some dragons could breathe fire, and others couldn't.

Dragons symbolized different things. In Mesopotamia, the original female goddess who gave birth to the other gods was a dragon. The Egyptian god Apepi was a dragon-god who ruled the world of darkness and evil. In Greek myths, the dragons — which the Greeks called *drakontes,* the origin of the name — were often clever, magical creatures from inside the earth. Athena had a snake (*drako* in Greek) that was her pet and helper. The Chinese thought of the dragon as the male half of the universal order — the "yang" in "yin-yang." And in the Hebrew Bible, the "serpent" who talks to Eve in the Garden of Eden is "the most subtle of God's creatures."

Because the pre-Christian world of Europe and the Mediterranean was so full of images of dragons, medieval Christianity used the dragon as a symbol of the non-Christian, pagan world. But dragons were too interesting to give up — the dragon often appeared as a symbol for Saxon England, and the Welsh coat-of-arms today has a dragon on it.

Unicorn

The nicest and most cuddly of the mythological "monsters" was the *unicorn.* It looked like a horse with a single horn growing from the center of its forehead. Unicorns appear in the art of Greece and Rome, and even earlier in the art of Mesopotamia. The Greek writer Ctesias, who lived in the fifth century BCE, described a *monokeros* (or "one horn," which in Latin is *unicornis*) with a purple head (with blue eyes) on a white body and a red, black and white horn. (Some older translations of the Hebrew Bible mention unicorns, but the references are the result of a mistranslation — the Hebrew word is *re'em,* which actually refers to a kind of ox.)

From antiquity onward, people thought that the unicorn's horn had the magical ability to purify and heal — medieval Christians saw the unicorn as a symbol of the Christ because of its mild nature and its healing powers. The unicorn could purify a polluted spring by dipping its horn in it. Medicines made from the horn supposedly had all sorts of healing properties. "Unicorn horn" was worth twenty times its weight in gold in medieval Europe — what was sold was actually the long, spiral horn of the narwhal, a whale that lives in the cold northern seas.

Griffon

The *griffon* had a lion's body, wings (sometimes), and an eagle's head. Some of them had ears like horses, too. The earliest images of griffons come from Mesopotamian art of around 1800 BCE, but by 1500 BCE, the creature had spread all around the Middle East and Mediterranean world. The Minoan Greeks on the island of Crete — a rich and artistic civilization during the Bronze Age, around 1400 BCE — painted griffons with fancy, curled manes around their beaky heads.

Later Greeks liked to portray griffons with their beaks open to show long, curling tongues. Griffons (sometimes spelled "griffins" or "gryphons") seem to have been important symbols, because they show up on art associated with kings, with temples, and with the burials of wealthy people.

Sphinx

The most famous sphinx is The Sphinx, the big statue at Giza in Egypt, with a lion's body and the head of a man. The head is that of Pharaoh Khafre, who ruled around 2500 BCE. The sphinx is a very, very old mythological monster.

Sphinxes showed up in Greek art starting around 1600 BCE and were common all around the ancient world ever after. The Greeks thought the name *sphinx* came from the Greek verb that means "to strangle," but modern scholars are dubious about this. Greek sphinxes were female monsters with human heads, lion bodies, and snakes for tails. They appeared in all kinds of art, but were especially common on official seals — small, carved stones used for pressing into wax or clay to make something official. These seal-sphinxes were usually sitting with one paw raised, like a dog shaking hands.

The most famous story involving a sphinx is the story of Oedipus. Mostly because of this story, which the tragedian Sophocles turned into a very famous play (check out Chapter 8 for more about it), the sphinx has long been a symbol of deep wisdom.

Chapter 24

Ten Mythological Places

. . . .

In This Chapter

▶ Playing in the (Elysian) Fields of Dreams

▶ Getting drunk on goat liquor in Valhalla

▶ Submerging Atlantis

. . . .

Any tour guide in Central America, or Japan, or Greece, or Egypt can take you to places where, according to myth, gods once spoke to humans or heroes fought monsters. But some mythological locations are, themselves, mythological. Some of these places are real enough — places on the map — but have gained mythological status through stories told about them, usually by people who had never been there. Others may have once existed, but their locations are long forgotten and only the mythology remains. Others are entirely fictional, but nevertheless have a real existence in the world of mythology. And not all of these mythological places are especially old!

Elysium, or Elysian Fields

Elysium was the closest thing the ancient Greeks had to a "heaven." In Homer's tales, Elysium was a mystical land, far off in the West, near the great river Oceanos that circled the world. The poet Hesiod later placed it in the west, near the river Oceanos (which is now the Atlantic). Only the very best dead people got to go there. According to Homer, Zeus's mortal sons went straight to Elysium without having to die first, and they lived there in perfect happiness forever. See Chapters 3 and 4 for more on the Greeks' view of the world.

The place most people went wasn't especially bad — no burning fires or devils with pitchforks — but it wasn't especially fun either. When the hero Odysseus, who got to visit the land of the dead, asked the great (but dead) Achilles how he liked his "life" among the dead, Achilles said: "I would rather be a hired hand, working for a poor man, than king down here." It was preferable, though, to the eternal torment of Tartarus, where the worst sinners went. See Chapters 7 and 8 for the stories of Odysseus and Achilles.

By Roman times, Elysium had relocated to some undefined place under the earth, but the blessed dead still got to go there. According to the Roman poet Virgil, they kept doing whatever job they had done in life and continued to enjoy doing it forever.

Brigadoon

Brigadoon is a mythological fishing village in Scotland that appears for one day every century, then disappears again. On that day, any outsider who finds the village is welcome to stay there, but if any of the residents leave, then the magical spell would be broken forever. Great myth . . . but this "myth" is less than one hundred years old!

In 1947, Alan Jay Lerner and Frederick Loewe wrote a musical play for Broadway, called *Brigadoon;* it was later made into a movie starring Gene Kelly. The play and movie were both immensely successful, and so the story of this magical Scottish town has become as firmly planted in the list of "mythological places" as, well, Elysium.

But Lerner and Loewe made it up — there's no old Scottish story about Brigadoon. Actually, they probably didn't make it up from scratch. Though the writers denied it, many people assume that they based their play on a German short story by Friedrich Gersacker about a German village called Germelshausen, which appeared only one day every 100 years. The name "Brigadoon" comes from a real place, the "Brig-o-Doom" (Bridge of Doom), which appears in a famous poem by the Scottish poet Robert Burns.

Xanadu

In 1797, the English poet Samuel Taylor Coleridge moved to the countryside to recover from some sickness or other. He helped his recovery along by taking doses of laudanum — a liquid made from poppies, the eighteenth century's version of Prozac that was really more like opium. One day he fell into a laudanum-induced stupor while reading a book about Asia, and had a vision. When he woke up, he quickly started writing down the verbal image that remained in his brain.

The poem described a marvelous palace and park, with cliffs and caverns, rivers and waterfalls all around it. When he had written about 50 lines, someone knocked on his door. By the time that Coleridge had gotten rid of the visitor, his vision had faded.

Though unfinished, the poem "Kubla Khan" put Xanadu on the mythological map. The place is a real place — Shang-tu, or Shangdu, a city in China that was founded by the Mongol ruler Kublai Khan in the year 1256. Marco Polo (or his family) visited it around 1265. The historical Shang-tu was a huge city with walls surrounding many public buildings and a large central park. But the mythical Xanadu — the product of a warm afternoon, a dose of opium, and a brilliant poet — has become the more famous of the two today.

Shangri-La

Like Elysium (see the "Elysium" section), Shangri-La is a mythological place of perfect happiness. Like Brigadoon (see the "Brigadoon" section), most people know of it because of a twentieth century work of literature. And like Xanadu, it's Asian and (probably) an idealized, mythologized version of a real place.

James Hilton wrote a novel in 1933 called *Lost Horizon,* about a place called Shangri-La high in the Himalayan Mountains in Tibet. It was a secret, hidden kingdom where people never grew old, but lived in harmony and happiness, guarding ancient, secret wisdom. Hilton's novel was based on a Tibetan Buddhist myth of Shambhala, the "Hidden Kingdom," the home of perfect humans who keep the highest form of mystical Buddhism. The place is hidden by mountains pierced with waterfalls. Behind those mountains, the kings of Shambhala rule for 100 years each. After 32 of these kings have ruled, the place will no longer be hidden and the people of Shambhala will emerge and reveal themselves to the world.

In 1998, an American explorer, Ian Baker, led a team searching for Shambhala in Tibet. Though he found some landscape features that seemed to correspond to places mentioned in ancient manuscripts, his expedition had to turn back early and so far the Chinese government has allowed no more. So the secrets of Shangri-La are, for the time being, still hidden.

Arcadia

Arcadia is a real place, located in the central part of the southern peninsula of Greece, the Peloponnesus. In ancient times, Arcadia was a mountainous backwater populated by poor shepherds just getting by.

To aristocratic Romans, though, the life of the people in Arcadia seemed ideal, compared to the stress of Roman politics in the big city. Roman poets invented a mythical "Arcadia" that was a peaceful place where simple folks lived simple lives in harmony with nature. The poet Virgil wrote a bunch of poems about happy shepherds and their girlfriends cavorting on the Arcadian hills. The Arcadia of myth is mountainous but green, filled with minor gods and happy peasants whose lives are plain but satisfying, who celebrate quaint festivals when they aren't dozing in a meadow while their flocks graze nearby.

The idea of Arcadia as an idyllic wilderness stuck around. Philip Sydney wrote about Arcadia in a very popular, somewhat pornographic novel in 1578. Perhaps it inspired Christopher Marlowe, who in 1599 wrote a (non-pornographic) poem called "The Passionate Shepherd to His Love." In Walt Disney's film *Fantasia,* the sequence set to the music of Beethoven's *Pastoral Symphony* is as good an image of the mythological Arcadia as anyone will find anywhere.

Valhalla

This was the Hall of Dead Warriors from Norse mythology. In Valhalla, the dead warriors ate the "bottomless boar," which was slaughtered every day, eaten, and reborn at the end of the evening. A goat's udder produced liquor for them. When they weren't feasting on pork and getting drunk, the warriors fought each other — why not, they were already dead! — and waited for the last battle of Ragnarok. See Chapter 13 for more on Norse myths.

Atlantis

The Greek philosopher Plato recounted the story of Atlantis in a *fictional dialogue* (that means it's not true!). This tale says there was once an island called Atlantis beyond the Pillars of Hercules (the ancient name for the Straits of Gibraltar), which was bigger than Libya and Asia combined and was the home of a powerful kingdom. The whole island sank into the sea after an earthquake.

During the Middle Ages, Europeans forgot about much of the learning of the Greeks but the Arab world didn't. The myth of Atlantis came back to Europe through the writings of Arab geographers. Europeans who heard the story wondered if Atlantis might have been the Canary Islands, or perhaps some-place in Scandinavia — or even the Americas. A popular modern theory is that the Atlantis story actually refers to the island of Thera (modern Santorini), which was blown almost entirely to bits by a volcanic eruption in 1500 BCE. Today, only a crescent-shaped island remains, with the center com-pletely gone.

The Kingdom of Prester John

In the year 1071 CE, the Seljuq Turks conquered Jerusalem. The Christians of Europe freaked out because their Holy City was now in the hands of Muslims. This began the period of the Crusades — a long unhappy period in the long unhappy history of a city that is sacred to three great religions.

The Europeans were eager to recapture the Holy Land and looked for help from wherever it might come. In 1145, the Pope received news of a certain Prester John, who was supposedly the descendent of one of the Magi, the Wise Men who visited the infant Jesus from the East. The report claimed that Prester John was a Christian king, lord of a powerful empire in Asia, who was marching west to help reconquer the Holy Land. A similar letter with promise of assistance arrived at all the powerful courts of Europe in 1165.

Pope Alexander III wrote back, but no army of Christian Asians ever showed up. Despite this disappointment, Europeans continued to wonder about the Kingdom of Prester John. A number of travelers journeyed to Asia looking for it — Giovanni da Pian del Carpini, Giovanni da Montecorvino, and of course, Marco Polo. None of them found it, but they did make profitable contacts with the real empire of China. When Europeans started sailing across the Atlantic, but before they realized that the continent on the other side wasn't Asia, they still hoped to find Prester John and his marvelous kingdom.

Avalon

Avalon was the magical island where King Arthur went after his last battle, where his wounds would be healed, and where he would remain until the time was ripe for his return. (See Chapter 15 for the Arthur story.) One tradition says that Avalon is not actually an island, but the town of Glastonbury, which was associated in some Celtic myths with the "land of dead heroes." But many people think that the monks who lived in Glastonbury invented that story to bring tourists to their area and help the local economy. Avalon is now a symbol of any mystical, happy place.

Index

deities *(continued)*
  Mesopotamian, 241–242
  Norse, 189–196
  Persian, 139, 156
  Roman, 153–154
  Roman and Greek equivalents, 144
  Vedic, 262–263
Delphi, 50, 69, 84, 119
Demeter, 25, 34, 49, 66–68, 124. *See also* Ceres
Description of Greece (Pausanius), 78
Deucalion, 41, 245, 246
Devas, 262–263
Devi, 268–269
dharma, 266
Di Penates, 137, 146, 147–148
Diana, 144, 175, 176. *See also* Artemis
Dictys, 79, 81–82
Dido, 136, 162, 165–166
Diomedes, 19, 99
Dione, 33
Dionysus, 49, 50, 55, 57–59, 88, 114–115. *See also* Bacchus
Discord, 30
disease
  Egyptian treatments for, 256–257
  introduction of, 12–13
  Mata and, 269
Disney, Walt, 181
Divine Comedy (Dante), 23
Diwali, 271
dolphin, 51
Doom, 30
dragons, 333
dreams, 259
Dukas, Paul, 181
Dunciad (Pope), 24
Durga, 268, 271
dwarves in Norse mythology, 188, 189, 194, 197

• E •

Ea, 238–239, 242
Earth, 30, 37–38
earth goddess, 66
Ector, Sir, 218, 221–222
Egypt, 20, 21, 138, 247–248, 255–260. *See also* Egyptian mythology
Egyptian mythology, 249–255
Egyptologist, 248
Ehecatl, 310
Eight Immortals, 280–283
Elaine, 219, 220, 224–225, 227
Elaine (Maid of Astolat), 223–224
elders, respect for, 284
Electra, 21, 116, 127, 128
Electra (Euripides), 118, 127
Electra (Sophocles), 127
Electryon, 82
elves in Norse mythology, 197
Elysium or Elysian Fields, 335–336
end of world myth, 13, 200–202
Enkidu, 234–235
Enlil, 241
Enûma Elish, 233, 236–237
epic poems, 94, 162. *See also Iliad* (Homer); *Odyssey* (Homer)
Epimetheus, 35, 39, 41
epithet, 44, 94
Erato, 74
Erebus, 30
Ereshkigal, 242
Eris (Strife), 63, 72, 95
Eros, 30, 33, 54, 65. *See also* Cupid
Eteocles, 122, 123, 134
eternal year, 119
Ethiopia, 38
Etruscans, 133–134
Eumenides (Aeschylus), 76
Euphrosyne, 74

• *H* •

• P •

Notes

Notes